The Canadian Forces and Arctic Sovereignty:
Debating Roles, Interests, and Requirements, 1968-1974

Compiled and Introduced by

P. Whitney Lackenbauer and Peter Kikkert

LCMSDS Press of Wilfrid Laurier University

0 1 2 3 4 5 6 7 8 9

Printed in Canada

Library and Archives Canada Cataloguing in Publication

The Canadian Forces and Arctic Sovereignty
Debating roles, interests, and requirements, 1968-1974 / compiled and introduced by P. Whitney Lackenbauer and Peter Kikkert.

Collection of documents from the Department of External Affairs, Department of National Defence, and from the House of Commons.

Includes bibliographical references and index.
ISBN 978-1-926804-00-2

1. Canada. Canadian Armed Forces--History--20th century--Sources. 2. Canada--Military policy--History--20th century--Sources. 3. Canada--Defenses--History--20th century--Sources. 4. National security--Canada--History--20th century--Sources. 5. Canada, Northern--Strategic aspects--Sources. 6. Arctic regions--Strategic aspects--Sources. 7. Canada--Boundaries--Arctic regions--Sources. 8. Arctic regions--Boundaries--Canada--Sources. I. Lackenbauer, P. Whitney II. Kikkert, Peter III. Canada. Dept. of External Affairs IV. Canada. Dept. of National Defence V. Canada. Parliament. House of Commons

UA600.6.A7C35 2010 355'.03357109719 C2010-900493-0

Printed and bound in Canada
Designer: Geoff Keelan
Cover Design: Matt Symes
Map Design: Matt Symes
Distributed by: Wilfrid Laurier University Press/University of Toronto Press

LCMSDS Press
Wilfrid Laurier University
Waterloo, ON
N2L 3C5 Canada
www.canadianmilitaryhistory.com

Mixed Sources
Product group from well-managed forests and other controlled sources
www.fsc.org Cert no. SW-COC-002206
© 1996 Forest Stewardship Council

Table of Contents

Acronyms

ACND	Advisory Committee on Northern Development
ASW	anti-submarine warfare
AWAC	Airborne Warning and Control
AWPPA	Arctic Waters Pollution Prevention Act
CAF	Canadian Armed Forces
CANUS	Canada-United States
CCGS	Canadian Coast Guard Ship
CDS	Chief of the Defence Staff
CDSAC	Chief of the Defence Staff's Advisory Committee
CFB	Canadian Forces Base
CFHQ	Canadian Forces Headquarters
CFNR	Canadian Forces Northern Region
CFS	Canadian Forces Station
CGS	Coast Guard Ship
DC Plans	Director Continental Plans (DND)
DConP	Director Continental Policy (DND)
DERMS	Director Equipment and Readiness Maritime Sea (DND)
DEW Line	Distant Early Warning Line
DEXAF	Department of External Affairs
DFR	Defence Relations Division (DEXAF)
DGCES	Director General Communications and Electronics Systems (DND)
DG INFO	Director General Information (DND)
DGIS	Director General Intelligence and Security (DND)
DGOPSA	Director General Operations Air (DND)
DGOPSL	Director General Operations Land (DND)
DGOPSM	Director General Operations Maritime (DND)
DHH	Directorate of History and Heritage
DIAND	Department of Indian Affairs and Northern Development
DIP	Director Intelligence Production (DND)
DMIL	Director Militia
DND	Department of National Defence

DOT	Department of Transport
DRAE	Defence Research Analysis Establishment
DRB	Defence Research Board
DREA	Defence Research Establishment, Atlantic
DREO	Defence Research Establishment, Ottawa
DREP	Defence Research Establishment, Pacific
DREV	Defence Research Establishment, Valcartier
EMR	Department of Energy, Mines and Resources
FDO	Force Development Objective
FLE	Legal Division (DEXAF)
FLO	Legal Operations Division (DEXAF)
FLP	Bureau of Legal and Consular Affairs (DEXAF)
HMCS	Her Majesty's Canadian Ship
ICBM	Intercontinental Ballistic Missile
IRLS	infra-red line scanning equipment
JAG	Judge Advocate General (DND)
JIC	Joint Intelligence Committee
LAC	Library and Archives Canada
LORAN	Long Range Aid to Navigation
MARCOM	Maritime Command
MIA&ND	Minister of Indian Affairs and Northern Development
MOT	Ministry of Transport
NATO	North Atlantic Treaty Organization
NCHQ	Northern Command Headquarters
NCO	Non-Commissioned Officer
NRHQ	Northern Region Headquarters
NORAD	North American Air Defence
NORPLOY	Northern Deployment
NWT	Northwest Territories
OMD	North American Defence and NATO Division (DEXAF)
OPI	office of primary interest
PSI	Security and Intelligence Division (DEXAF)
pt.	part
RCAF	Royal Canadian Air Force
RCCs	Rescue Co-ordination Centres
RCN	Royal Canadian Navy

RCMP	Royal Canadian Mounted Police
RG	Record Group
SAC	Strategic Air Command
SAR	Search and Rescue
SOSUS	Sound Surveillance System
SPADATS	Space Detection and Tracking System
STOL	Short Take Off and Landing
U.S. or USA	United States of America
USSR	Union of Soviet Socialist Republics
VCDS	Vice Chief of the Defence Staff
vol.	volume

Acknowledgements

Terry Copp, the director of the Laurier Centre for Military Strategic and Disarmament Studies, supported this project from the onset for which we are most appreciative. We are also grateful to the Balsillie Fellowship program through the Centre for International Governance Innovation which provided funding that allowed us to collaborate on this project over the past year, as well as the Social Sciences and Humanities Research Council of Canada for a standard research grant (held by Whitney Lackenbauer and Matthew Farish) which facilitated access to documents in Ottawa.

Compiling a document collection like this can be onerous, and we benefitted from support offered by other scholars and public servants. Thanks to Jennifer Arthur-Lackenbauer for her comments on various drafts of the introduction, as well as to Philip Isard who assisted with transcribing several documents. Dr. Greg Donaghy of the Historical Section at the Department of Foreign Affairs and Dr. Stephen Harris of the Directorate of History and Heritage at the Department of National Defence helped us to decipher difficult acronyms. Dr. Rob Huebert of the Centre for Military and Strategic Studies, who recently produced a report for the Canadian International Council about sovereignty and control issues, agreed to write the afterword. A final thanks to Paul Kelly, Matt Symes and Geoff Keelan for their work in layout, final copy-editing, and the cover design.

P. Whitney Lackenbauer and Peter Kikkert
Waterloo, Ontario
30 June 2009

Introduction

Speaking in Winnipeg on a cold winter's day in December 2005, Prime Minister Stephen Harper placed the responsibility for protecting Canada's sovereignty in the Arctic squarely on the shoulders of the Canadian Forces. "You don't defend national sovereignty with flags, cheap election rhetoric or advertising campaigns," he proclaimed. "You need forces on the ground, ships in the sea and proper surveillance." Since his election to the prime minister's office in January 2006, Harper has promised a broad array of military measures, including the creation of a deepwater Arctic docking and refueling facility in Nanisivik, the establishment of a Canadian Forces Arctic Training Center in Resolute, offshore patrol vessels, and the expansion and enhancement of the Canadian Rangers. The Canadian Forces have been assigned a more robust role in "defending" Canada's sovereignty and asserting effective control over Canada's northern regions. In a speech delivered in Whitehorse on 11 March 2009, Minister of Foreign Affairs Lawrence Cannon re-affirmed the Harper government's intentions to create a more extensive role for the Canadian Forces in the North, concluding that military exercises are required to "demonstrate a visible Canadian presence in the Arctic."

In placing such a strong emphasis on the importance of the Canadian Forces in asserting sovereignty in the Arctic, the Harper government is mimicking the actions of past governments that have turned to the military when faced with northern sovereignty "crises." In response to the 1969 Manhattan voyage, Prime Minister Pierre Trudeau and his defence planners highlighted the need for a persistent presence in the North and argued that surveillance was essential to the preservation and strengthening of Canada's legal claims over the area. The American Coast Guard cutter *Polar Sea*'s 1985 transit of the Northwest Passage led Brian Mulroney's Conservative government to declare its intent to improve surveillance capabilities in the Arctic, build a Polar class icebreaker, and even develop a fleet of nuclear submarines to patrol under the ice. Both Mulroney and Trudeau released White Papers on Defence that shifted the primary focus of the Canadian military to the maintenance of Canadian sovereignty, particularly in the Arctic.

The goal of bolstering Canada's military capability in the Arctic has never been about intimidating the United States and the other circumpolar powers to submit to our national will. No defence planner has seriously envisioned a Canadian naval ship opening fire on an American counterpart or taking other aggressive and 'un-Canadian' actions to safeguard its sovereignty. Therefore, when Trudeau and Mulroney called for a stronger military presence in the Arctic, critics questioned what the armed forces could actually accomplish. In response to Mulroney's northern defence initiatives, Douglas Frith, the Liberal Party defence critic, argued:

> Take it from the sovereignty standpoint. Joe Clark has said that sovereignty in the Arctic is essentially a legal question. If so, I question why we're having a military response to a legal problem. I put a question in the House which was not answered except in a silly way: Suppose our sub in the Arctic runs into an American or a Soviet or a British submarine and we say 'You're in Canadian waters,' and they say, 'No, we're in international waters.' What do we expect the sub to do about this anyway? The response is, 'We'll log it and document it, in case we go to the World Court.'[1]

Similar opinions were voiced during the 1970s and are echoed today by the Opposition parties and other critics of Harper's defence policy. Without a probable, conventional military threat in the Arctic, do the Canadian Forces have something to contribute to the region?

Canada does not need to earn a seat at the Arctic negotiating table through military capacity. By the 1970s Canada recognized that it was meeting the requirements of effective occupation throughout its North and that it had uncontested ownership of the Arctic islands. Analysts noted that Canada would solve boundary disputes through international law, not with armed forces. Legal scholar Donald McRae has recently explained that Canada needed defence capabilities in the Arctic because "a responsible government provides policing, surveillance, search and rescue, and other services throughout its territory."[2]

Symbolic "presence" is less important than functional capabilities according to this logic. The Canadian Forces need to operate in all parts of the country and play a supporting role to other government departments, such as the Canadian Coast Guard and Royal Canadian Mounted Police. These roles, however, have been confused by alarmist rhetoric that has dominated Canadian dialogue about Arctic sovereignty since the end of the Second World War. Government speeches, from Trudeau to Harper, often emphasize the need for showing the flag, sovereignty patrols, and "standing up for Canada." It is striking that these rallying cries have been used most frequently to justify increased defence expenditures for the Arctic, rather than to emphasize governance, resource development, and other forms of human capacity-building.[3]

The role of the Canadian Forces in asserting sovereignty is often tied to the old maxim that possession is 9/10th of the law. Surveillance capability and "boots on the ground" are often tightly bound to Canada's credibility in "defending its sovereignty." As talk of a polar race intensifies and new concerns arise over the continental shelf, boundaries, pollution, melting ice and that tiny piece of rock called Hans Island, a more robust Canadian Forces presence is perceived as essential to "using or losing" the Canadian Arctic. Where is the justification to validate this accepted wisdom? A country must be able to control activities in its territory, but does a military presence really strengthen Canada's sovereignty over the Arctic?

One of the central problems in grappling with these questions is defining the concept of sovereignty. "Stripped of all rhetoric and emotion that normally surrounds this issue," political scientist Rob Huebert notes, "sovereignty is about controlling the actions of others within the boundaries claimed by the Canadian Government."[4] How does a military presence play into demonstrating effective occupation? What is the nature of the threats facing Canada, and how are expanded and enhanced military capabilities expected to meet them? Is there a distinction between what is essential to maintain Canada's sovereign title in legal terms, and desirable government activities that address the myriad political, socio-economic and environmental problems in the North?[5] The defence planners who wrote the White Paper on Defence in 1971 believed that establishing a military presence and showing the flag strengthened Canada's legal claim to Arctic lands and waters. It is difficult to ascertain whether the current defence build-up in the

Arctic is simply to demonstrate a presence or if the Canadian Forces will be given specific military tasks to improve Canada's control. Equally unclear is how Harper's government perceives the connection between sovereignty and security. If the need to assert sovereignty is the primary impetus for military activities in the region, how do Canadian Forces surveillance and presence enhance our sovereignty?

The Harper government has not publicly defined or discussed these core concepts. Recent government legal opinions are classified and cannot be analyzed, but history can help to illuminate core considerations and debates. Discussions during the first Trudeau administration on the role of the Canadian Forces in preserving sovereignty – the military's first priority according to the then-prime minister, just as it is to the current one – suggest that improved military capabilities do not translate into stronger, legal sovereignty claims. The insights that documents from this period reveal about the nature of Canada's sovereignty in the Arctic and the role of the armed forces in the region remain as relevant today as they were in the early 1970's. Defence planners and policy analysts employed by Trudeau were dealing with many of the same issues facing decision-makers today and their dialogue contains warnings and solutions that the present government must consider in developing its own northern strategy.

Sovereignty and Security in the Early Cold War

In the interwar years, the Arctic was seen as a strategic desert. Military historian C.P. Stacey noted in his 1940 study of Canadian defence policy that in the north "Generals January and February mounted guard for the Canadian people all year round" which helpfully narrowed, "for practical purposes, Canada's actual area of defence."[6] By the end of the Second World War, however, the geostrategic equation had changed. The Japanese invasion of the Aleutian Islands during the war, coupled with the growing awareness that the Russo-American wartime alliance would not survive in peacetime, prompted defence activities in remote regions of the continent. As early as 1945 the Canadian army undertook a number of exercises in the North to determine its capacity to operate in this frigid region. The results were disappointing, but Canadians could take some solace in the knowledge that no one else would be able to operate more effectively. As the wartime alliance dissolved, however, the United States encouraged active and aggressive steps to counter any possible attack over the Arctic front. Polar projection maps were unrolled and the difficult strategic position of Canada became readily apparent, sandwiched as it was between the two superpowers. Geography made Canada a necessary component in North American continental security, and its defence relationship with the United States made it a willing ally.

From the late 1940s to the early 1960s the Canadian North became the scene of large-scale cooperative military activity, culminating in the establishment of the massive Distant Early Warning (DEW) Line. Although the Canadian government expressed grave sovereignty concerns as the American presence grew in its remote northern regions, Canada's position was strengthened through careful bilateral negotiations and the willingness of the United States to allay Canadian worries about de facto control. Both sides made concessions, and these defence projects represented a major coup for Canadian sovereignty: the Americans officially acknowledged that the Arctic islands north of the Canadian mainland belonged to Canada. According to Canadian strategist R.J. Sutherland, "Canada secured what the United States had up to that time assiduously endeavored to avoid, namely, an explicit recognition of Canadian claims to the exercise of sovereignty in the Far North."[7]

Concurrently, the federal government ordered the Canadian Forces to "show the flag" and demonstrate presence in the North. Accordingly, the Canadian navy commenced annual summer Arctic cruises in 1948 and started to play a larger role in northern re-supply operations. In the mid-1950s it operated an icebreaker, the HMCS *Labrador*, in the region. The Royal Canadian Air Force engaged in aerial reconnaissance missions, while the army continued to conduct exercises across the Arctic and sub-Arctic. Whenever new defence projects were initiated in remote areas, qualified Canadian Forces personnel participated. The Canadian government did not authorize these actions to simply improve continental security; it was part of a "re-Canadianization" program with the objective of "keeping the Canadian Arctic Canadian."[8] Although the government saw little intrinsic value in the Arctic, the fear of continuing American penetration into the region brought the Canadian military onto the scene.[9] Sovereignty, though still largely symbolic, was now vested in the Canadian Forces, who replaced the Royal Canadian Mounted Police as the primary uniformed symbols of Canadian authority to safeguard the north – from friend and foe.

DEW Line stations, built from 1955-57, stretched across the North American Arctic to provide advance warning of a Soviet air attack. (LAC)

As continental defence priorities shifted to missiles and satellites, Canada's concerns about American sovereignty threats to its Arctic territory diminished. By the mid-1960's the strategic picture held little incentive for the Canadian Forces to remain active in the region.[10] Naval patrols and army exercises were cancelled, surveillance flights were scaled back, and the Canadian Rangers (a Reserve force of local residents created in 1947) were virtually abandoned.[11] With no direct military threat to the Canadian North, and without the looming presence of the American military causing Ottawa officials to worry, the Canadian Forces retreated from the area. The 1964 White Paper on Defence did not contain a single reference to the Arctic.[12] Four years later, a defence paper on the role of the armed forces in maintaining Canadian sovereignty noted that "the sovereignty of a great majority of modern states is in fact protected, not by their military power, but by international law and a somewhat more nebulous but important factor referred to as 'world public opinion.'"[13] Soon, however, the Canadian Forces returned to the Arctic in the early 1970s to counter sovereignty threats prompted by hydrocarbon development and the interests of Canada's closest neighbour and ally.

Quiet Diplomacy and the Arctic Waters

After the conclusion of the DEW Line agreement in 1955, the federal government's primary *de jure* sovereignty concerns shifted from the mainland and archipelagic islands to the water (ice) between and around the islands. "Since World War II Canada has, for all practical purposes, acquired another ocean," political scientist Thomas Tynan observed in 1979. "Before that time the Arctic Ocean was impassable and unchallengeable. Now it is a major pathway for the exchange of hostilities between the two great superpowers, Russia and the United States, and Canada is caught in between. Moreover, the fragile environment of this region opens up the possibility that commercial pollution could cause it irreparable damage."[14] The unique geography of the Canadian Arctic made it an interesting and complicated case. "The Arctic Archipelago is really a prolongation of the main mass of [the] Canadian mainland North of the Hudson Bay in the direction of the North Pole, and the whole Archipelago is a clear unity with the continental mass," a British diplomatic document stated in 1958. Rather than far-flung, scattered islands, Canada's Archipelago was more of "an island fringe off a mainland coast" far removed from the main commercial shipping routes or lanes. Its symmetrical, unitary appearance – "practically a solid land mass intersected by a number of relatively narrow channels of water"– distinguished it from other archipelagos around the world.[15]

That same year, External Affairs' legal expert Gilles Sicotte wrote that the properties of Canada's Arctic waters made them unique. They were not open to navigation without extensive Canadian assistance, and because of their ice cover resembled land more than the open seas that covered much of the globe:

> A further consideration is that for most of the year the waters within the archipelago are completely frozen and form an integral part of the land areas. The sea ice is lived on and moved over in precisely the same fashion as the land masses. In fact, the sea ice is used to a greater extent for surface transportation and for hunting by the local

> inhabitants. For practical purposes the waters within the archipelago are, therefore, completely indistinguishable from the land during most of the year.

The Arctic archipelago was physically, geographically and economically tied to the mainland. "The local inhabitants depend almost entirely on the resources of these waters for their livelihood," Sicotte noted.[16] Yet as late as the 1950s senior Canadian officials acknowledged that Canada had not clearly formulated its position with regard to sovereignty over the waters of the Arctic basin and the channels between its Arctic islands, both from "narrow national" and international points of view.[17] This clarification would take decades to realize.

The nature and extent of Canada's claims to the waters had always been ambiguous. The sector theory introduced in the early twentieth century – which theoretically extended Canadian control over all the lands and waters in a pie-shaped wedge between the 141st and 60th meridians running up to the North Pole – never became official government policy, but was held in reserve as a possible way to bolster Canada's case.[18] The voyages of British explorers formed the original basis for Canada's claims in the far north, and at the time their concern was with land, not water. Joseph-Elzéar Bernier's 1909 declaration also referred only to lands and islands.[19] Over time, however, Canada became increasingly preoccupied with how far its jurisdiction could extend over northern waters.

While postwar military activities bolstered Canada's legal claims to the mainland and islands of the archipelago, there was no foreign recognition of Canadian sovereignty over Arctic waters beyond the three mile territorial sea. Resource constraints severely impeded Canadian naval operations in the Arctic in the early postwar period; meanwhile, U.S. Navy and Coast Guard icebreakers (sometimes with Canadian observers aboard) gained operational experience in northern waters carrying supplies and materials to new defence projects in the region.[20] The Department of External Affairs (DEXAF) worked diligently to ensure that these annual naval re-supply missions did not threaten Canadian control. Canadian officials also carefully monitored all publicity emanating from these missions, lest it create some public doubt about Canadian sovereignty.[21]

By agreement, U.S. vessels supplying the DEW Line had to apply for and receive Canadian waivers under the Canada Shipping Act before they could proceed with their missions.[22] In 1957, Captain T. H. Pullen, then serving as the commanding officer of the Canadian military icebreaker *Labrador*, was appointed as U.S. Navy task group commander for the annual sealift. One of his jobs was to ensure that three U.S. coast guard ships safely navigated the Northwest Passage. "In those days, Canadians did not react as they would now to foreign encroachment in their Arctic waters," he reminisced thirty years later; "but they had no cause. Great care was taken by the United States to respect Canadian interests. The joint security interest in the DEW line provided a shared incentive to devise arrangements that would avoid injury to either national position."[23] Indeed, journalists heralded Canada's supply efforts as a "big gain for sovereignty" that "immeasurably strengthens our claim to the waters between the islands."[24] The simple fact that these vessels had to pass through Canadian coastal waters to supply DEW Line stations on Canadian land made this a relatively uncontroversial arrangement.

After the question of territorial waters was raised in the House of Commons on 5 April 1957, DEXAF lawyer Jim Nutt explained that the seaward boundary of the internal and contiguous water boundaries of the Archipelago remained unclear. "There would seem to be no question about the territoriality of Bellot Strait between the Boothia Peninsula and Somerset Island since I understand it is only about a mile wide," he noted. "On the other hand Lancaster and Viscount Melville Sounds constitute the main waterway through the Arctic Archipelago and are approximately 70 miles wide at the eastern entrance and 100 at the western entrance. The establishment and recognition of the territoriality of these waters would seem to be tantamount, at least by implication, to the establishment and recognition of a claim to all the internal waters of the Archipelago." Although Canada had insisted on a U.S. waiver for transit of its Arctic waters, Nutt carefully observed that this was "not inconsistent with the waters of the Archipelago being high seas outside the normal territorial limit, for instance three miles from the baseline, since I understand that the ships in question would be entering waters within the three-mile limit and so in any event would technically require to apply for a waiver under the *Canada Shipping Act*."[25]

What waters did – or could - Canada actually claim? Senior government officials in Ottawa scrambled to find out. Before Canada formulated an official position, it had to ponder national goals and the international implications of claiming the waters and ice, as well as the underlying seabed and air space above. "In addition to any advantages," chairman of the Advisory Committee on Northern Development Gordon Robertson explained, "sovereignty would imply certain obligations including the provision of such services as aids to sea and air navigation, the provision of any necessary local administration, and the enforcement of law"—in other words, the expenditure of public money. In response, the Soviet Union might either reject the claim or use it as a pretext to assert sovereignty over an even larger sector north of its mainland, and other countries would likely also refuse to recognize a Canadian claim.[26] Indeed, reporters cautioned that "the Russians would like nothing better than to stir up a row between Uncle Sam and Canada over who owns the Arctic ice and sea on our side of the North Pole."[27]

External Affairs officials knew that pushing for clarity and trying to secure American and other countries' acquiescence to Canadian claims was not a straightforward matter. The legal division reported to the acting undersecretary on 23 February 1954 that:

> it is not necessary to solicit formal admissions of our sovereignty from other governments. In fact, such solicitation carries an implication that we may have some doubts regarding our sovereignty in the absence of formal recognition by foreign states. Since our intention has already been sufficiently demonstrated, Canadian sovereignty over Arctic areas only remains to be perfected by the continuous and actual exercise of state activity in this region. In time, this will be sufficient to confer an absolute title in international law.... From our point of view, it would seem to be desirable and advisable to rely on this peaceful and effective method of perfecting our claim to sovereignty over the whole of our Arctic region and avoiding any possibility of provoking communications from foreign governments which might deliberately refuse ... to recognize our formal claim to

> sovereignty over the whole or part of this region.... [It] would seem to be unwise on our part to run the risk of provoking another government to assert such a denial or register a reservation with respect to our claim.[28]

Provoking protests from foreign countries would hardly serve Canada's national interests, and the longer Canada exercised authority the stronger its claims would become. "It is almost a certainty that the United States would not concede such a claim and that the world at large would not acquiesce in it," a legal appraisal at External Affairs explained in 1958. "It would therefore seem preferable not to raise the problem now and to implicitly reserve our position in granting permission for the U.S. to carry out work in Canadian territorial waters." It made more sense for Canada to reach agreements with the U.S. on "the unstated assumption that 'territorial waters' in that area means whatever we may consider to be Canadian territorial waters, whereas the U.S. does likewise." The difference of opinion would not create difficulty "until something happens which might involve Canada asserting jurisdiction over an area which the U.S. considers to be high seas. Then, and only then, would it be necessary for Canada to state its claim or by implication from silence, relinquish it or seriously weaken it."[29]

When Ivan Head, a lawyer with the Department of External Affairs, surveyed the official record in 1963, he was dismayed. "Few Canadian policies have been so inconsistently or unhappily interpreted over the years as that pertaining to the Arctic frontiers," he lamented. In 1946, Lester Pearson, then Canadian ambassador to the US, had written that Canada's northern territory included "the islands and frozen seas north of the mainland between the meridians of its east and west boundaries extended to the North Pole." A decade later, Jean Lesage, the Minister of Northern Affairs, stated that Canada's sovereignty extended to all the Arctic islands, but that "the sea, be it frozen or in its natural liquid state, is the sea; and our sovereignty exists over the lands and over our territorial waters." Did this include the Arctic waters? Prime Minister Louis St. Laurent responded a few months later that his government considered the waters between the Arctic Islands to be "Canadian territorial waters."[30]

The election of John Diefenbaker's Conservatives to a minority government in 1957 and a majority in 1958 suggested that the federal government would pay more attention to establishing a Canadian position on the Arctic waters. In June 1958, Conservative Minister of Northern Affairs Alvin Hamilton clarified the position and claimed that "the area to the north of Canada, including the islands and waters between the islands and areas beyond, are looked upon as our own, and there is no doubt in the minds of this government, nor do I think in the minds of former governments of Canada, that this is national terrain." On 7 July 1958, Hamilton told the House of Commons that Canada could only retain control of the region through effective occupation.[31] Important questions remained unanswered. What were the actual boundaries? Who was effectively occupying the Arctic waters? Would the military again be tasked to show the flag? In the mid-1950s, the Royal Canadian Navy pondered whether, to bolster Canada's claims, it should or could build nuclear-powered submarines or icebreakers.[32] Instead, the Navy decided to get out of the Arctic game altogether. The RCN's priorities lay with NATO anti-submarine operations and investing in Arctic capabilities would be costly and require a significant change in focus. In April 1958 the Navy transferred its icebreaking responsibility to the Department of Transport and forgot about the Arctic waters. Had a naval capacity in the northern waters been developed at this point the threat posed by the Manhattan voyages would have been greatly diminished.

Prime Minister John Diefenbaker reiterating his Northern Vision in the new town of Inuvik, 1961 (LAC)

The growing strategic importance of these waters also created some complex problems for Canada and its attempt to assert its sovereignty over the area. In 1958, the nuclear-powered submarine U.S.S. *Nautilus* crossed under the polar ice cap in its voyage from Pearl Harbor to

Iceland. International law expert Maxwell Cohen wrote in Saturday Night magazine:

> now that the *Nautilus* has made the full undersea voyage that Jules Verne visualized for his readers and Sir Hubert Wilkins actually planned a few years ago - with much less manageable equipment – the Arctic seas have become another arena among the many that now provide military and strategic vantages in the continuing contest of East and West. For it will not be lost upon the Russians that atomic-fueled submarines can roam beneath the ice pack, not only under that portion of the pack regarded as the North American "sector" but also within the Soviet angle of "presumed" authority as well. How dangerous this may be to either side, with submarine-launched missiles such as the Polaris having a 1,500-mile range - and perhaps in the near future a 2,000 and 3,000-mile range – requires no great military imagination to understand. So the Arctic waters, now with Arctic air-space, are all a potential battleground while the romance of exploration and dog-team yields to the cruder demands of polarized power.[33]

Canada could not pretend to exist in a vacuum, its sovereignty issues divorced from geostrategic considerations. Friend and foe alike were taking a greater interest in the Arctic waters.

Soon U.S submarines along with other allied and enemy submarines were traveling under the Arctic ice, undoubtedly transiting waters claimed by Canada, including the Northwest Passage. The Arctic Ocean, covered by a dense (and noisy) ice pack, offered protection from aerial surveillance and sonar detection. Commander James F. Calvert of the U.S.S. *Skate* told public audiences that the U.S. could "best hold its world leadership by gaining superiority in the Arctic," and that the Arctic waters would soon become an "entirely nuclear sub-ocean."[34] Although Calvert did not speak for the United States government and this was not official policy, it reflected U.S. strategic interests in the region.

The status of the waters within Canada's "sector" (between 60° and 141° west longitude running up to the pole) was catapulted to the forefront of internal discussions about Canadian sovereignty. Canada had not adopted a clear position on the status of these waters beyond the territorial sea (having adopted a longstanding practice to neither affirm nor disaffirm the sector theory in explicit terms), but would benefit the most if these waters were internal and subject to their complete control. No country disputed that Canada held rights to territorial waters extending seawards from either its coast or baselines that enclosed its internal waters, but there was potential for conflict about how far these extended. In the nineteenth century, the U.S. and Britain adopted a three nautical mile (3.45 miles or 5.55 km) limit on territorial waters, which became a standard in many parts of the world. By the 1960s, however, most states were attempting to claim territorial waters of 12 nautical miles (22.22 km) or more, a move supported by Canada. Under this regime, foreign ships still had the right to "innocent passage" through territorial waters, which would limit Canadian control.

In the late 1950s, External Affairs saw "little advantage and numerous disadvantages to the assertion by Canada of the claim to the waters of the [Polar Basin lying north of the Canadian mainland], at least at the present time" because "it would undoubtedly stir up international controversy." International law did not justify it, and the conditions in the region and the lack of Canadian capacity made such a claim almost impossible to enforce. The United States insisted on "free navigation" through the Northwest Passage, but optimists suggested that "quiet negotiations with the United States leading to the granting of special privileges in … these waters might achieve reluctant acquiescence from them." The Undersecretary of State for External Affairs "thought that it would be in no nation's interest to invite an international wrangle, comparable perhaps to the one now going on concerning the Antarctic, by laying controversial claims to the waters and ice of the Arctic Basin."[35] Multilateral and bilateral negotiations were the key to eventually asserting Canadian sovereignty over the Arctic waters, not unilateral action predicated on a military presence.

Gordon Robertson, the deputy minister at Northern Affairs and National Resources, conceded in 1959 that "the main interest in the Northwest Passage and other routes through the Canadian Arctic Archipelago is military" - by both the US and the Soviet Union - but he envisioned three possible events that could generate more non-military interest:

> The discovery of major resources, such as petroleum, in the archipelago itself.
>
> The closing of the Panama Canal, or even the development of a difficult political situation in Panama.
>
> The development of an open polar sea. The average thickness of ice in the Arctic Ocean appears to have decreased significantly since the drift of the 'Fram', and the development of an open polar sea within the next century, while improbable, cannot be considered impossible. This would give the polar regions an importance for shipping similar to the importance that is now becoming recognized in connection with international air services.[36]

Robertson's analysis remains as pertinent today as it was a half century ago. It was, of course, inherently speculative. Hypothetical threats to national sovereignty rooted in questionable legal claims to water (as opposed to physical security threats) were unrealistic reasons to expect an ally to concede on core legal principles. With the voyage of the S.S. *Manhattan* a decade later, however, Canadian politicians believed that they had little choice but to take unilateral action.

In the 1960s, Lester Pearson's Liberal government continued to officially endorse a three-mile territorial sea but it also announced its intention to expand its control beyond those limits. Canada decided to declare a nine-mile fishing zone adjacent to its three-mile territorial sea using straight baselines on the east and west coasts, but a sharp reaction from the United States kept the Canadians from doing the same in the Arctic. Indeed, Canada did not officially issue any geographical co-ordinates to delineate its claim to baselines in the Arctic for another twenty-three years.[37] "With the North seemingly secure, the sovereignty question could wait. Time seemed to be on Canada's side," political scientist Edgar Dosman noted in the mid-1970s. "As the years went by *de facto* occupation would result in an even more irrefutable claim to the Arctic, along with diminishing U.S. resistance to a Canadian initiative enclosing the waters of the Canadian Arctic archipelago as internal waters."[38] New challenges, however, pushed the federal government to adopt a more activist stance.

Commercial Interests and Canadian Jurisdiction

The prospect of resource development led the Canadian government to take action to secure its control over the region. The search for petroleum began during the Second World War, and large-scale exploration in the Queen Elizabeth Islands started in 1959. By the mid-1960s, an exploration boom drew unprecedented attention to the Beaufort Sea north of Canada and Alaska, as well as to the Mackenzie Delta and the Sverdrup Basin.[39] Oil companies and economists began to look at the isolated Canadian Arctic as a source of untapped wealth and potential. Great riches rested underneath the ice just waiting to be exploited. Oil companies secured exploration permits, conducted geological mapping and geophysical prospecting, drilled at a few sites, and began to prepare for the possibilities of shipping oil in the Canadian Archipelago. "This has presented the first opportunities for use of part of the Northwest Passage for strictly commercial shipping," Trevor Lloyd predicted in the prominent American journal *Foreign Affairs* in 1964. "Even if oil in commercial quantities were to be discovered shortly, there might well be considerable delay before it could reach world markets as the method of transportation is still to be determined."[40]

Four years later, the discovery of massive petroleum deposits on the north slope of Alaska by the Atlantic Richfield Company suddenly and dramatically changed the situation in the Arctic. How could the estimated ten billion barrels of oil extracted from the north slope be transported thousands of kilometers to southern markets in the United States in a cost effective and expedient manner? The oil industry immediately began exploring the option of using tankers to transport oil through the Northwest Passage to east coast refineries. In 1969, Atlantic Richfield, British Petroleum, and Standard Oil laid out a plan to send an ice-strengthened vessel through the Passage, explaining that "if successful, the test could result in the establishment of a new commercial shipping route through the Arctic region with broad implications for future Arctic development and international trade."[41] Historically, the prospect of using the Passage for shipping and commercial gain had driven countless explorers into the icy waters of the Canadian archipelago. All had failed to transit the dream passage through the Arctic waters, which theoretically would cut the distance and time to reach the markets of the Orient. Roald Amundsen made the first successful all-water transit of the Northwest Passage in a small vessel in 1906, but it was more than a half century before the exigencies of oil extraction rekindled serious interest in opening the Northwest Passage for large-scale commercial shipping.

The plans for a commercial oil tanker transiting the Northwest Passage caught the Canadian government off guard. Although the Advisory Committee on Northern Development (ACND) offered an appropriate platform for interdepartmental discussions between key federal stakeholders, such as the Departments of National Defence and External Affairs, the committee met infrequently and had done little to explore the implications of the oil and gas activities.[42] At the same time, neither the committee - nor any other arm of the government - comprehended the technological advancements that made mineral extraction and commercial navigation plausible. Dosman argued that the failure of the ACND to see these developments looming just over the horizon "must be counted as one of the great lost opportunities for a coherent foreign and defence policy in the North." At the 71st meeting of the ACND in December 1967, for example, the committee discussed a report that a hunt for oil was imminent in the Arctic waters. The report recommended that Canada develop a control system to regulate incoming foreign-owned ships and form an interdepartmental committee to review possible options and departmental roles. This group was never formed, however, and no regulatory actions were taken.[43]

In September 1969, the ice strengthened S.S. *Manhattan* slowly made its way through the Northwest Passage with a small load of oil. The voyage had broad implications for both Canadian-American relations and Canadian defence policy. Whereas Canada's past approach to Arctic diplomacy had been marked by quiet negotiations, this commercial intrusion into its Arctic waters prompted a more activist approach. "In an era of heightened concern with Canadian sovereignty across the board, matters affecting the Arctic were drawn into the public sector and

Prime Minister Pierre Trudeau dons Arctic gear in Igloolik, 1970. (Glenbow)

brought to high visibility," political scientist Thomas Tynan explained. "They could no longer be suitably dealt with through simply informal, or closed, diplomatic channels. A bold statement of national interest in the Arctic was needed to replace a merely quiet affirmation of it."[44] The voyage came at a time of increasing nationalism and ecological awareness, and it aroused "concerns that Canada's manifest destiny might be lost in the North to American multinational corporations."[45] Accordingly, the new prime minister faced a dilemma as he defined Canada's Northern interests within a broader national economic and political framework. Dosman asked:

> What priorities would be chosen in the last great area of the country not yet possessed and exploited? Would Canada seize the opportunity now denied it in the South, to lessen Canadian dependence on the United States, to undertake a truly Canadian development of the North? Would Ottawa exercise leadership in the high Arctic to maintain national jurisdiction and to develop an

> internationally acceptable approach to activity in the polar area as a whole? Or would it follow the line of least resistance: foreign ownership of resources, exploitation with massive government subsidies paying only lip-service to environmental and native objections; transportation of raw materials to foreign markets; the abandonment of historic claims in the face of American diplomatic pressure? What was once the remote periphery was now central to the mainstream questions of Canadian development and Canadian-American relations.[46]

As the "media-created perception" of an American challenge to Canada's sovereignty in the Arctic grew,[47] so did the indignation of the Canadian public. This caught Trudeau's government by surprise.[48] "Apart from the general question of Canada-United States economic and cultural relations and their meaning for the future of Canadian decision-making autonomy and identity," Maxwell Cohen observed in 1970, "perhaps no other subject has so polarized the idea of the national interest as its continuing debate over Canada's Arctic claims and plans for its future."[49] After the *Manhattan* made its way through the Passage many Canadians supported an activist approach to counter what they believed was an inevitable American challenge to Canadian sovereignty. The federal government felt pressured to create the means necessary to defend its territory and explicitly state its sovereignty over the Northwest Passage.[50] Activists wanted the abilities of the military to be improved so that it could operate in the Arctic and enforce Canada's sovereign title. Despite the loud cries of those who supported these aggressive actions, there were others, both in the government and in the general public, who supported a gradualist approach. They looked at the quiet diplomacy of the past and saw a United States that was willing to negotiate to allay Canadian concerns. Furthermore, they did not anticipate a significant amount of shipping through the Passage. Accordingly, Canada could pursue "special status" for the Passage rather than deploying its military to the Arctic for sovereignty-fulfilling reasons. According to political scientist Franklyn Griffiths, the common gradualist opinion was that "success resides not in the commitment to pursue confrontation through to the bitter end, but in avoiding a confrontation in the first place."[51]

At first, the Canadian government attempted to portray the voyage of the *Manhattan* in a positive light. Prior to the voyage the oil companies requested information on conditions in the Passage, and as the tanker made its voyage a Canadian icebreaker accompanied it through Canadian waters -- facts overlooked by many in the opposition and general public. Mitchell Sharp, the Canadian Secretary of State for External Affairs (SSEA), explained his frustration in the *Globe and Mail* at this misrepresentation, stating that "the Manhattan project would not have been possible without ... extensive Canadian input, consisting of preparatory studies extending for many years over a vast area of the North.... It is wholly misleading, therefore, to portray the Manhattan passage as a test of Canada's sovereignty in the Arctic, the issue simply does not arise." He emphasized that this was "no time for wide-ranging assertions of sovereignty - rather Canada must concentrate on specific objectives, the most important of which is the opening up of the Canadian Arctic region for development."[52]

Despite the reassuring words, fears abounded; particularly after the owners of the *Manhattan* began planning a second voyage the following year to test an alternate route. Again Sharp attempted to alleviate Canadian concerns, this time in the House of Commons. When asked if the owners of the *Manhattan* had sought Canadian permission for a second voyage through the Arctic on 16 February 1970, the SSEA noted:

> When ships pass through our waters, wherever these are, they do not seek the specific approval of the Canadian government. They are assumed to be on innocent passage and we do not question them. We assume that the Manhattan, if it is to go again, will undertake an innocent passage. Indeed the purpose of the voyage would be to find out, by way of this experiment, what conditions are like in the north. That is why we welcome it and have cooperated and given our permission in the past.

The Opposition was not convinced. Former prime minister John Diefenbaker interjected his views on sovereignty during parliamentary sessions, answering Sharp's statement with the cry: "What price Canadian sovereignty! Heaven help us!"[53] Faced with a strong public outcry and incisive political criticism, the government changed its tune and prepared a response to what had become a national crisis.

Trudeau and his advisers sought an alternate solution to a vexing political problem. The ecologically delicate nature of the Arctic and the severe risks posed to the fragile environment by oil filled tankers traveling in ice filled waters now became a convenient reason to extend Canadian jurisdiction northward. In his October 1969 Throne Speech to Parliament, Trudeau explained that:

> Canada regards herself as responsible to all mankind for the peculiar ecological balance that now exists so precariously in the water, ice and land areas of the Arctic Archipelago. We do not doubt for a moment that the rest of the world would find us at fault, and hold us liable, should we fail to ensure adequate protection of that environment from pollution or artificial deterioration. Canada will not permit this to happen....
>
> Part of the heritage of this country, a part that is of increasing importance and value to us, is the purity of our water, the freshness of our air, and the extent of our living resources. For ourselves and for the world we must jealously guard these benefits. To do so is not chauvinism, it is an act of sanity in an increasingly irresponsible world. Canada will propose a policy of use of the Arctic waters which will be designed for environmental preservation..., as a contribution to the long-term and sustained development of resources for economic and social progress.[54]

The prime minister's innovative use of environmental concerns to strengthen Canadian jurisdiction in the Arctic helped to ease lingering nationalist concerns. Trudeau's government chose to cast foreign activities, especially the actions of its closest ally, as threats to Canada's territorial integrity and the fundamental right of all humans to live in a safe and healthy environment, rather than pushing the internal waters versus international strait debate.

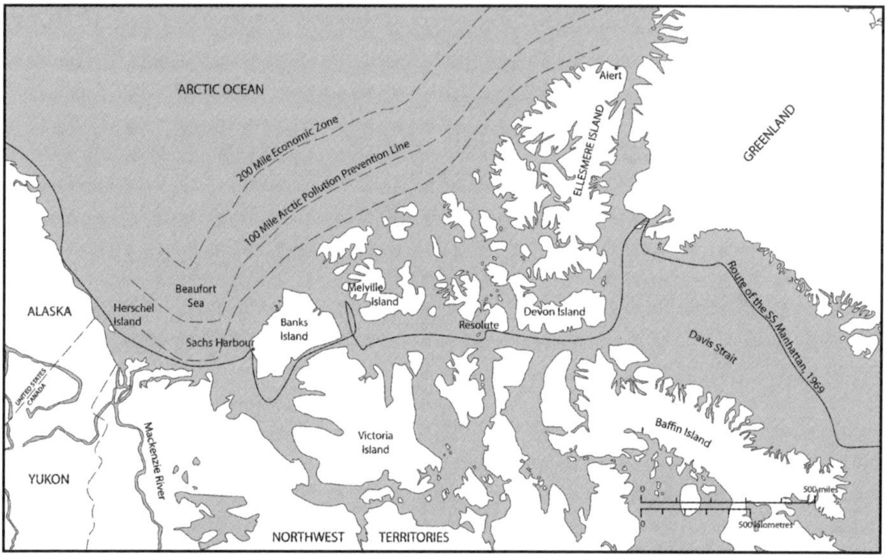

For a larger version of this map, visit www.wlu.ca/lcmsds/arctic_sovereignty_security

The Canadian emphasis on the environment had strong international and moral appeal, and the government quickly adopted extraordinary measures to protect its environmental interests. In April 1970, the Liberal government introduced two bills into Parliament that heralded a new "functional" approach to Canadian sovereignty. Bill C-202, the *Arctic Waters Pollution Prevention Act* (AWPPA), created a pollution prevention zone one hundred nautical miles (115 miles or 185 km) outside the archipelago which also covered the waters between the islands. This allowed Canada to regulate and control future tanker traffic through the Northwest Passage. "The Arctic Waters bill represents a constructive and functional approach to environmental preservation," Sharp asserted in the House of Commons. "It asserts only the limited jurisdiction required to achieve a specific and vital purpose." While not a formal assertion of sovereignty, Canada still claimed jurisdiction over the area.[55] Bill C-203, the *Territorial Sea and Fishing Zone Act*, extended Canada's territorial sea from three to twelve miles. The new 12-mile limit in the Arctic created a Canadian controlled eastern gateway in the Northwest Passage between Young and Lowther islands in the Barrow Strait. A similar western gateway already existed through the Prince of Wales Strait, which was covered by the traditionally-recognized the three-mile limit.[56] With the enactment of Bill C-203, a ship could not even transit the Passage using the ice infested M'Clure Strait without violating Canadian regulations, because it needed to travel through Canadian territorial waters at some point. Although Canada could not deny the right of innocent passage in these territorial waters, it could temporarily suspend the right of passage if its security was challenged by a threat, even an environmental one.[57]

In explaining the bills in the House of Commons, Trudeau argued that "the important thing is that we ... have authority to ensure that any danger to the delicate ecological balance of the Arctic to be prevented or preserved against by Canadian action.... It is not an assertion of sovereignty, it is an exercise of our desire to keep the Arctic free of pollution."[58] International lawyer Leonard Legault of External Affairs elaborated on the bills, stating that "Canada cannot abdicate its responsibility for the protection of its territory, and Canada cannot wait for the slow and difficult development of international law to afford that situation. Canada moreover has thoroughly tested the climate for international action against marine pollution...and has found it seriously wanting."[59] Parliament passed both bills unanimously.

Rather than risk a full assertion of Canadian sovereignty over the Northwest Passage, which likely would have been rejected by the United States to the detriment of the Canada's position, Trudeau's government embraced functional sovereignty: jurisdiction to regulate certain activities in Arctic waters. Because the *Arctic Waters Pollution Prevention Act* did not assert full Canadian sovereignty, its critics alleged that the government was actually weakening Canada's sovereignty claim. Trudeau refused to concede to the "ultranationalists": his course was that of "legal moderation" with a clear focus on the popular issue of environmental protection.[60] After all, the prime minister explained, "to close off these Arctic waters would be as senseless as placing a barrier across the entrance to Halifax or Vancouver harbour." Instead, the government committed to actively monitor the passage to ensure safe navigation by any vessel that followed Canadian regulations and safety standards.[61] Canada made the dumping of wastes illegal in the newly created pollution prevention zone, established safety control zones for shipping, set personnel qualifications, stipulated navigational aids, and insisted on standards for ship hull construction.[62] By embracing this functional approach, the government was actually laying the groundwork to apply straight baselines to the Arctic archipelago. Indeed, as international lawyer Donald McRae observed, the legislation was a "manifestation of sovereignty" that was ultimately accepted by the international community, thus helping to consolidate Canada's authority over its archipelagic waters.[63]

Commentators at the time noted that, if Canada was going to act unilaterally, it needed adequate enforcement capabilities to assert control over its northern waters. How would Canada enforce its laws if foreign vessels decided to mount a direct challenge? Would Canadian weakness not encourage foreign interests to challenge its jurisdiction? While the opposition parties supported the Trudeau government's initiatives, they worried about Canada's capacity to enforce these new regulations. During the parliamentary debate on the AWPPA, Robert Stanfield, the Leader of the Opposition, stated:

The destroyer HMCS Margaree and a Tracker aircraft patrol Canada's Arctic waters. (LAC)

> Having accepted the responsibility of controlling pollution in this area, and I agree that we should accept the responsibility, we must now make certain that we discharge this responsibility, I and the hon. members of this house will expect this government to prepare itself to discharge its responsibilities and, incidentally, to tell us how it intends to enforce these measures it proposes.... This is what this government is asking Parliament to define. If we accept that responsibility, than we must carry it out. We must not fail, not only because we do not want to look silly but because we have accepted a heavy responsibility.

In response to Stanfield's question of how Canada would enforce its new regulations, members of parliament mockingly cried out "through flower power" and "through Jamieson's navy."[64]

The Role of the Canadian Forces in Sovereignty Assertion

In the late 1960s the Canadian military undertook a defence policy review which studied the possible role of the Canadian Forces in protecting and maintaining sovereignty. Defence planners became convinced that persistent presence and surveillance were essential to the affirmation of Canada's legal claims in the Arctic. A 1968 paper on the role of the Canadian Forces in the maintenance of Canadian sovereignty stated:

> In uninhabited regions, a government should at least be able to maintain effective surveillance, if only for the purpose of asserting its authority if the need should arise. India's claim to Ladakh, never too strong in any case, has not benefited from the fact that the Chinese were able to occupy 12,000 square miles of it, and build a road across it, without the Indian Government becoming aware of what was happening for several years.

Even in areas where little direct military threat existed, the Canadian Forces needed to maintain some kind of presence for 'insurance' purposes and to assist in the maintenance of law and order, disaster relief, search and rescue, and the prevention of violations against Canadian territory. While there was already a government presence in the Arctic,

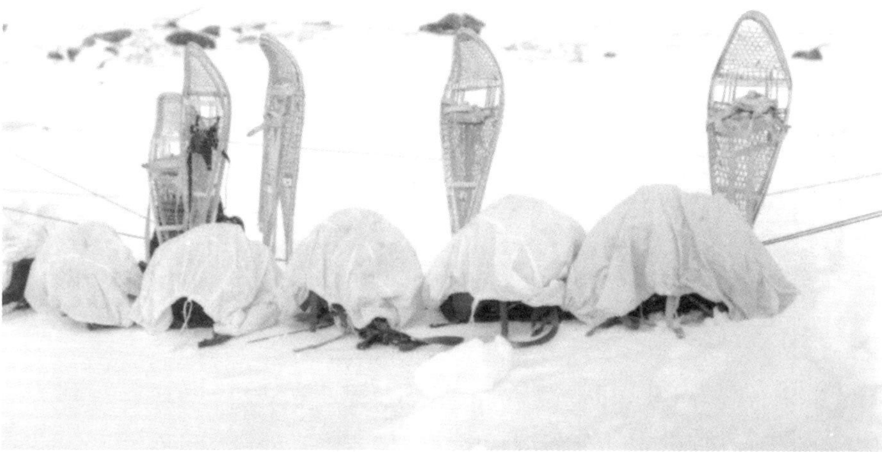

Base camp for 3rd Battalion Royal 22e Régiment during Patrouille Nocturne 72, Frobisher Bay, 2 February 1972. (LAC)

defence planners believed that the establishment of regular patrol flights in the region could reinforce Canada's claim to sovereignty.[65] In short, surveillance was considered key to asserting sovereignty.

By the spring of 1969, Trudeau started to promote the Canadian Forces' new focus by publicly declaring that his government's "first priority in our defence policy is the protection of Canadian sovereignty."[66] This was followed by Mitchell Sharp's claim that the new defence policy would be centered on "the surveillance of our own territory and coastlines in the interests of protecting our sovereignty."[67] While Lester Pearson's government had funneled the lion's share of defence resources and attention into NATO responsibilities and United Nations peacekeeping, Trudeau adopted a 'Canada first' approach with particular emphasis on the North.[68] Although the Canadian forces had the task of defending Canada's sovereignty, the specific nature of this role was ambiguous and doubts existed about the extent to which the government was ready to commit men and resources.[69]

In the following years the Departments of National Defence and External Affairs attempted to define this new role for the Canadian Forces and to determine the most effective way for the military to fulfill its duties. By 1970, Michael Shenstone of External Affairs' North American Defence and NATO Division still could not understand the rationale for the government's defence policy, and recommended that defence planners begin a comprehensive assessment of the threats to the Arctic. "We are not aware of any current intelligence estimates forecasting a need for a greater level of military surveillance and capability in the North," he explained. Public announcements, however, seemed to suggest that "the Canadian Armed Forces are moving in the direction of a significant reallocation of resources towards the North and away from other areas such as NATO Europe."[70] Why? The government insisted that there was no challenge to Canada's northern lands, territorial waters, and seabed, and that the only likely challenge was to the Northwest Passage – one that would be commercial and peaceful. "At the same time, Canada's Armed Forces had been given the primary mission of protecting sovereignty," strategist Ken Eyre later explained. "Yet, by the government's own admission, the only possible challenge to Canadian claims - and that in a very specific and restricted area - was mounted not by an international rival or threat, but by the United States, Canada's closest ally and major trading partner." Given this confusion, Eyre was not surprised that both the Canadian Forces and the broader public had difficulty discerning what the military's role should actually be in the North.[71]

"If Canada is serious about asserting its sovereignty in the Arctic, it must be prepared to pay a fantastically high price," Vice Admiral J. C. O'Brien, the commanding officer of Maritime Command, proclaimed in a March 1970 speech. He insisted that the Canadian military not take half measures in the Arctic that would only waste limited resources in pointless exercises to assert Canada's sovereignty. The admiral estimated that it would cost 2.5 billion dollars for six nuclear powered attack submarines, greatly increased air surveillance, the installation of a vast network of navigational aids, and a naval capability to escort merchant ships in the Arctic – all platforms required to ensure that the military had the minimal capability necessary to deal with potential

Canadian Forces personnel unload a Bombardier at Resolute Bay. (LAC)

challenges. "It's pretty obvious there's only one nation we need to worry about encroaching on our sovereignty," O'Brien noted in reference to the United States. "The only way to combat it is to be there and prove you care."[72]

Defence planners did not share O'Brien's appetite for investing in expensive northern capabilities, but emphasized the importance of a military presence and surveillance to strengthen Canada's legal claims. In turn, international lawyers questioned whether these military contributions actually bolstered sovereignty. In April 1969, Erik Wang, who was then at Canadian Forces Headquarters but would soon move to the Defence Relations Division at External Affairs, commented that "it is difficult to see what expanded role the Canadian Armed Forces could usefully play in support of Canada's claim to sovereignty over water between the Arctic islands." He described the problem of sovereignty in the Arctic as being based in legal, economic and political considerations. "It is not a military problem," Wang concluded. "It cannot be solved by any amount of surveillance or patrol activity in the channels by Canadian forces." There had to be a firm military rationale for the involvement of the Canadian Forces in the North, not "presence of the sake of presence."[73] In peacetime, what was the advantage in having the military take responsibility for law enforcement already covered by civil departments in the Arctic?[74]

Wang suggested that to develop any military role merely to satisfy the "optical demands" of political sovereignty "would be to build on shifting sands.... It would not be long before somebody noticed that one visit of the Governor General, accompanied by an enthusiastic press corps, can provide a sovereign presence to a remote area much more effectively and much more cheaply than 100 [Canadian Forces] surveillance overflights."[75] In July 1970 the Canadian government seemed to take this advice to heart, and invited Queen Elizabeth II to pay her first official visit to the Arctic. During her trip, the Queen was greeted by the Prime Minister and Governor General at Frobisher Bay and visited Inuit communities all the way up to Resolute Bay. The government also organized annual trips to the Arctic for foreign diplomats stationed in Ottawa. "These trips gave foreign representatives visible demonstrations of the Canadian presence in the North," political scientist P.C. Dobell noted in 1976; "even more the diplomats' acceptance of the invitations confirmed Canada's sovereignty in the area."[76]

Throughout the early 1970s the Legal Division at External Affairs continued to take issue with DND reports and policy statements that confused the "the problematic enforcement of Canada's jurisdictional claims in the Arctic waters with the problem of the legal basis for those claims." Although defence planners implied that an increased military presence in the North was necessary to assert Canada's sovereignty, External Affairs argued that this did nothing to establish the "legal validity of Canada's claims" in the Arctic.[77] DND seemed to overlook the most important question: "whether an increased level of military surveillance or patrols in the area of the archipelago waters could help to strengthen Canada's legal claim to these waters, for example, if the dispute were ever referred to arbitration in the International Court."[78]

The idea of presence developed by military officials seemed to be a misapplication of the doctrine of effective occupation, which had long been the foremost Canadian objective for the Arctic.[79] International courts had clarified the definition of effective occupation, ruling "that the display of state activities required to establish 'effective occupation' and sovereign title need not be continuous but may be intermittent."[80]

Legally, Canada did not have to furnish military forces to prove its effective presence in the Arctic; government policies had been meeting the requirements of effective occupation since the beginning of the twentieth century. If Canada's legal case was as solid as government legal opinions suggested, External Affairs lawyers noted that "there was no need for increased presence of military forces in the North merely for the sake of presence in order to bolster our legal claim to the real estate."[81] Political scientist John Gellner opined:

> Canada has established in the lands and the waters it claims as its own an organization capable of making Canadian laws respected. No other power has at present that capability. The people living in the area, whether permanently or temporarily, consider themselves governed by Canadian law. What physical presence there is of representatives of the state is no doubt sufficient, at least at the present stage of development of the region. It would appear, then, that challenges to Canadian sovereignty would have to be based not on the lack of 'effective occupation,' but rather on general principles of international law – or though this would be difficult to imagine – on historical rights.[82]

Arguably, Canada already had effective occupation of the North, regardless of its military presence.

Legal experts also suggested that while surveillance "may well be a necessary function of sovereignty," it "could not be considered a basis for or sine que non of sovereignty." Although surveillance may be required for the purposes of control, enforcement and protection, the department disputed the idea prevalent in the military that "he who is best informed has the best case."[83] In February 1971, Leonard Legault sharply criticized the sovereignty aspects of the Draft White Paper on Defence and called the emphasis on defence as solution for all of Canada's sovereignty concerns "confused and deficient."[84] He asserted that the White Paper "sometimes seems to view 'surveillance' as a sort of mystic rite rather than a functional requirement to meet well defined needs." The very suggestion that comprehensive surveillance or an increased presence was needed to protect Canada's title unnecessarily called into doubt Canada's sovereignty over the Arctic, an idea prevalent in External Affairs documents published in this volume.[85]

Although External Affairs officials were critical of the attempts by defence planners to lay out a sovereignty-assertion role for the Canadian Forces in the Arctic, most agreed with the main thesis emanating from National Defence: that northern developments called for a new and expanded role for the military. The rationale and basis for this role, however, needed to be clearly formulated.[86] In documents reproduced in this volume, External Affairs reiterated that the military needed to embrace functional roles "in specific areas where a useful job can be performed in support of other government agencies with operational responsibilities in the North."[87] Erik Wang concurred and noted that the consistent reference to:

> presence in the Defence Objectives seemed to me to be misleading in another sense. It seemed to connote something static and symbolic whereas the Government's approach to questions of sovereignty had been a functional approach, seeking to define and indentify where Canadian sovereignty interest lay (i.e. anti-pollution and safety of navigation) and shaping policy and legislation to meet what needed to be done to protect those interests.... A pre-occupation with 'presence' for the sake of 'presence' would be inconsistent with this approach."[88]

A military presence, surveillance, and simply having "boots on the ground" could do little to strengthen Canada's sovereignty in the Arctic. Indeed, emphasizing the need for these measures only cast doubts about the validity of Canada's existing claims.

Implementing the Plan

Despite interdepartmental differences of opinion, the defence planners maintained their focus on presence and adopted a strategy for the Arctic based on the premise that military activities inherently bolstered sovereignty. The new motto for Canada's Arctic patrols was "to see and be seen.[89] In 1970, naval vessels sailed into Arctic waters for the first time in eight years, initiating annual northern deployments or

"NORPLOYs" that continued through the decade. Maritime Command began Arctic surveillance patrols using medium- and long-range patrol aircraft, performing tasks such as surveying northern airfields, examining ice conditions, monitoring wildlife and pollution, and documenting resource extraction and fishery activities. The army began regular, small unit "Viking" indoctrination patrols, as well as elaborate paratroop assault exercises in the archipelago involving the Canadian Airborne Regiment. All of these activities were short-term, as were long-range air surveillance patrols (which were often limited by weather and the lack of northern airfields) and naval activities confined to select waters only in ice-free months. To provide a permanent presence, the Canadian Forces set up a new Northern Region headquarters in Yellowknife in May 1970, which boasted that it was responsible for "the largest single military region in the world." To cover forty percent of Canada's land mass, the resources at Northern Region's direct disposal in the early 1970s consisted of a small headquarters staff, less than two hundred active Rangers in units that were being resurrected after their abandonment during the 1960s, and a few hundred personnel at communications research and radar stations.[90] These modest measures provided fodder for the opposition parties in Ottawa, who chastised the government for doing too little.[91]

The benefits of defence initiatives were not confined to the Department of National Defence. The government's integrated northern strategy promised, in addition to maintaining Canadian sovereignty and security, to enhance the northern environment "with due consideration to economic and social development."[92] Concurrently, the mandate of Northern Region Headquarters to "serve as a link between [the Canadian Forces] and the northern settlements in which they operate and exercise"[93] obliged military authorities to balance traditional security needs with socially and environmentally responsible programs. At a special facility near Inuvik, for instance, the military investigated communication difficulties in the Arctic, solving technical problems to the benefit of remote northern communities. National Defence cooperated with other government departments such as the Department of Indian Affairs and Northern Development, working to build remote airstrips and bridges that facilitated community access to year-round administration and health services. These activities are documented in excerpts from annual reports reproduced in this volume.[94]

While these initiatives were helpful, the capacity of the military to act in the North was severely hampered by a budget freeze in the early 1970s. "The Minister is willing to pay lipservice to the priorities in the 1971 White Paper, but since sovereignty tasks are considered quasi-military they are deemed of secondary importance when compared to the more traditional military functions," political scientist R.B. Byers observed in 1976. Without ice-capable ships or submarines, and with no special reconnaissance aircraft or surveillance equipment, the military could fulfill few of the functional roles that External Affairs had urged it to undertake. The Forces also had limited capability to detect and combat oil spills or any other forms of pollution. By 1972, no units had been posted to the Arctic to police the new pollution control zone.[95] The government's failure to deliver on the bold plans hatched by Brigadier Ramsay Withers, the young general commanding Northern Region Headquarters, proved in the minds of two prominent historians "that the emphasis on sovereignty in the north … was a political and a military sham."[96]

Ken Eyre has observed that "the programs and projects undertaken by the military during the 1970s were traditionally symbolic but on a more intense level than heretofore attempted but still, in the final essence—symbolic."[97] Defence scholar Douglas Bland observed:

> Sovereignty missions and national development tasks, though they did not amount to much activity in reality, heaped more demands on the defence budget. [Vice Chief of the Defence Staff] Admiral [Robert] Falls recalled that following the minister's demands, "We conducted superficial acts. We flew aircraft in the north on monthly patrols… they never made contact … we flew in complete darkness, figuratively and literally, most of the time. We sent ships into the north and damaged their hulls, they weren't made for that type of action. It was a complete waste of time, but it satisfied the politicians." The CDS reluctantly ordered the CF to undertake these domestic missions and tried to plan for Canada's alliance

Prime Minister Stephen Harper, in one of his annual trips to the territorial north, outlines his plans to "defend" Canada's Arctic sovereignty. (DND)

> commitments, but no one had any idea how these old and new tasks were to be accomplished "in the teeth of a budget freeze."[98]

Army and Navy exercises had less to do with establishing a capability to operate in the North than with demonstrating "the capability to establish a presence," and it seemed less important for aircraft on long-range northern patrols to actually conduct effective surveillance that to allow the government to claim that it was conducting a rational program aimed at protecting Canadian northern interests.[99]

Although public (and thus political) concern about Arctic sovereignty wound down when the resource sector moved from tankers to pipelines in the mid-1970s, the Canadian government's symbolic program appeased the public and cost little. "In some inchoate way," Ken Eyre observed, the idea that Canada needs to have a military "presence is adequate for Canadian governments and the Canadian population at large. That presence does not imply a significant operational capability has either not dawned on the nation, or, again in the absence of a northern imperative, it does not seem to matter."[100]

In the early twenty-first century, political rhetoric has heated up once again, this time prompted by climate change, an alleged "race for resources" in the circumpolar north, and persistent uncertainty about Canada's hold on its piece of the Arctic. The Harper government has mobilized strong nationalistic rhetoric to promote Canada's interests in the region, promising to "stand up for Canada" and to exercise our Arctic sovereignty on the basis that we "use it or lose it." Using logic and language reminiscent of that adopted by defence planners during the Trudeau era, Harper has made the military the lynchpin of his northern strategy. The issues that are re-shaping the Arctic in the twenty-first century, however, are even more complex than those that generated the "sovereignty crisis" of the early 1970s. Once again, a central issue relates to the appropriateness of a military response to what most believe are non-military challenges in the Arctic.[101]

Like Trudeau, Harper's government has inextricably tied the assertion of sovereignty in the Arctic to the Canadian Forces. Simply claiming, however, that any investment in CF capabilities in the North or an increase in military activity strengthens our sovereignty is tenuous. This political messaging may be designed to evoke a strong image of government action and resolve for voters, but the simplistic equation that improved defence capabilities equals more sovereignty is in need of modification. As External Affairs urged in the early 1970s, announcements of new military infrastructure, vessels, and activities promised by the government should be evaluated according to the functional contributions they can make to meeting Canada's broad range of responsibilities in the region. If not, pessimists will have grounds to anticipate that, once the immediate perception of sovereignty crisis passes, the government will have little political basis to justify implementing a defence-driven agenda based upon the rhetoric of presence and sovereignty protection. This, after all, was the case in the past.

After Trudeau introduced his controversial new measures in the House of Commons in 1970, Walter Dinsdale (the Minister of Northern Affairs and National Resources from 1960-63) stated:

> As I hear hon. Members beating their breasts with patriotic fervour and saying that we must resist any intrusion on Canada's fundamental rights in the Arctic

> – the Minister of National Defence said just a moment ago that we are reinforcing our military in the Arctic to the tune of some 50 personnel – I received an impression similar to that which Don Quixote created when he was tilting at windmills.[102]

As the federal government again leans on the Canadian Forces to "defend" Canada's Arctic sovereignty, politicians, defence planners, scholars, and journalists should be cognizant of earlier debates that both complicated and clarified core issues. "Sovereignty is not a magic word which automatically requires or justifies a certain military set-piece," Erik Wang noted. "It is rather the political and territorial framework within which a state exists and functions. It is not made up of, or protected by symbols, tokens or gestures."[103] If Canada wants to situate the Canadian Forces in an integrated Northern strategy that supports security, sovereignty, and sustainable development in the region, the military's role must be clearly articulated. Is the rationale of the need for a military "presence" justified, or is it prejudicial to Canadian sovereignty? What functional roles should the Canadian Forces assume within the broader suite of government responsibilities in the Arctic? How can investments in the military support and contribute to governance and development in the region? If pithy political rhetoric like "use it or lose it" is allowed to frame the issues and justify military involvement, Canadians may not engage the substantive issues raised in earlier debates. The stakes are too high, and the circumpolar world is changing too rapidly, for Canadians to tilt at windmills in the twenty-first century.

The Documents

This documentary collection is intended to introduce scholars and policy makers to the main contours of the debate about the Canadian Forces' role, mission, and contributions to Arctic sovereignty from 1968-1974. Recently declassified documents, which reveal insight into subjects about which subsequent documentation remains classified, are separated thematically rather than chronologically to show the evolution of ideas, expectations, and proposed solutions that dominated discussions leading up to and surrounding the release of *Defence in the 70s* (the 1971 White Paper on Defence). Although the majority of the documents are from the Department of External Affairs and the Department of National Defence, excerpts from parliamentary committee and House of Commons debates also reveal political thinking on Arctic sovereignty and security.

The first section, "A New Focus for the Canadian Armed Forces," includes three foundational documents on the role of the Canadian military in the maintenance of Canadian sovereignty from 1968 and the influential criticism of the military's new focus that E.B Wang wrote in April 1969. These papers include initial attempts to define sovereignty and the possible roles the armed forces could play in strengthening Canadian claims. They acknowledged that the nature of sovereignty changed, at least in the Western world, as nations rejected old forms of gunboat diplomacy in favour of diplomatic alternatives. National Defence documents also attempt to detail Canada's position vis-à-vis the United States and promote the idea that any violations of Canadian territory would be prevented by the United States. There is little mention of the type of threat posed by the commercial interests of Canada's southern neighbour.

The second section, "The *Manhattan*, Sovereignty and the Canadian Response," includes documents that cover the reaction to the voyage of the *Manhattan* and the long term implications it would have on Canadian sovereignty. The different options available to Canada for the protection of its sovereignty are also presented, including the pros and cons of taking unilateral action in the Arctic. "Preparing a Plan for the Canadian Armed Forces," the third section, presents the wave of defence planning that followed Trudeau's announcement that the primary role of the Canadian Forces would be protecting Canadian sovereignty. These documents discuss threat assessments, possible responses, and military resources. They also propose roles that the Canadian Forces should assume, as well as cooperation with other federal departments. Concurrently, External Affairs officials explored the rationale for increased military activity in the Arctic, particularly the alleged necessity of maintaining an armed forces presence in the region. They also debated meanings of sovereignty and jurisdiction. Although official assessments agreed that Canada needed to enforce its new regulations and jurisdiction, there was no clear consensus on how to go about doing this.

The fourth section, "The Canadian Armed Forces, Government Departments and the Functional Requirements of Sovereignty," reveals interdepartmental discussions on the need for what is now called a "whole of government" approach, and includes a list of functional requirements for Arctic sovereignty. The fifth, "The White Paper on Defence," illuminates reactions from External Affairs to the draft federal policy document on defence. These sources lament defence planners' imprecise definitions of sovereignty and their loose treatment of concepts like security, effective control and effective occupation. "Deploying the Forces," the sixth and final section, includes excerpts from House of Commons debates and reports on what the military actually did in the Arctic before and after the release of the 1971 White Paper.

Arctic security specialist Rob Huebert has provided a provocative afterword that, we hope, will initiate the discussion about what the lessons derived from the documents in this volume can contribute to Canada's responses to present and future security challenges. We disagree with his emphasis on traditional security threats, given that the threat analyses that we have seen from 1968-74, like those in the public arena today, do not anticipate a significant short-term military threat to Canadian sovereignty in the Arctic that would demand a unilateral response. We also recognize the value of critically analyzing what is presented from various perspectives, and are pleased that he agreed to contribute.

Some important documents remain classified. For example, drafts of the "Role of Canadian Armed Forces in the Protection of Sovereignty," a DND document circulated in 1970, remain unavailable because of "Defence of Canada and International Relations" provisions in the *Access to Information Act*. While the absence of this document is unfortunate, given how central it is to the debate over the roles of Canadian Forces in asserting sovereignty, the detailed commentary from External Affairs provides a strong indication of its contents. Furthermore, E.B. Wang noted on 20 March 1970 that this paper was "a slightly edited version of the paper I did in CFHQ before I left" – which is reproduced in this volume as document 1-4. Given the sensitivity of the subject matter, and the decision by the Department of Foreign Affairs to not publish sections on Arctic sovereignty in the most recent volumes of its

Documents on Canadian External Relations series, we do not anticipate that additional classified documents will be released soon. The same holds true for Cabinet conclusions from the 1968-74 era, which are only partially open on the subject of Arctic sovereignty.

Accordingly, this edited collection is intended to serve as a partial but revealing source on the role of the Canadian Forces in defending, strengthening, and exercising sovereignty. Although the documents are from the late 1960s and early 1970s, the points that they raise should contribute to ongoing debate about what Canadians expect from their military in the Arctic. A more robust understanding of previous thinking on sovereignty will also help to ensure that the Canadian Forces have reasonable support and tasks when they are asked to serve in the twenty-first century Arctic.

Notes

1 Barry Stevens, "The Defence White Paper: Six Comments," *Peace Magazine* (August-September 1987), 24.

2 Donald McRae, "Arctic Sovereignty: What is at Stake?," *Behind the Headlines*, vol. 64, no. 1 (2007), 3.

3 On these themes, see P. Whitney Lackenbauer, *From Polar Race to Polar Saga: An Integrated Strategy for Canada and the Circumpolar World* (Toronto: Canadian International Council, 2009).

4 Rob Huebert, *Canadian Arctic Sovereignty and Security in a Transforming Circumpolar World* (Toronto: Canadian International Council, 2009).

5 Erik Wang, "Canadian Sovereignty in the Arctic," *Canadian Yearbook of International Law 1976* (Vancouver: UBC Press, 1976), 311-12.

6 C.P. Stacey, *The Military Problems of Canada: A Survey of Defence Policies and Strategic Conditions Past and Present* (Toronto: Ryerson Press, 1940), 5.

7 R.J Sutherland, "The Strategic Significance of the Canadian Arctic," in *The Arctic Frontier*, ed. Ronald MacDonald (Toronto: University of Toronto Press, 1966), 271.

8 Colonel Bernd Horn, "Gateway to Invasion or the Curse of Geography? The Canadian Arctic and the Question of Security, 1939-1999," in *Forging a Nation: Perspectives on the Canadian Military Experience*, ed. Bernd Horn (St. Catharines: Vanwell, 2002), 121.

9 Kenneth C. Eyre, "Forty Years of Military Activity in the Canadian North, 1947-1987," *Arctic*, vol. 40, no. 4 (1987), 294.

10 Colin Gray, *Canadian Defence Priorities: A Question of Relevance* (Toronto: Clarke, Irwin, 1972), 185.

11 Eyre, "Forty Years of Military Activity," 296.

12 Horn, "Gateway to Invasion or the Curse of Geography?," 322.

13 Doc. 1-1.

14 Thomas Tynan, "Canadian-American Relations in the Arctic: The Effect of Environmental Influences Upon Territorial Claims," *The Review of Politics*, vol. 41, no. 3 (1979), 424.

15 W.G. Lamarque to G. Sicotte, 5 March 1958, Library and Archives Canada (LAC), Record Group (RG) 25, vol. 7118, file 9057-40, pt. 9-2. Donat Pharand calculates that, in Canada's case, the close link between land and sea necessary to draw straight baselines is very strong. The sea to land ratio is 0.822 to 1, much better than the 3.5 to 1 ratio for the Norwegian Archipelago upon which the original legal decision was based. Furthermore, he notes that "that the quasi-permanency of the ice over the enclosed waters bolsters the physical unity between land and sea." "Arctic Waters and the Northwest Passage: A Final Revisit," *Ocean Development and International Law*, vol. 38, nos. 1&2 (2007), 18.

16 G. Sicotte to W.G. Lamarque, 14 April 1958, LAC, RG 25, vol. 7118, file 9057-40, pt. 9-2.

17 G.W. Rowley, Memorandum for the Advisory Committee on Northern Development, "Canadian Sovereignty in the Arctic Basin and the Channels Lying Between the Islands of the Arctic Archipelago," 16 September 1958, LAC, RG 25, vol. 7118, file 9057-40, pt. 9-2.

18 Legal Division to Legal Adviser, 7 March 1955, LAC, RG 25, vol. 4253, file 9057-40 pt. 5, notes the official position: "Canada has never publicly or diplomatically 'proclaimed' the sector theory but does regard it as one argument in support of its claims to sovereignty over the Arctic islands." The *Canada Year Book 1954* asserted that "northward Canada extends to the North Pole and includes the Arctic Archipelago between Davis Strait, Baffin Bay and the connecting waters northward to and along the 60th meridian on the east and the 141st meridian on the west." It also quoted Louis St. Laurent's comment in the House of Commons on 8 December 1953 that "We must leave no doubt about our active occupation and exercise of our sovereignty in these northern lands right up to the pole." Wershof noted on the memo that "I think the quoted articles go much too far, but I don't know what to do about it." He suggested a meeting, the minutes of which are still classified, to discuss Canada's strategy. DEXAF, memorandum re: Arctic Sovereignty, Legal Division to Mr. Wershof, 5 November 1954, LAC, RG 25, vol. 4253, file 9057-40 pt.4.

19 Pharand, "Arctic Waters and the Northwest Passage," 10.

20 Thomas Pullen, "What Price Canadian Sovereignty?," *U.S Naval Insitute Proceedings*, vol. 113, no. 9: (1987), 67.

21 For a detailed study of early postwar relations, see Peter Kikkert, "Pragmatism and Cooperation: Canadian-American Defence Activities in the Arctic, 1945-1951," (M.A. thesis, University of Waterloo, 2009).

22 J.M. Leeming, "HMCS Labrador and the Canadian Arctic" in *RCN in Retrospect*, ed. James A. Boutilier (Vancouver: UBC Press, 1982), 286-307; Louis St. Laurent, House of Commons Debates, 6 April 1957, excerpted in "Public Statements regarding Arctic Sovereignty," c. June 1960, copy on LAC, RG 25, file 9057-40, acquired under Access to Information.

23 Pullen, "What Price Canadian Sovereignty?," 68.

24 Leslie Wilson, "Canada Supplying Arctic: Big Gain for Sovereignty," *Financial Post*, 27 September 1958.

25 J.S. Nutt, Legal, DEXAF, Memorandum for File: Arctic Territorial Waters, 9 April 1957, LAC, RG 25, file 9057-40 pt. 6-2.

26 R.G. Robertson, draft letter, c. fall 1958, LAC, RG 25, file 9057-40 pt. 5.

27 "Arctic Sovereignty: Canada Ownership of Polar Islands Tacitly Recognized," *Montreal Star*, 8 August 1958.

28 DEXAF Legal Division to Acting USSEA, 23 February 1954, LAC, RG 25, f.9057-40 pt. 4.

29 Memorandum for file 500-370-40, "U.S. Request for Permission to Make Submarine Installations off Cape Dyer, Baffin Island in connection with the BMEWS Cable to Thule," 29 July 1958, LAC, RG 25, file 9057-40 pt. 7.

30 Ivan L. Head, "Canadian Claims to Territorial Sovereignty in the Arctic Regions," *McGill Law Journal*, vol. 9 (1963), 200-226.

31 Head, "Canadian Claims to Territorial Sovereignty," 200-226.

32 Norman Robertson to External Affairs, Ottawa, 1 August 1958, and reply, 8 August 1958, LAC, RG 25, file 9057-40, acquired under Access to Information.

33 Maxwell Cohen, "Polar Ice and Arctic Sovereignty," *Saturday Night*, 30 August 1958, 12-13.

34 Diplomatic telegram Washington DC to External Affairs, Ottawa, 10 October 1958, LAC, RG 25, file 9057-40 pt. 7, acquired under Access to Information.

35 USSEA to R.G. Robertson, 17 December 1958, LAC, RG 25, vol. 7118, file 9057-40 pt. 8. General Charles Foulkes, the Chairman, Chiefs of Staff, also raised concerns about foreign "sector" claims that could deny Canada "freedom of passage by sea to parts of our northland and Arctic reconnaissance would be very limited." Draft, Foulkes to Chairman, Advisory Committee on Northern Development, 12 December 1958, *ibid.*

36 Memo, R.G. Robertson for Deputy Minister, "Arctic Sovereignty," 3 July 1959, LAC, RG 25, file 9057-40 pt. 6-2.

37 Gordon W. Smith, "Sovereignty in the North: The Canadian Aspect of an International Problem," in *The Arctic Frontier*, ed. R. St. J. MacDonald (Toronto: University of Toronto Press, 1966), 236-37; and Elizabeth B. Elliot-Meisel, *Arctic Diplomacy: Canada and the United States in the Northwest Passage*, (New York: Peter Lang, 1998), 140.

38 E.J Dosman, "The Northern Sovereignty Crisis, 1968-1970," in *The Arctic in Question*, ed. E.J Dosman, (Toronto: Oxford University Press, 1976), 35.

39 Dosman, "The Northern Sovereignty Crisis," 35.

40 Trevor Lloyd, "New Perspective on the North," *Foreign Affairs*, vol. 42, no. 2 (1964), 293-308.

41 Christopher Kirkey, "The Arctic Waters Pollution Prevention Initiatives: Canada's Response to an American Challenge," *International Journal of Canadian Studies* 13 (Spring 1996), 41-42.

42 Dosman, "The Northern Sovereignty Crisis," 36.

43 Dosman, "The Northern Sovereignty Crisis," 37.

44 Tynan, "Canadian-American Relations in the Arctic," 426-27.

45 J. L. Granatstein, "A Fit of Absence of Mind: Canada's National Interest in the North to 1968," in *The Artic in Question*, 30.

46 "National Jurisdiction and International Responsibility: New Canadian Approaches to International Law," *American Journal of*

International Law, vol. 67 (1973), 15, quoted in Dosman, *The National Interest*, xii.

47 Donald Rothwell, "The Canadian-U.S. Northwest Passage Dispute," *Cornell International Law Journal*, vol. 26, no. 2 (1993), 337.

48 Elliot-Meisel, *Arctic Diplomacy*, 141.

49 Maxwell Cohen, "The Arctic and the National Interest," *International Journal*, vol. 26, no. 1 (1970-71), 52-81.

50 Franklyn Griffiths, "Canadian Sovereignty and Arctic International Relations," in *The Arctic in Question*, 144.

51 Griffiths, "Canadian Sovereignty and Arctic International Relations," 148.

52 Quoted in Tynan, "Canadian-American Relations in the Arctic," 415-16.

53 Doc. 2-11.

54 Doc. 2-9.

55 D.M. McRae, "Arctic waters and Canadian sovereignty," *International Journal*, vol. 38, no. 3 (1983), 478.

56 R.B Byers, "Sovereignty and Canadian Foreign Policy: The Need for Enforcement Capability," in *The Arctic in Question*, 64.

57 Elliot-Meisel, *Arctic Diplomacy*, 142.

58 Larson, "United States Interests in the Artic Region," *Ocean Development and International Law*, vol. 20 (1989): 167-91. Pharand explains that even foreign warships still had the right to innocent passage through these "gateways" because they were territorial and not internal waters. Pharand, "Arctic Waters and the Northwest Passage," 11.

59 Cited in Byers, "Sovereignty and Canadian Foreign Policy," 73.

60 Tynan, "Canadian-American Relations in the Arctic," 419.

61 Quoted in Evan Browne, "Sovereignty questions remain after century in the Arctic," *International Perspectives*, (July/August 1980), 8.

62 Elliot-Meisel, *Arctic Diplomacy*, 142. Eventually parliament would create sixteen safety zones and thirteen categories of ships to regulate when and where ships could travel in the Passage.

63 McRae, "Arctic Sovereignty: Loss by Dereliction?"

64 Doc. 2-6.

65 Doc. 1-1.

66 *Globe and Mail*, 4 April 1969.

67 *Globe and Mail*, 18 September 1969, A7.

68 Horn, "Gateway to Invasion or the Curse of Geography?," 324.

69 Eyre, "Forty Years of Military Activity in the Canadian North," 296.

70 M. Shenstone, "Joint Intelligence Committee 1970-71 Work Programme: the Canadian Arctic," 10 June 1970, LAC, RG 25, file 27-10-2-2 pt. 1.

71 Eyre, "Forty Years of Military Activity in the Canadian North," 297.

72 Vice Admiral J. C. O'Brien, "Address to Canadian Naval Officers Association," *Montreal Star*, 2 March 1970.

73 Quoted in P. Whitney Lackenbauer, "Research Note: The Role of Canadian Armed Forces in Defending Sovereignty," *Journal of Military and Strategic Studies*, vol. 11, no. 3 (Spring 2009).

74 Doc. 2-10.

75 Doc. 1-4.

76 P.C Dobell, "The Policy Dimension," in *The Arctic in Question*, 127.

77 Doc. 3-12.

78 Doc. 3-7.

79 This accounted for the RCMP posts that had extended further northward along the Arctic coast and on the Arctic islands during the interwar years See William R. Morrison, *Showing the Flag: the Mounted Police and Canadian Sovereignty in the North, 1894-1925*, (Vancouver: University of British Columbia Press, 1985).

80 Doc. 2-10.

81 Doc. 3-14.

82 J. Gellner, "The Military Task: Sovereignty and Security, Surveillance and Control in the Far North," in *The Arctic in Question*, 95.

83 Doc. 3-12.

84 Doc. 5-2.

85 Docs. 5-1, 5-2, and 5-4.

86 Doc. 3-12.

87 Doc. 3-8.

88 Doc. 3-14.

89 Wain King, "New Look for Arctic Patrols: To See and Be Seen," *Ottawa Journal*, 3 April 1971.

90 Ron Purver, "The Arctic in Canadian Security Policy, 1945 to the Present," in *Canada's International Security Policy*, ed. D.B. DeWitt and D. Leyton-Brown (Scarborough: Prentice-Hall, 1995), 87-89; Eyre, "Forty Years of Military Activity in the Canadian North," 297. In April 1974, the effective strength of the Canadian Rangers in the Yukon and NWT was 163 – a sharp contrast to the documented strength of 407 which Mobile Command had suggested on handover in 1971. Northern Region Headquarters to Director Militia (DMIL), 11 April 1974, Canadian Rangers National Authority file "Canadian Rangers 1974."

91 See, for example, docs. 2-16 and 2-17.

92 *Northern Canada in the 70's*, (Ottawa, 1970). For a comprehensive reflection on the overlapping aims between DIAND and DND in this era see James Scott Bryce, "Security Considerations in the Canadian Arctic," (M.A. thesis, Queen's University, 1975).

93 Major-General David Huddleston in *The Arctic: Choice for Peace and Security*, ed. Thomas R. Berger (West Vancouver: Gordon Soules Book Publishers, 1989), 179. See also G.G. Bell, "The Armed Forces and the Civil Authority: 2 Aiding National Development," *Behind the Headlines*, vol. 31, nos. 7-8 (December 1972).

94 Docs. 6-2, 6-3, 6-5, 6-6, 6-8, 6-9, 6-15.

95 House of Commons Debates, 12 June 1972.

96 J.L. Granatstein and Robert Bothwell, *Pirouette: Pierre Trudeau and Canadian Foreign Policy*, (Toronto: University of Toronto Press, 1990), 257. On Withers' plans, see doc. 6-1.

97 Kenneth C. Eyre, "Custos Borealis: The Military in the Canadian North," (Ph.D. thesis, University of London-King's College, 1981).

98 Douglas Bland, *Chiefs of Defence*, (Toronto: Canadian Institute of Stratetgic Studies, 1995), 232-33.

99 Eyre, "Custos Borealis."

100 Eyre, "Custos Borealis."

101 Eyre, "Forty Years of Military Activity in the Canadian North," 297.

102 House of Commons Debates, 17 April 1970.

103 Doc. 3-12.

1 A New Focus for the Canadian Armed Forces

1-1. Arthur Kroeger, DND, "The Canadian Forces and the Maintenance of Canadian Sovereignty," [6 August 1968].[1]

Aim

In the context of the current review of Defence Policy there has been a certain amount of discussion of the requirement for Canadian armed forces that arises from the need to maintain Canadian sovereignty. The purpose of this paper is to examine, first, the concept of "maintaining sovereignty", and secondly, the extent to which this concept can provide a guide to Canada's requirement for various kinds of armed forces.

Sovereignty and the Use of Force

The concept of sovereignty is a complex one, with ramifications that extend to some of the more difficult aspects of political theory and international law. Some authorities consider that, with the evolution of various forms of Liberal democracy and close interdependence among nation states, sovereignty has lost much of its usefulness as a concept, and that it is generally preferable to think in terms of rights and obligations of governments. In the contemporary era, sovereignty has become a relative rather than absolute concept. Whenever a state assumes obligations in relation to other states, whether by joining an international organization, signing a treaty, or even giving an oral undertaking that it regards as binding, it thereby reduces its sovereignty. It follows from this that there is today no such thing as a fully sovereign

1 Copy attached to J.S. Nutt, Legal Division to Defence Liaison Division, DEXAF, "Department of National Defence on the Canadian Forces and the Maintenance of Canadian Sovereignty," 2 August 1968, LAC, RG 25, vol. 10322, file 27-10-2-2 pt.1. Originally classified as "Confidential." There is no date on the original document, but Captain (Navy) J.P. Coté noted the date of the paper in a subsequent letter. Coté to J. Harris, Politico-Military Affairs, Department of External Affairs, 6 May 1969, LAC, RG 25, vol. 10322, file 27-10-2-2 pt.1.

state. While it may be true, as the present French Government maintains, that a state can never be absolutely bound, and retains a formal right to repudiate its obligations, common prudence and the dictates of national interest place sever limitations on the extent to which this right can in practice be exercised.

For the purposes of this paper, the following definition of sovereignty has been adopted:

> The right of a state freely and at its own discretion to decide its internal and external affairs without violating the rights of other states or the principles and rule of international law.[2]

Under the doctrine of the sovereign equality of state, every state possesses this residual right in equal measure and is entitled to have its rights respected by other states. In practice, of course, the extent to which states are able to exercise their right to determine their own affairs varies considerably from case to case, depending upon the constraints of national interest and the resources – financial, technological, military, and other – at the disposal of any particular state. Nevertheless, it is a notable feature of the post-war world that states have been somewhat more willing to observe at least the forms of international conduct, and to refrain from forcibly violating the rights of others, than in most previous period of history. Wars are still common enough in various parts of the world but overt gunboat diplomacy has to some extent fallen into disrepute. The sovereignty of the great majority of modern states is in fact protected, not by their own military power, but by international law and a somewhat more nebulous but important factor commonly referred to as "world public opinion". A supplementary and somewhat more traditional source of protection is the risk to a would-be violator that his action may attract the intervention of some powerful third country.

The function of national armed forces is to enable a government to exercise its rights internally and externally, in situation when law, convention, and the protection of others prove inadequate. Most

2 C. Wilfred Jenks: *Law in the World Community*. Although Jenks quotes this definition with approval, he acknowledges that its wording is mainly drawn from the text book on *International Law* of the Institute of Law and Science of the U.S.S.R.

commonly, of course, armed forces are maintained to defend against attack, insurrection, or military blackmail, which represent – singly or in combination – the most serious possible challenges to the sovereignty of a government. Where no such threat exists, a government may still find it worthwhile to maintain some kind of armed forces – although probably on a fairly small scale – for insurance purposes, and to perform certain functions such as assisting in the maintenance of law and order, disaster relief, search and rescue, and preventing casual violations of national territory.

In most Western countries, problems related to the maintenance of sovereignty are generally of fairly limited dimensions. In Western Europe and Japan, for example, such problems would be viewed primarily in terms of internal security, and a number of these countries maintain special paramilitary forces to deal with riots and civil disorders. A comparable role is carried out in the U.S. by the National Guard. Canadian Governments to date have not considered it necessary to create forces for the express purpose of maintaining internal security and have relied on the armed forces in those situations when there was a need to supplement the regular police forces. While there have fortunately been relatively few such situations in the past 30 years, it is a reasonable assumption that Canadian Governments would generally consider it desirable to be able to maintain some kind of forces – whether militia or regular – to assist in making their authority effective if the need should arise.

Canadian Territorial Sovereignty

Aside from the requirement to maintain internal security, there are two general reasons why it is necessary for considerations of sovereignty to receive special attention in a Canadian context. The first was summed up in Prime Minister [William Lyon Mackenzie] King's remark that, "if some countries have too much history, Canada has too much geography." Canada's geographic limits include vast areas that are virtually uninhabited, and there are obvious reasons why it is desirable for Canadian Governments to exercise some measure of surveillance over them. Additional factors are extensive continental shelf off Canada's coast – the resources of which are legally Canada's – and the regular use of waters adjoining Canada by foreign fishing fleets.

In order for a state to maintain its territorial claims, it is desirable if not essential for one or more of the following conditions to have been met:

a. An effective national presence should have been established in the territory in question. No one is likely to lay claim to the Province of Alberta for the very good reason that it is indisputably populated by Canadian citizens. If Canada had similarly been in possession of the parts of the Alaskan panhandle that it claimed at the turn of the century, it would have been in a much stronger position in its dispute with the U.S. As further examples, the first entry of Canadian warships into Hudson Bay in 1948, the establishment of weather and research stations in various remote regions, and the presence of RCMP [Royal Canadian Mounted Police] detachments in the Arctic could all be construed as being, in different ways, assertions of Canadian sovereignty.
b. In uninhabited regions, a government should at least be able to maintain effective surveillance, if only for the purpose of asserting its authority if the need should arise. India's claim to Latah, never too strong in any case, has not benefited from the fact that the Chinese were able to occupy 12,000 square mile of it, and build a road across it, without the Indian Government becoming aware of what was happening for several years.
c. A government should be able to bring to bear at least a certain minimum of force if a violation of its territory is attempted. There are two aspects to this point. So far as violations by individuals – smugglers and fishermen, for example – are concerned, the degree of forces that is required to repel them is relatively small and well within the capabilities of virtually all states. The situation with regard to violations by other governments is rather different. Unless sufficiently large military forces can be brought to bear to defeat the violation, the only point of using force at all is to prevent a fait accompli and to call into play "non-military" factors such as world opinion or intervention of third countries. In effect, this is a sort of "plate glass window" concept for the use of armed forces. Belgium's

> resistance in 1914 was a major factor in turning sentiment against Germany in a number of counties, with consequences that were particularly important in relation to British participation in the war. India was deterred from seizing Goa for a number of years because, although the Portuguese forces in the colony were relatively weak, their mere existence meant the Indians would have to shoot and kill to achieve their objective.

So far as Canada is concerned, the likelihood that another state would try to seize Canadian territory by force is remote. Some kind of national presence – civilian more often than military nowadays – exists even in the more remote regions such as the Arctic islands, and Canada's present territorial claims are not disputed by any state, notably including the USSR. The institution of regular patrol flights over the Arctic could also be said to reinforce Canada's claim to sovereignty in the region. Perhaps the most important deterrent of all is the knowledge of other governments that any advantage that could possibly be gained by the seizure of Canadian territory would be heavily outweighed by the risk of provoking the intervention of the United States. Because such intervention would be dictated by the interests of the U.S. itself in most circumstances of which one can conceive, it is unlikely that Canada needs "plate glass window" forces to prevent territorial seizure from even being attempted.

Canada's problem, therefore, is mainly one of preventing occasional intrusions, whether by other governments or by foreign nationals. So far as the latter are concerned, the principal requirement is for territorial surveillance, backed up by the appropriate kinds of police forces. With regard to willful violations by foreign governments, which would most probably involve only Canadian territorial waters or air-space, these might not be an overly-serious problem so long as they were limited to rare isolated cases. A good deal of diplomatic heat might be generated now and then, but the incident would eventually be settled or simply fade away. Whether a Canadian Government should maintain more than police-type forces to guard against the possibility of such violations by other governments would be a matter of choice in the light of prevailing circumstances. Iceland, for example, eventually succeeded in having its 12-mile fishing limit respected by the British, even though it had no armed forces at its disposal during the dispute between the two countries. On the other hand, it could be argued that the British would have respected Iceland's proclaimed limits from the outset if their only alternative had been to sink Icelandic naval vessels that were enforcing it.

Theoretically, of course, it is possible that a foreign government would undertake a program of regular and systematic violations of Canadian territorial waters and air-space if Canada were completely disarmed. Presumably such violations would have military purpose and be directed against the United States. However, if such systematic violations were overt in character, there is no question that the U.S. would if necessary take forcible action to stop them (the implications of this for Canadian sovereignty are discussed later). So far as systematic clandestine activities were concerned, these could today be carried out only below the surface of the water. It is difficult at present to see what the objectives of such activities would be, or how they could have more than a marginal effect on the security of either Canada or the U.S. There is nothing that a missile-firing submarine could do from the Gulf of the St. Lawrence that it could not do equally well from off the coast of the U.S., nor is it easy to imagine what could be accomplished by missile batteries on the floor of Hudson Bay that could not be done with less hazard and expense by missiles now sited in Siberia.

One cannot of course foreclose the possibility that this situation will change at some point in the future, and that a requirement will develop for more intensive and extensive under-water surveillance than is practiced at present by either the Canadian or U.S. governments at present. This however is primarily a military question, and is most usefully discussed in terms of the alternative ways of meeting a threat rather than in terms of sovereignty – except in so far as co-operative military arrangements may involve a compromise of Canadian sovereignty. The relevant point in the present context is that there is no particular size or type of forces that one can say a priori that Canada needs for the purposes of maintaining its territorial sovereignty. The requirement varies depending upon the circumstances prevailing at any given time – as indeed the level and kinds of forces that Canada has maintained for purposes specifically related to its territorial sovereignty have varied over the past 50 years or more. All that can be said is that a requirement for some kind of forces will exist in most of the circumstances that it is possible to foresee.

Canada and the United States

The second general problem that needs to be examined is the maintenance of Canadian sovereignty vis-a-vis the United States. It is reasonably clear from the preceding discussion that, while Canada does have a basic requirement for police-type forces to prevent casual intrusions and to assist in the maintenance of internal security, the threat to Canadian territorial sovereignty from governments outside North America is relatively marginal. On the other hand, because of direct threat to North America that has existed in the past 20 years, and Canada's geographic position in relation to the U.S., Canadian Governments have been concerned to minimize the limitations on their sovereignty arising out of the defensive measures that were taken.

During the late 1940s and early 1950s, Canadian concern about the U.S. coincided with concern about Canada's territorial sovereignty. The dimensions of the emerging bomber threat were still a matter for conjecture, and fears were expressed in some quarters that the U.S. would have to establish extensive air defence installations throughout the Arctic on a more-or-less permanent basis, with the result that Canada would lose control of the regions in question. Worse still, Canada's long-term existence as an independent country might be jeopardized by U.S. pressures on Canadian Governments. From the vantage point of the present, and particularly since the bomber threat has begun to decline, it is clear that many of the fears that were expressed 15 years ago were seriously exaggerated. On the other hand, there is no doubt that Canada's strategic situation does in fact place certain limitations on the freedom of Canadian Governments to decide their own policies – i.e., on their sovereignty, in the sense in which the term was defined at the beginning of this paper.

The principle limitation on Canadian freedom of action – and it is a permanent one – is that Canada must never become a threat, direct or indirect, to the basic security of the United States. This limitation is inevitable for any small country that is situated next to a powerful one. Admittedly, some powerful countries are prepared to be more tolerant than others in relation to the actions of their weaker neighbour, as is clear from a comparison of the degree of independence enjoyed by Canada (and Mexico) with that of Finland or Poland. It is also true that the precise point at which Canadian actions would evoke forcible action on the part of the U.S. is virtually impossible to define. Nevertheless, the principle enunciated by Dr. [R.J.] Sutherland [a strategist with the Operational Research Establishment, Defence Reserch Board] remains valid: a Great Power must take whatever action is necessary to protect its basic security or it must cease to be a Great Power. This situation represents a limitation on Canadian sovereignty, and there is nothing we can do about it. Fortunately, this limitation is not a very onerous one because of the close identity of the interests of Canada and the U.S. in so far as the physical security of North America is concerned. The second limiting factor that must be singled out relates, not to Canadian freedom of decision per se, but rather to the marginal significance of Canadian defence policy decisions in relation to Canadian security. Regardless of what policy it decides to adopt, Canada is not the master of its own fate. This is partly because of the magnitude of the prevailing threat, and partly because in the present state of military technology no defence – in the classic sense – is possible against an opponent armed with modern weapons systems. Moreover, because of the predominant power of the U.S. the only critical defence decisions are those taken by the United States. If the U.S. decides that it needs an ABM [anti-ballistic missile] system against China, and a fleet of hunter-killer submarines for defence against Soviet boats, these will become major components in the defence of North America, including Canada, regardless of whether Canada participates in them or not. Conversely, there would be little point in Canada deciding to maintain a system of air defences if the U.S were not prepared to do so, since it would be beyond Canadian resource to mount an effective defence alone against a major threat.

The third factor limiting Canadian freedom of action, and probably the most important of all in practical terms, is Canadian interests. This factor is not of course unique in its application to Canada. Every country, including the United States, has a complex of interests that constrain it from adopting various policies that might otherwise be attractive to it. The weighing of possible advantages and disadvantages of alternative courses of action by theoretically "sovereign" states is an every-day feature of international life. So far as Canada is concerned, it has two general interests that have a major bearing on its continental defence policies: the interest of being as secure as possible, and the interest of maintaining good relations with the United States. It would be an exaggeration to say that, because of these interests, Canada must acquiesce in whatever the U.S. wishes to do. The United States also has interests, and one of them is to avoid bad relations with Canada. Nevertheless, Canada is the weaker partner, and its freedom of action is undoubtedly limited.

The three major limiting factors outlined above must be taken as constants in any assessment of the relationship between Canada's continental defence activities and the maintenance of Canadian sovereignty vis-à-vis the U.S. In practical terms one may take it as given that, because of these factors, Canadian Governments in the post-war period have had no real alternative but to accept the protection of the U.S. and to extend to the U.S. at least a certain minimum measure of co-operation. Unlike Mexico, however, Canada has chosen to participate actively in continental defence and to make a contribution of forces. The question that arises so far as the purposes of this paper are concerned is whether the policy course adopted by Canada is of significance in terms of Canadian sovereignty.

To the extent that a policy of active participation gives Canada a greater influence than it would otherwise have on the shape of North American defence arrangements, such participation could be said to increase Canadian sovereignty, in the sense that Canadian decisions would have a greater effect on Canada's security. There is room for a good deal of doubt, however, about the amount of influence that really does accrue to Canada as a direct result of its defence policy. On the positive side, it would not be easy to substantiate a claim that Canada has contributed many creative ideas that have been of major significance in shaping continental defence arrangements. It would be unrealistic, of course, to expect that Canada's role could be anything like as important as that of the U.S. Nevertheless, the record lends some support to the criticism that Canada at times places more emphasis on the formality of consultation than on the substance of what it is consulted about.

In terms of negative decisions, Canadian influence has admittedly been greater. There have been a number of instances in which, because Canadian territory was involved, Canada was able to exercise a veto power. The significance of these decisions should not be under-estimated, since they probably did contribute – in ways that will be examined later - to the maintenance of Canadian sovereignty. It would, however, be a rather extraordinary argument to claim that Canada's ability to prevent various defence arrangements from being made on or over Canadian territory is actually greater because Canada makes an active contribution to North American defence. This line of argument would imply that the U.S. is less respectful of the sovereign rights of its passive allies than it is of the rights of those countries that co-operate with it actively. There is little in the peacetime record of the U.S. dealings with countries such as Spain, Iceland, Mexico, or Japan to suggest that this is so. It would in fact be reasonable to assume that the U.S. would if anything be more careful to respect the formal sovereignty of those countries whose willingness to continue as allies could not be taken for granted. The most that can be claimed, therefore, is that Canada's occasional refusals to accept U.S. proposals may in some cases have caused less ill-will because of Canada's demonstrated willingness to bear a part of the burden of defending North America. Generally speaking, however, the limits on Canada's veto power are dictated mainly by Canadian interests, and are only marginally related to Canada's contribution to joint arrangements.

It seems fair to say that the influence Canada gains by its policy of active rather passive co-operation with the U.S. in continental defence is of significance mainly in relation to points of detail, and at best serves only to mitigate the effects of the three general factors limiting Canadian sovereignty that were identified earlier. What Canada does accomplish by its policy of active co-operation, however, is:

a. To minimize the extent of the U.S. military presence in Canada, and to provide for the defence of a substantial part of Canadian territory and approached by Canadian forces. This is done, not only by the provision of military units such as air squadrons, but also by providing trained personnel to man certain installations such as the SOSUS [Sound Surveillance System][3] and SPADATS [Space Detection and Tracking System][4] units that the U.S. considered it desirable to establish in Canada.

b. To underline the fact that U.S. activities involving Canadian territory – e.g., the operation of the DEW [Distant Early Warning] line stations, which are nominally under Canadian command – are being carried out with the consent of the Canadian Government.

c. To provide a Canadian element to participate in certain joint activities such as air defence in which the U.S. role is predominant

There is no real doubt that the three functions summarized above are important ones. By playing the part of an active ally, Canada is able to avoid appearing to the rest of the world as a mere military extension of the United States. It has also been useful for Canadian Governments to be able to reassure the public that U.S. defence activities in Canada are subject to Canadian control – particularly on those occasions when major new activities have had to be undertaken. Finally, the fact that Canada makes a contribution to its own defence is a factor of some importance in maintaining Canadian self-respect.

On the other hand, the exact relationship of these functions to Canadian sovereignty is rather difficult to define. In a general sort of way, it could no doubt be said that the three functions summarized above help to make Canadians maîtres chez eux. The foreign military presence in Canada is kept to a minimum and various institutional arrangements serve to remind the foreign residents – as the have sometimes needed to be – that they are here with Canadian consent. All of this is reasonable enough. Most countries are sensitive about preserving the externals of their sovereignty, and military relationships are generally regarded as having particular significance for the sovereignty of a state. The extent to which appearances are essential for the preservation of the reality of sovereignty is uncertain, however, and it is very doubtful whether any invariable rule can be laid down. The experience of the United States with recalcitrant allies in various parts of the world during the past

3 *Editors' note:* SOSUS was a chain of underwater listening posts across the GIUK (Greenland-Iceland-United Kingdom) gap used for deep sea ocean surveillance during the Cold War.

4 *Editors' note:* SPADATS is a worldwide system for the detection, tracking and identification of all objects in space. It was transferred to NORAD operational control, with operational command to Continental Air Defense Command, on 7 November 1960.

twenty years indicate that there is no necessary connection between the presence of foreign military bases in a country and the ability of the host government to pursue independent policies.

One of the reasons for the controversy that has surrounded Canada's co-operation with the U.S. is that the optical effect achieved by Canadian defence activities is not entirely convincing in so far as the preservation of Canadian sovereignty is concerned. Canada's contribution of interceptors represents only 5% of the total available for the defence of the North America, and the defence of a substantial part of Canadian air-space is in fact assigned to the U.S. units. The difference between the control of Canadian forces exercised by NORAD, and the actual command exercised by the Canadian authorities, has been emphasized in any number of public statements, but the distinction tends to be too subtle to be very widely understood outside official circles. A further source of confusion is apt to be that, while a Canadian contribution to the air defence forces is held to have a bearing on the maintenance of Canadian sovereignty, no such connection is perceived to exist in respect of the 20-or-so over flights of Canada every day by the U.S. Strategic Air Command – despite the fact that SAC [Strategic Air Command] has a good deal more to do with Canada's real security than do the air defences of North America. There are of course good reasons for these and other anomalies that could be cited. What they particularly illustrate is that considerations of sovereignty do not in practice play a particularly large role in determining either Canada's general defence policy or its specific contributions to continental defence. Whether this is a desirable situation or not is a matter for Canadian Governments to judge. It is open to question, however, whether the reality of Canadian sovereignty – in the sense of freedom to determine internal and external policies – would be significantly enhanced even by a major increase in the resources that Canada allocates to continental defence (whether such an increase might be desirable for other reasons is a separate matter). As was pointed out earlier, the real degree of Canada's freedom of action is determined mainly by several fundamental factors, notably including Canadian interests. The principal problem, therefore, is that of the extent to which Canadian Governments wish to be seen to be independent – by their own people, by the U.S. and by the rest of the world. This problem is not a negligible one; on the contrary, some of its political ramifications are of considerable importance. Solutions to it, and specifically to the problem of what priority should be assigned to visible independence, must however be decided in the light of particular circumstances; there is no pre-determined formula that can be applied.

Conclusions

The conclusions that emerge from the foregoing discussion may be summarized as follows:

a. In common with most states, Canada has a requirement for police-type forces to maintain internal security.
b. The geographical limits claimed by Canada are not disputed by any country at present. Canada does however have a general interest in maintaining a national presence in, and surveillance over its remote regions to deter other countries from devising claims in the future.
c. Canada could probably rely on international law and/or the protection of the Untied States for the purposes of preventing major violations of its territory, including forcible seizures, by other countries. The ability to prevent casual violations, particularly by fishermen and smugglers, would be useful.
d. Canada's co-operation with United States has more to do with the appearance than the reality of Canadian sovereignty. Considerations of sovereignty are only one determinant, and probably not the most important one, of the kind of activities Canada engages in for the defence of North America.

Because sovereignty has the nature of an abstract right, it is a somewhat elusive concept to work with. It is particularly difficult to define the concrete acts or circumstances that would necessarily detract from or enhance this right. What, for example, are the specific effects on Canada's sovereignty if a foreign aircraft enters Canadian air-space without authorization? To what extent are the motives for any particular violation relevant to its consequences for Canadian sovereignty? How much control must Canada have over foreign military installations on its territory if its sovereign rights are to be unimpaired?

A second source of difficulty is that the possession of sovereign rights is not necessarily the same thing as the ability to exercise them. A newly-independent country might have exclusive sovereignty over its natural resources and still lack the technology ability to exploit them. More commonly, states are constrained in the exercise of their rights by considerations related to their own interests. The British Government may have the right to criticize the role of the U.S. in Vietnam, but it must still take into account its requirement for U.S. support in maintaining the parity of sterling.

Because of these conceptual problems, it is probably more useful, particularly for purposes of military planning, to think in terms of specific situations and the steps necessary to meet them, rather than to address the abstract problem of maintaining sovereignty for its own sake. With regard to territorial violations, for example, it is necessary to weigh the likelihood of any particular kind of violation against the cost of being able to prevent it. There are some kinds of violation that it is clearly in Canada's interests to be able to prevent by force, others for which the use of force is only one of several possible solutions, and still others that could be prevented only at a cost out of all proportion to the identifiable benefits of doing so. That sovereignty cannot be treated as an absolute interest is most clearly illustrated by the field of continental defence, where it is potentially in conflict with security – an interest that has an equally strong claim to be treated as an absolute. What is required in practice, of course, is a reconciliation of these two, together with whatever other interests may be at stake in any particular issue. The substance, and also the externals of sovereignty are undoubtedly factors that must be taken into account in the forming of national policies, including defence policy, but they do not in themselves provide a formula for the solution of difficult problems.

1-2. DEXAF, W.M. Weynerowski to C.J. Marshall, re: DND Paper: "The Canadian Forces and the Maintenance of Sovereignty," 9 August 1968.[5]

You will recall that two copies of the attached paper were passed to us "under the table" by DND in order that we might comment on it. We sent a copy to Legal Division last Friday. That Division was asked to let us have their observations by today. Mr. [J.S.] Nutt has asked me to examine the paper in consultation with you. My comments follow.

2. The paper is divided up into three sections. The first, entitled Sovereignty and the Use of [Force], examines sovereignty as a concept. This section, which will presumably be scrutinized closely be Legal Division, appears to be a satisfactory introduction and I have no comments on it.

3. The second section entitled Canadian Territorial Sovereignty makes a straight forward and convincing case for the existence of armed forces sufficient to safeguard internal security and to protect this country's territorial sovereignty against such minor intrusions as those made by smugglers, foreign fishing fleets operating in Canadian coastal waters, etc. The observations made by this section of the paper do not appear to raise serious difficulties.

4. The third section, which takes up the question of Canadian sovereignty vis-à-vis the United States, deals with a much more hypothetical subject. In essence, the argument advanced in this section is that for purposes of defence against large scale aggression, Canadian armed forces can make only a limited contribution to continental defence or to the continental defence system of the United States which is designed to protect the whole continent against such aggression. Whether the present size of this limited contribution can be justified in terms of effectively enhancing Canadian contribution, with its strictly limited military significance, should not be increased beyond its present size in an effort to augment still further Canadian sovereignty since:

5 LAC, RG 25, vol. 10322, file 27-10-2-2 pt.1. Originally classified as "Confidential."

a. our sovereignty is at any rate compromised or at least precarious as a result of Canada's strategic position on this continent, and since
b. the concept of national sovereignty cannot justifiably be regarded as absolutely desirable but should rather be regarded as only one of several important determinants of our defence policy.

5. The paper thus argues that Canadian sovereignty in the North American context necessarily leads a compromised existence since the United States will do all it decides it must do to ensure the defence of the entire continent. Departing from this premise, which is sound enough in principle but has never been fully tested and therefore must at least partly remain hypothetical, the third section of the paper attempts to justify Canadian defence policy by stating that Canadian active military co-operation with the United States has minimized the presence of American forces on Canadian soil and has therefore increased Canadian sovereignty, and has made Canada more sovereign in the eyes of the world than it would have appeared if Canada had been a passive ally of the United States.

6. What would have been the consequence for Canadian sovereignty had Canada adopted a third option by acting as a difficult or at any rate a more independent ally is not considered. The paper tends to assume that a certain amount of sovereignty should be sacrificed for the sake of good relations with the United States. However, the paper does not explain why a more sovereign or more independent stance vis-à-vis the United States should necessarily harm our relations with that country.

7. The paper leaves a good deal unstated. …[I]t is said that Canada has "two general interests that have a major bearing on its continental defence policies: the interest of being as secure as possible and the interest of maintaining good relations with the U.S." The paper concludes that certain consequences must follow from this fact; above all that it restricts Canada's freedom of action. Perhaps the paper should have been more frank and explicit by pointing out that "being as secure as possible," i.e. maximum security, involves a substantial degree of co-operation with the United States and this co-operation in turn requires

good relations, so that security and good Canadian-American relations are complementary interests.

8. The paper also argues that Canadian defence policy serves both our security and our good relations with the U.S. Furthermore, while it is true that Canadian defence policy also accepts a limitation on our national sovereignty this limitation is only realistic in view of Canada's strategic situation which necessarily imposes such a limitation irrespective of the modalities of our defence policy. Since the reality of Canadian sovereignty is at any rate compromised (indeed the paper implies that Canadian sovereignty in the context of North America defence is a contradiction in terms), Canadian sovereignty is relevant to Canadian defence policy only insofar as that policy succeeds, or does not succeed, to enhance or preserve the appearance of Canadian sovereignty. The paper implies that a more independent stance could perhaps increase the appearance of Canada's sovereignty but that such a more independent stance is one which calls for a far reaching policy decision which can only be taken at the political level.

1-3. A Paper on DND Policy in the Canadian North, 27 November 1968 (updated 14 March 1969).[6]

Introduction

1. The DND has, primarily for financial reasons, withdrawn from most of its activities in the Canadian Arctic during the past 10 years. Concurrently there has been increased civilian interest and activity in this area. Several major exploration parties are now active in the Arctic and the new Canadian Government has affirmed that there will be an acceleration of interest in the area. It is timely, therefore, for DND to review Canada's national objectives in the North to determine what the DND objectives in the North should be and to determine what activities are worthy of consideration in the attainment of these objectives.

Aim

2. The aim of this paper is to identify DND objectives in the Canadian Arctic and Middle North and to determine what studies are required to decide the DND activities which would best fulfill these objectives. A sub-aim of this paper will be to determine the best procedure to follow within CFHQ [Canadian Forces Headquarters] to ensure that DND Arctic and Middle North policy progresses in a coherent and efficient manner.

National Policies

3. The Department of Indian Affairs and Northern Development has provided a statement of national policy for the Canadian North. This broad policy has, as its primary objective, the effective occupation and implementation of Canadian sovereignty in the Canadian territory lying generally between the 141st and 60th west meridians, northward from the 60th north parallel to the North Pole including all the islands within the Arctic Archipelago. Specific responsibilities of the Minister of Indian Affairs and Northern Development (MIA&ND), as stated in the Government Organization Act, 1966, include:

6 Directorate of History and Heritage (DHH) 79/527, Folder 2F (Sutherland Papers).

a. Co-ordinating the activities in the Northwest Territories and the Yukon Territory of the several departments, branches and agencies of the Government of Canada.
b. Undertaking, promoting, and recommending policies and programs for the further economic and political development of the Northwest Territories and the Yukon Territory.
c. Fostering, through scientific investigation and technology, knowledge of the Canadian North and of the means of dealing with conditions related to its further development.

4. The programs of the MIA&ND are therefore directed toward occupation of this territory, on meaningful economic activity and on the advancement of the people socially and politically. Specific programs have as their aim, to:

a. Stimulate and accelerate the development of natural resources.
b. Create employment and investment opportunities.
c. Ensure that the indigenous population has an opportunity to participate on equal terms with the more sophisticated transient population.

A Canadian Forces helicopter lifts off in front of a small group of Northerners. (LAC)

Defence Responsibilities

5. The policy and objectives of the Defence Department must be in harmony with the broader national policy and objectives which are essentially those of the department with primary responsibility, i.e. Indian Affairs and Northern Development. However, Defence responsibilities are not restricted by geographical boundaries as defined in paragraph 3 above. Rather, Defence interests are nation-wide and Arctic and Middle North aspects must be considered in the context of overall National Defence policies and objectives. The Advisory Committee on Northern Development, of which the CDS [Chief of the Defence Staff] is a member, has a responsibility to advise the Government on questions relating to civilian and military undertakings in the North. This committee, in its report of Government activities in the North in 1967, described the responsibilities of the Canadian Armed Forces as follows:

a. Support of Canada's external and Defence policies in the North by contributing to the maintenance of Canadian sovereignty in the Arctic.
b. All aspects of maritime, land and air defence of the North. In some areas of the North, these tasks are done in co-operation, or shared with the USA under joint agreement.
c. Defence mapping of the North.
d. Provision of search and rescue services, and assistance to other government agencies in areas where normal commercial services are not available.
e. Research into the problem of Arctic communications, techniques and equipment.

Defence Objectives

6. In the light of national policies in the North and the DND responsibilities stated by the Advisory Committee on Northern Development, the following DND objectives may be identified:

a. Maintenance of sovereignty in the Canadian Arctic.
b. Maintenance of territorial integrity.
    (1) through surveillance of Canadian Arctic territory, airspace and national waters

(2) through the ability to identify incursions into Canadian airspace and national waters by sea or air.

(3) through an active defence capability to prohibit free access into the North by land, sea or air.

c. Developing and maintenance of military techniques and expertise for conducting land, sea and air operation in the Arctic and Middle North.

d. Support of other Federal Government activities toward development of the Arctic and Middle North.

Threat

7. CANUS 68, "The Military Threat to North America," is a total appreciation of the threat of Soviet and Chinese capabilities for offensive action against North America. A detailed analysis of the findings contained in CANUS, in so far as they concern the Arctic and Middle North area, must be carried out to lay the foundations for any subsequent studies on this subject. In this regard the threat must be examined in, but need not be restricted to the each of the following areas:

a. A Direct Threat

(1) The Arctic as one of the possible routes to be used by hostile bombers.

(2) The Arctic as a possible [submarine-launched ballistic missile] launch area for operations against the North American continent.

(3) The Arctic and Middle North as an enemy landing area with an aim of tying down disproportionate numbers of the Canadian Forces.

b. Indirect Threat

(1) The Arctic as a submarine transit route for Atlantic and Pacific Ocean Operations.

(2) Intelligence gathering in preparation for future hostile operations.

(3) Clandestine exploitation of Canadian natural resources.

Levels of Defence Activities

8. The following levels of defence activities will be considered:

a. A Minimum Level to meet the military threat by the maintenance of sovereignty and territorial integrity through surveillance of Canadian Arctic and Middle North Land, Air and National Waters.

b. A Moderate Level to include the activities outlined for a medium level plus the ability indentify incursions into Canadian Airspace and National Waters. A reasonable level of activity should also be undertaken to:

(1) prohibit free access into the Arctic and Middle North by air or sea.

(2) develop and maintain expertise for conducting land, sea and air operations in the Arctic and Middle North;

(3) support other Federal Government activities with a view to furthering National Policy in the Arctic and Middle North.

c. A Significant Level which will include the minimum and moderate levels plus a significant effort to prohibit free access and to develop expertise in Arctic and Middle North operations. An increased level of support to other Federal Government activities should also be undertaken.

Activities Required for the Minimum Level

9. The activities to meet the minimum level should be considered under two categories; those activities which, it is considered, are now being performed adequately and accordingly require no further study and; those activities which do not meet the minimum level and therefore require further study:

a. Activities Requiring No Further Study

(1) those relating to Air Surveillance, in the DEW Line context,

(2) our present Arctic Search and Rescue capability in relation to the present level of commercial activities.

b. Activities Requiring Further Study

(1) The need to continue and expand research in the areas of under-ice acoustics, sea ice coverage and structure.

(2) The desirability and feasibility of providing a detection system in the vicinity of possible surface and submarine transit

routes… to obtain an indication of submarine activity in the area.

(3) The desirability and feasibility of establishing a DND liaison office with the Northwest Territories Government,

(4) the possibility of conducting frequent unit and force training exercises in all areas of the Canadian North. These activities could serve a twofold purpose by expanding service knowledge of operating in the area and at the same time exercising sovereignty rights by establishing a military presence.

(5) The desirability of disbanding or expanding and revitalizing the Canadian Rangers so that this organization may be employed in a manner to further DND objectives.

(6) Those areas in the field of Arctic communications which require further research to solve current internal and external communications problems. This study should also include consideration of the possibility of the DND contributing toward the establishment of a more satisfactory communications system.

(7) To determine what increase in Search and Rescue capability will be required to keep pace with known developments in the Arctic and Middle North.

(8) To determine the means of utilizing, to a greater extent, DND capabilities for the support of other federal agencies and commercial operators in the Arctic and Middle North.

Activities Required for a Moderate Level

10. Some of the activities listed below are now being studied. However, all require detailed study in the Northern context. Those activities requiring study are:

a. Possible Canadian participation in Airborne Warning and Control (AWAC) operations.

b. The desirability and feasibility of increased national participation in DEW Line operations.

c. Pending the results of studies required for the minimum level the desirability and feasibility of establishing some form of permanent maritime detection and identification capability in the vicinity of likely or possible transit routes.

d. The desirability of expanding the DND liaison office, possibly by creating a northern defence headquarters to co-ordinate defence activities and provide and seek advice on possible military expansion in the Arctic and Middle North.
e. The possibility of expanding facilities at existing far northern airfields to enhance our identification capability and other activities in the Arctic and Middle North.
f. To determine the advisability of establishing a militia organization to serve the area.

Activities Required for a Significant Level

11. The following activities would provide a significant level of the DND participation in furthering defence objectives in the Arctic and Middle North. However, as with those activities listed under moderate level they also require extensive study:

a. The practicability of positioning a mobile air interceptor force in the Arctic region to extend our air defence capability, particularly in the light of increasing civil as well as military air traffic in the Arctic regions.
b. On the premise that a satisfactory detection and identification system has been devised, determine the requirements for, and means of acquiring, a suitable range of Arctic ASW [anti-submarine warfare] weapons.
c. To determine the desirability of developing a series of operational bases, manned by regular forces, at strategic locations in the region, to support extensive land, sea and air operations in the Arctic and Middle North.
d. To determine the possibility of developing and maintaining overland routes, not only to improve our operational deployment capability, but also to assist in the industrial expansion.
e. To determine the means of expanding DND support to other federal agencies through the provision of air, sea and surface transportation, utilization of Canadian Forces Bases, medical

assistance and making available DND specialized knowledge of the Arctic area.

Timing and Priorities

12. DND activity in the Canadian Arctic and Middle North is now at a very low level and does not meet the minimum requirements stated in this paper. Clearly, first priority should be given to the task of meeting this minimum level of activity.

13. The studies required by the moderate and significant levels are in large measure contingent on the conclusions reached in the detailed analysis of the threat and in establishing the minimum DND level of activity. Therefore these studies should proceed as the findings of the minimum level of studies permit.

Staff Responsibilities

14. Before integration, each of the Services had staff officers within their headquarters who specialized in the northern operations and considerable information and expertise was developed. Although our present headquarters organization does not reflect any specific agency charged with Arctic problems, there are activities which can be associated with agencies in the present organization. These agencies should be tasked to conduct specific studies. In order to ensure the effectiveness of DND activity in the Arctic and Middle North, it is considered necessary that one group be appointed to coordinate and provide impetus to a further examination of this field. This group, which would be in the form of a steering committee, will be required to work with other government departments and research bodies.

15. There will also be a requirement for direct participation in the DND studies by other agencies and Departments of Government. The Arctic Institute of North America will likely be of great assistance in several of the studies and their assistance should be sought as required.

Conclusions

16. A minimum level of DND activity to meet the objectives has been identified. Some of these activities can be precisely stated but the remainder require additional study. These studies are required on a first priority basis.

17. The studies listed under moderate and significant levels should be undertaken on a second priority bases.

18. Staff responsibilities for Arctic and Middle North matters should be assigned to agencies within the CFHQ in a logical manner and these agencies should strive to develop expertise in their particular field of endeavour.

Recommendations

19. It is recommended that:

a. The defence objectives be accepted as outlined.

b. The studies of the threat as it pertains to the Arctic and Middle North and those directed toward the minimum level of activity commence immediately with OPI's assigned as follows:

Study	OPI
The Threat	DGIS
Environmental Factors Affecting Military Operations	DRB
Submarines and Detection	DERMS
Reconnaissance and Maneuvers	DGOPSL, DGOPSA, DGOPSM
Assistance to other agencies	DGOPSA, DGOPSM, DGOPSL
Increase SAR Activities	DGOPSA, DGOPSM
Rangers	DGOPSL
Arctic Communications	DGCES

c. The steering committee, to be known as "The Steering Committee on the Canadian North" under the chairmanship of the Director of Continental Plans and with representation from CFHQ branches,

DRB [Defence Research Board] and [the deputy minister's] office as required be formed. The Steering Committee on the Canadian North will monitor and coordinate the assigned studies as well as undertake those "minimum level" studies which have not been assigned to other agencies.

d. In carrying out the above studies OPI's [offices of primary interest] be authorized to obtain assistance from other government departments and research bodies and the Arctic Institute of North America as required. Authority to commit funds for outside assistance would be sought through normal channels and procedures.

1-4. E.B. Wang, memorandum, "Role of Canadian Armed Forces in Defending Sovereignty," 30 April 1969.[7]

ROLE OF CANADIAN ARMED FORCES
IN DEFENDING SOVEREIGNTY

1. The P.M.'s [Pierre Trudeau's] defence policy statement of 3 April [1969] indicates a change of emphasis from the present role of Canadian Forces within a collective security framework in Europe to a new role in Canada in protection of our sovereignty. "The protection of our sovereignty" is identified as the first of the four priorities for Canadian defence forces and the pre-occupation with sovereignty is reflected elsewhere in the same policy statement. Indeed, in his Calgary speech of 12 April [1969] the P.M. stated that Canada was to remain aligned in NATO but that "our first priority in our defence policy is the protection of Canadian sovereignty, in all the dimensions that it means."

2. If the Defence Staff is to proceed with its military planning on a realistic basis, it is important to understand what sovereignty means and how Canadian Forces can protect it. What are the "dimensions" the P.M. referred to?

3. Sovereignty can be taken to mean two quite distinct things which present different problems and must be treated differently in any realistic government policy for the use of the Canadian Forces. These two principal dimensions which this paper will examine are territorial sovereignty and political sovereignty.

Territorial Sovereignty

4. It is often stated by press commentators, and in fact sometimes reflected in CFHQ military guideline documents, that one of the objectives of the CAF [Canadian Armed Forces] is to maintain territorial sovereignty. For this purpose it is sometimes stated that the forces should have the capability to maintain an acceptable level of surveillance of Canadian territory and air-space, combined with

7 LAC, RG 25, vol. 10322, file 27-10-2-2 pt.1. Originally classified as "confidential."

an interception or "kill" capability. The problem is thus often seen as a problem of determining what level of forces activity is "acceptable" or "necessary" to maintain territorial integrity. This approach is based on a fundamental misunderstanding.

5. It is essential to recognize that Canadian territorial sovereignty is not in doubt, even in respect of Arctic islands. This claim has been made without challenge by successive Canadian governments over a number of years and was reiterated most recently by P.M. Trudeau in the House of Commons on 10 March 1969, in the following terms: "We have complete sovereignty over the islands in the Arctic and there is no equivocation about that."

6. As Prof[essor] Ivan Head points out (1963 McGill Law Journal, p. 210) Canada's claim to territorial sovereignty has broad foundations in discovery, acquisition by treaty and effective occupation. It is particularly well based in the latter, which has become the principal requirement of international law in determining sovereignty. A multitude of Canadian government activities in the North contribute to establish a pattern of effective occupation. These activities include postal and customs services, navigation, game protection, civil and criminal courts, scientific and meteorological services, resource developments, and welfare, including the monthly distribution of family allowance cheques to eskimos [sic] and other residents of the North. Even though large tracts of territory are uninhabited and rarely visited by Canadian Government personnel there is no doubt that these activities at their present level ensure for Canada good title to the Arctic mainland and the islands of the Archipelago. Under well established principles of international law it would be impossible for any other state to make a competitive claim to any of this territory and in fact no challenge has been made since at least 1900.

7. The present level of CAF activity in the North is very modest in relation to the non-military activities mentioned above. There are no more than 400 Canadian Forces personnel stationed in the North West Territories, almost all at two Canadian Forces Stations – Inuvik and

Alert. In addition there are [marginalia: infrequent search & rescue operations and] infrequent exercises: in 1968 only one, involving 40 Canadian military personnel at Fort Churchill.

8. If the present overall level of Canadian Government activities in the North are adequate to protect Canadian territorial sovereignty it is clear that these activities do not need to be bolstered by an increased level of CAF activity, for this purpose. A rationale for a new emphasis on the role of the forces "in the protection of Canadian sovereignty" must therefore rest on some other basis.

9. While the Canadian claim to sovereignty over the Arctic mainland and Archipelago islands is not in doubt, Canadian claims in respect of Arctic waters are subject to some uncertainty. Is there a legitimate role for Canadian Forces in helping Canada assert and consolidate sovereign rights over these waters?

10. The problems here should be viewed in three dimensions:
   a. Continental shelf and seabed resources;
   b. Archipelago waters; and
   c. Polar pack ice.

11. Exclusive Canadian rights to continental shelf resources are, like Canadian rights in respect to northern lands and islands, not in doubt. These rights depend not on assertions of discovery or "effective occupation" but on formal treaty provisions. The 1938 Geneva Convention on the Territorial Sea and the Contiguous Zone, which has been signed by Canada, U.S., USSR and (?) other nations, reserves for the coastal states exclusive rights of exploitation of the resources of the subjacent continental shelf to a depth of 200 meters. All of the seabed contiguous to and between archipelago islands lies within this depth. Should oil, for example, be discovered on the Canadian side of this continental shelf, as is strongly suspected, there can be no question of Canadian jurisdiction. There is accordingly no useful role for Canadian forces in protection of these rights already embodied in a formal treaty to which all interested parties are signatory.

12. Archipelago waters give rise to a problem as to whether they can or should be claimed by Canada as territorial waters or inland waters. Canada's long-standing claim to sovereign jurisdiction over a three-mile territorial waters belt has never been in question. Nor is the status of [Hudson] Bay – and the Gulf of St. Lawrence – which have been enclosed by drawing straight baselines across their mouths, thereby creating inland, as distinct from territorial, waters. There is, however, considerable doubt and even controversy as to whether, by drawing straight baselines around the outer perimeter of the Arctic Archipelago, Canada could assert jurisdiction over the passages through the Archipelago as inland waters.

13. The practical consequences of such jurisdiction would be two-fold. Many passages are wider than the three-mile territorial limits and thus as high seas give unrestricted access to international shipping whether commercial or military and whether surfaced or submerged. If a claim to inland waters were to be successfully asserted all shipping would be subject to prior Canadian approval. Secondly, there would be no automatic right of innocent passage as there now is in respect of traffic through territorial waters from one area of high seas to another area of high seas.

14. In 1963 the Canadian Government informed the U.S. Government of our intention to enclose the channels of the Arctic islands within straight baselines. This action followed upon a public assertion of the Canadian claim to these waters by Mr. Alvin Hamilton, Minister of Northern Affairs and National Resources, in the Standing Committee on Mines, Forests and Waters on 10 June, 1958. During discussions on law of the sea matters between Canada and the U.S. in 1963 and 1964 Canada advanced the claim as consistent with the straight baseline system of the 1958 Geneva convention and the earlier decision of the International Court of Justice in the Anglo-Norwegian fisheries case. The Americans expressed very strong objections to the course of action proposed by Canada on grounds that it would be legally invalid and, if unopposed by the USA, would constitute a precedent for more sweeping

claims by the Philippines and Indonesia, to the serious detriment of vital strategic interests of the USA. In light of the adverse U.S. reaction, no steps have yet been taken to implement the decision to draw baselines around the Arctic archipelago. The claim has not, however, been abandoned. Government departments have been cautioned against taking any action which might compromise Canada's claim to these waters.

15. A public confrontation has so far been avoided and a sort of modus vivendi has developed for the entry of U.S. Government or naval vessels into these waters so that it has generally been possible to avoid forcing this issue of their status, whether territorial or internal. For example, the "Manhattan" project as it has developed so far does not necessarily admit or deny Canada's claim. A Canadian Coast Guard icebreaker, the "John A. MacDonald", is scheduled to take part in this trial run of a reinforced oil tanker through the Norwest Passage this summer. The great interest and publicity centered on this project may make it difficult for Canada to continue the attempt to safeguard its claim to sovereignty while avoiding a possible confrontation with the U.S.

16. It is difficult to see what expended role Canadian Armed Forces could usefully play in support of Canada's claim to sovereignty over waters between Arctic islands. The historic basis for this claim has been adequately safeguarded by the activities of the Department of Transport over many years of supply, survey, icebreaking, and hydrographic operations dating back to 1903 when this Department charted the "Neptune" to show the flag in Northern waters. If it is decided to reinforce the Canadian claim by a substantial degree of Canadian participation in the "Manhattan" trial run, this could best be served by the [Department of Transport] icebreaker "John A. MacDonald," by [Department of Transport] aerial reconnaissance of ice conditions and by other, non-military forms of participation.

17. If it is decided to assert the Canadian claim publicly by proceeding with the implementation of the straight baseline system around the Arctic islands it would have serious legal, political and economic

implications in Canada's relations with the U.S. If the dispute could not be settled by diplomatic negotiations or by an agreement to refer the issue to the International Court of Justice (as was done in the 1951 Anglo-Norwegian fisheries case) the U.S. might react by instructing its ships and aircraft to disregard Canadian claims in this respect and/or by resorting to direct economic retaliation, for example, by denying Canada oil import concessions. But it is difficult to envisage how such a dispute could have any military implications. It is inconceivable that any Canadian government would wish to resort to force to deny access to U.S. vessels and aircraft in the disputed area. Iceland resorted to force in asserting an exclusive twelve-mile fishing zone against Britain (without having naval forces, and deploying only fishery protection vessels). This action was, however, taken in protection of vital national interests by a country wholly dependent for its livelihood on what were then diminishing fishery resources. There are no comparable interests at stake for Canada in the North. Moreover Canada is firmly committed to a policy of seeking resolution of differences with the U.S. by peaceful means only, and there is no indication of any change of Government policy in this regard.

18. The problem of sovereignty over archipelago waters is thus a legal, political and economic problem. It is not a military problem. It cannot be solved by any amount of surveillance or patrol activity in these channels by Canadian forces. Nor would any increased military (or non-military) activity by Canada strengthen Canada's legal case or undermine that of the U.S., since the U.S. has formally reserved its rights.

19. Canada has never asserted a definitive claim to sovereignty over the Polar pack ice or Polar Basin lying to the north of Canadian land. The so-called "sector" theory has been referred to by Government leaders from time to time over the last 50 years, but in uncertain and ambiguous terms. Most jurists agree that this theory has a weak foundation in international law. Only the USSR has officially proclaimed the principle (in 1926) and in doing so applied it only to lands known or unknown lying within its sector. The U.S. has stated (most recently in an Aide Memoire of 4 April, 1969 from the U.S. Embassy in Ottawa) that it

does not recognize the sector theory as constituting a valid principle for claiming jurisdiction over floating ice in the polar high seas. An interdepartmental study in 1960 concluded that a claim to the Polar Basin would entail few advantages of consequence and attract strong opposition by the U.S. and perhaps other countries concerned about freedom of air and submarine navigation in polar regions. In these circumstances where no claim has been made and where no claim is likely to be made by Canada, it is clear that any plans for an expanded level of military surveillance of the Polar Basin would be completely unjustified and misplaced.

20. (As an aside, it may be worth noting that the latest map of Canada published by the Department of National Defense in January, 1959 excludes the Polar Basin from the Canadian Forces command region demarcated by a broken red line around the Arctic Islands. One could infer from publication of this map that Canada has abandoned any claim to sovereignty of this area extending to the North Pole. This could be a source of some public sensitivity if attention were drawn to the apparent inconsistency (in fact, of course, there is no inconsistency) between the new Government emphasis on protection of sovereignty and the Department's map making activities).

21. From the foregoing it can be concluded that there would be no useful purpose or justification for any expansion of the present modest but adequate level of Canadian forces activity in the North, out of concern for the protection of Canadian territorial sovereignty.

Political Sovereignty

22. Canadian forces can, however, play an important role, along with other agencies of government, in protecting and promoting the greatest possible measure of "political sovereignty", which is a matter of effective control by the Canadian Government over activities taking place on or over Canadian territory. This is not a legal problem but a problem of exercising authority and mobilizing all available resources to enable the

Government to determine Canadian policies in the light of Canadian interests. It is a political problem.

23. It is important, however, to recognize that in a highly interdependent world the notion of absolute sovereignty is a fiction and a mirage. According to Stanley Hoffman's definition: "sovereignty, rather than being a reservoir which can only be full or empty, is a divisible nexus of powers of which some may be kept, some limited, some lost". Or to quote Mr. Justice Holmes, "Sovereignty is a question of power, and no human power is unlimited". Sovereignty in this sense may be regarded as the exercise of political power in a dynamic international context where relative strength as between two countries is measured not only in terms of military power, but in large measure by the basic resources of the countries concerned in terms of geography, population, economic resources, industrial capacity, national character and morale, quality of government and quality of diplomacy.

24. The major outside limitation or influence on Canadian sovereignty is the predominant presence of American power in our political, economic, social and cultural life. The same is true of our defence posture. Any realistic appraisal of Canadian foreign and defence policy must begin with a recognition of a very high degree of interdependence with that of the U.S. There is little cause for Canadians to lament this high degree of interdependence - it reflects not coercion or subordination, but our willing consent to identify our interests and values closely with those of the U.S.

25. Canadian – U.S. joint defence arrangements in Canada do not detract from Canadian sovereignty in law; on the contrary they confirm that sovereignty.[8] They do, however, pose difficult questions for Canadian terms of two further Canadian requirements:

a. A reasonable degree of policy influence and operational control by the Canadian Government over all military activities taking place in, or closely affecting Canada; and
b. Canadian self-esteem and patriotic feeling.

8 Marginalia: "In addition, of course, they make essential contributions to our security."

26. The Canadian military role in enhancing the Canadian Government's influence and control has been stated in realistic terms by the Report of the Standing Committee on External Affairs and National Defence dated 26 March 1969 (page 9); "Canada must be prepared to incur reasonable expenditures for its own defence in order to maintain its independence and freedom of action as a nation, and to ensure that Canadian interests are taken into account when continental defence reassures are being considered". What level of expenditures would be "reasonable" is ultimately a matter of political judgment to be weighed against other measures which might be taken by Canada to enhance its independence vis-à-vis the U.S. (for example, by allocations to a Canada Development Cooperation, to "buy back" Canadian resources and industries owned or controlled by U.S. investors).

27. Other countries opt for a different "mix" of military and non-military expenditures, depending on their particular security needs and resources. Iceland, for example, makes no force contribution to its own security and is prepared to rely entirely upon U.S. and NATO allies to provide the necessary defences. In so doing, the Icelandic government has had to pay a large price in terms of a delegation of sovereign authority to the U.S. base commanders stationed in Iceland, who have virtually complete autonomy (subject of course to direction from Washington) in the administration and operations of those bases. This "price" is acceptable to the government and people of Iceland because their painfully limited resources are needed in non-military fields and because the adverse side-effects of a large autonomous foreign military presence in their midst are limited by the very strong cultural and linguistic identity and unity of the local population.

28. Canada has vastly greater resources than Iceland but it would nevertheless be beyond our capacity to provide from our own resources the continental defence systems which need to be located in Canada. Nor do we wish to leave the entire burden of North American defence to the U.S. and give them large scale access to Canadian bases and Canadian air-space for training and operational purposes. The objection to this

course was expressed as follows by the Minister of External Affairs, Mr. Paul Martin on 7 March, 1968:

> "This would keep the cost to Canada to a minimum but it would tend to erode our sovereignty as well as any influence we could otherwise have on the development of air defence policies- policies which would inevitably have a significant impact on us."

Canada has in fact adopted a third course in our defence relations with the U.S. since the beginning of World War II: cooperative arrangements for continental defence.

29. This policy has been based on the recognition that the security of North America from outside attack is indivisible, and that there is no threat to the territorial integrity of Canada apart from the threat of a general nuclear war involving the whole of North America. In other words the problem of "the defence of Canada" has been seen by successive Canadian governments as an inextricable part of the problem of "the defence of North America" and of "the defence of the North Atlantic area". Apart from a modest investment in forces for purely national roles and tasks such as aid to the civil power, search and rescue and "insurance" against the highly implausible risk of minor territorial intrusions by a 3rd power, all Canadian forces have been developed for roles in cooperative defence arrangements with the U.S., with NATO allies, and, on an ad hoc basis, with other countries in peacekeeping activities.

30. Does the policy statement of 3 April [1969] imply any change in this fundamental view of Canadian defence needs? In the absence of any change in the strategic balance of forces in the world and in the absence of any new threat to Canada, it would be absurd to interpret the statement as implying any change in these basic roles for Canadian forces.

31. The more logical interpretation and, indeed, the only reasonable interpretation is that the new emphasis on "surveillance of our territory and coastlines, i.e., the protection of our sovereignty" means a new emphasis on Canadian participation in joint continental defence

activities taking place in, or closely affecting Canada. This is entirely consistent with the guideline that "to the extent that it is feasible we shall endeavor to have those activities within Canada which are essential to North American defence performed by Canadian forces". It does not mean a requirement for an additional Canadian military presence in remote areas merely for the sake of showing the flag. It does not mean a requirement for additional air and maritime surveillance or reaction forces outside the framework of joint North American defence programs. Such activities would be pointless since, as we have seen, there is no legal need for the protection of Canadian sovereignty and there is no new threat to Canadian security.

32. There is, however, a political need to ensure adequate cooperation and coordination of joint continental defence activities on Canadian territory. To influence planning and to ensure a high level of operational control over these activities Canada must make an adequate force contribution. The requirements of political sovereignty cannot be met by merely attempting to impose directives from the outside on the plans and operations of U.S. forces operating on a regular basis in Canada. Experience has shown that even with the greatest goodwill and cooperation from the U.S. authorities, full participation by Canadians in plans and operations can be guaranteed only by an integral Canadian force contribution in the activities concerned, together with adequate cost-sharing and command arrangements.

33. How do we determine what contribution is "adequate" or "feasible"? This is the difficult question since we cannot do everything. We must be selective in the allocation of our military resources. In the past this has been an ad hoc process, as Mr. Paul Martin acknowledged when speaking about cooperative defence projects in North America:

> "... it has been found that, for a variety of reasons, the actual provision of the necessary manpower and equipment can best be handled through individual national contributions made on an ad hoc basis as requirements are defined."

It is clearly impossible to lay down any firm guidelines on how much is enough to ensure adequate Canadian influence and control. Decisions on individual joint programs must depend on a variety of factors including use of specialized Canadian resources or skills and the cost-effectiveness of a Canadian vis-à-vis an American input. In addition, it might be possible to define certain guidance principles in terms of financial resources and the functional impact of the activity concerned on Canadian life. For example, one benchmark which could be applied along with others (but not rigidly) would be a ratio of Canadian to U.S. contribution in roughly the same proportion as the Canadian G.N.P. to the U.S. G.N.P., or 1 to 10. This might provide some rational, for example, to the scale of our effort in [anti-submarine warfare] in relation to the overall [Standing Naval Force Atlantic – Western Atlantic deployment] effort, and of our effort in interceptor aircraft in relation to overall NORAD interceptor forces. Another benchmark might be the impact or "visibility" of a program in Canadian eyes. For example, it might be preferable to "pay our dues" to ensure Canadian influence, control and presence in highly visible activities such as interceptor or [Airborne Warning and Control System] operations even if it meant more token participation in manning remote communications links.

34. The objection might be raised: Canadian planning should not be concerned with questions of 'presence' and 'visibility' in the eyes of Canadians - this is a problem for public relations experts and political leaders. It would, however, be shortsighted for the Defence Staff to neglect this aspect. Political sovereignty is not only a matter of influence and control, it is also a matter of being seen in a position of influence and control. A prominent and constructive role for Canadian forces in defence partnership with U.S. forces helps contribute to Canadian self esteem. It can help foster a sense of common accomplishment, national self-respect and, indirectly, national unity. This should, however, be a bi-product of an effective defence posture. It should not be 'presence' for the sake of 'presence', in the absence of any military rationale. To build a role for Canadian forces merely to satisfy the optical demands of political sovereignty would be to build on shifting sands. It would not be long before somebody noticed that one visit of the Governor-General, accompanied by an enthusiastic press corps, can provide a sovereign

presence to a remote area much more effectively and much more cheaply than a 100 CAF surveillance over flights.

2 The *Manhattan*, Sovereignty, and the Canadian Response

2-1. Canadian Embassy in Washington to External Affairs Headquarters, re: Northwest Passage, 3 June 1969.[9]

NORTHWEST PASSAGE:
PROJECT MANHATTAN

1. We attended briefing arranged by Humble Oil Company on Manhattan Project on June 3. Simultaneous briefing was held in NY and two were connected by closed circuit TV. We will be reporting on questions of oil policy.... Briefing kit containing text of statements made by Humble officials together with other info material including set of TV clips following by bag.

2. Entire presentation was of greatest interest. Statements by Humble officials stuck closely to technical, organization, and economic aspects of project and gave acknowledgement of Canadian contribution. During question period following two Canadian press men (Bob Reguly of Toronto Daily Star and Terrence Wills of Globe and Mail) asked whether Humble regarded waters of Northwest Passage as being under Canadian sovereignty or being international waters and enquired whether Manhattan's voyage was intended to establish USA claim to right to navigate. Reply given by Stanley Haas project director, Marine Task Force was that question of sovereignty is not for Humble to determine but for State Department. Haas referred to statement by Prime Minister Trudeau in House of Commons on subject of sovereignty over Arctic waters. This aspect of matter was not raised by any other of the number of speakers during question period.

9 Raymont Collection, DHH 73/1223/987 box 52.

2-2. Canadian Forces Headquarters to Commander, Maritime Command, re: Manhattan Project Air Surveillance, 12 June 1969[10]

1. While air surveillance for subject project is DOT [Department of Transport] responsibility assisted by [US Coast Guard] this HQ understands any assistance which could be provided by Canmarcom during course of sovereignty flights this summer would be greatly appreciated. CFHQ telecom discussions to date have occurred between [the Director Operational Readiness Maritime] and Mr. D.C. Archibald, Chief of Basic Weather Division, Net Branch, Toronto.

2. CFHQ favours provision of support of DOT in project at maximum level consistent with your other operation commitments and obvious financial limitations. Assistance would be in keeping with increased emphasis to be placed on your Arctic role evolving from the defence review. It is not intended to charge DOT as experience and knowledge of Arctic operations to be gained by participating in this project considered most beneficial to DND.

3. Mr. W.E. Markham, meteorologist in charge Ice Central Halifax fully aware details of project and particularly air surveillance programme. He is aware MARCOM [Maritime Command] may provide assistance. Details of MARCOM participation should be discussed directly with Mr. Markham when he returns Halifax, Monday 16 June. This HQ would expect to be informed on continuing basis of your planned participation.

4. DOT through Mr. Markham will provide experienced ice observer for any MARCOM flights and will pay all his expenses. In this regard DOT particularly interested in providing ice observer for any Arctic flights planned for June provided route could include passage of interest to them.

10 Raymont Collection, DHH 73/1223/987 box 52. Originally classified as "Restricted."

2-3. Commodore P.F.X. Russell to Vice Chief of the Defence Staff, 12 June 1969.[11]

S.S. MANHATTAN
NORTHWEST PASSAGE PROJECT – SUMMER, 1969

1. As you are aware the MANHATTAN will attempt the Northwest Passage, through Parry Channel in July this summer as part of an attempt to prove the feasibility of year-round transit to and from the Prudhoe Bay oil discovery in Alaska. DOT is supporting the project with an icebreaker, CCGS [Canadian Coast Guard Ship] JOHN A. MACDONALD, and air surveillance by a specially equipped DOT Dakota. As it is highly desirable, from a sovereignty point of view, to keep US Coast Guard participation to a minimum, DOT was delighted when the possibility of some DND air surveillance assistance was mentioned.

...

3. You may be interested to know that arrangements are in hand to provide two naval elements officers to DOT to assist in the operations organization of the CCGS John A. Macdonald throughout the passage. The possibility of including an additional, technical, officer also is being explored.

11 Raymont Collection, DHH 73/1223/987 box 52. Originally classified as "Restricted."

2-4. House of Commons Debates, 15 July 1969.

CANADIAN SOVEREIGNTY: MAINTENANCE OF EFFECTIVE PRESENCE IN ARCTIC

Hon. Robert L. Stanfield (Leader of the Opposition): Mr. Speaker, I should like to ask the Minister of National Defence whether, apart from the intention to patrol the Arctic waters this summer, the government contemplates any measures extending beyond this summer to maintain an effective Canadian presence in the Arctic?

Hon. Léo Cadieux (Minister of National Defence): Mr. Speaker, I am gratified to note that the Leader of the Opposition approves the policy of the government which is to extend coverage to maintain Canadian sovereignty all around Canada, including the northern Arctic waters.

Mr. Stanfield: Mr. Speaker, I rise on a point of order. I did not express approval or disapproval; I asked a question. The minister is one of a few who try to answer questions and I hope he will not lose that reputation.

2-5. Cabinet Conclusions, "Arctic Sovereignty and The Manhattan," 11 September 1969.[12]

Hon. Mitchell Sharp, Secretary of State for External Affairs, showing off the booklet series Foreign Policy for Canadians which emphasized Canada's national interest and defined foreign policy as "the extension abroad of national policies." (LAC)

The Secretary of State for External Affairs [Hon. Mitchell Sharp] reported that the S.S Manhattan had encountered some ice difficulties which had led to the withdrawal of the accompanying U.S. icebreaker, but with the assistance of the Canadian icebreaker Sir John A. MacDonald was pursing its effort to traverse the Northwest Passage. As previously agreed, the Department of National Defence had provided transport for the members of the Parliamentary Committee who had overflown the Manhattan and conveyed a message which had been helpful in reinforcing the public impression that this was an area which Canadians regarded as their territory. The only possible basis for press reports that the Manhattan's voyage infringed Canadian sovereignty was the fact that Canada had not insisted upon its prior permission being sought, having publicly stated without being asked that it concurred in the proposal.

... [classified]

The Minister of Transport [Hon. Donald C. Jamieson] reported the view of his department that the Manhattan would probably be unable to complete the return passage to the Atlantic unless a second icebreaker

12 LAC, RG 2, vol. 6340. Available online at http://www.collectionscanada.gc.ca/archivianet/conclusions/001039-100.01-e.php.

should join the Sir John A. MacDonald to lend support. It happened that the St. Laurent was due to put to sea, and it was for consideration whether she should be sent to the area and if so whether any statement relating to the Manhattan should be made. After discussion, it was agreed that the St. Laurent should be sent to the general area but without any public announcement, while no denial would be made should the Press speculate that she was being sent to be available in case the Manhattan needed support.

Mr. Jamieson raised the further question whether his department should officially inform the Manhattan when the point in time was reached where the department could not assure the release of the Manhattan prior to the freeze-up if it were not immediately withdrawn. It was considered that this question should be re-examined in the light of developments.

Several ministers observed that if the voyage of the Manhattan established the feasibility of a commercial shipping route through the Canadian Arctic this would be bound to accelerate the development of the region, and in particular would provide the means of bringing to market such oil or other minerals as might be discovered in the area under Canadian jurisdiction. If, on the other hand, the voyage should be unsuccessful this would enhance the attractions of building a large pipeline to transport Prudhoe Bay oil to the continental heartland by way of the Mackenzie Valley. In either case Canada stood to gain important benefits.

... [classified]

2-6. Memorandum to the Cabinet, "Canadian Sovereignty over the Waters of the Arctic Archipelago," 15 September 1969.[13]

CANADIAN SOVEREIGNTY
OVER THE WATERS OF THE ARCTIC ARCHIPELAGO

Purpose of the Memorandum

The purpose of this memorandum is to examine various courses of action which may be open to the Canadian Government, in the wake of the S.S. "Manhattan's" voyage through the Northwest Passage, with a view to protecting or asserting the Canadian position concerning the status of the waters between the islands of the Arctic archipelago. The memorandum is addressed in particular to the advisability of Canada's adopting a 12-mile territorial sea as an immediate course of action for the protection of essential Canadian interests.

Possible Courses of Action

2. Four possible courses of action appear to be open to the Canadian Government with respect to the waters of the Arctic archipelago:

a. To abandon the Canadian claim;
b. To continue the present policy of maintaining the Canadian claim without asserting it in such a manner as to provoke a confrontation with the USA on this issue;
c. To assert the Canadian claim by implementation of the straight baseline system, either without the right of innocent passage or with this right;
d. To adopt a 12-mile territorial sea.

Course (A) – Abandoning the Claim

3. Canada could either explicitly or tacitly abandon its claim to the effect that all of the channels between the islands of the Arctic archipelago are internal waters of Canada. The major disadvantage, under existing domestic legislation, of abandoning the Canadian claim is that Canada would then have sovereignty over only the three-mile territorial sea (and fisheries jurisdiction over the nine-mile fishing zone)

13 LAC, RG 25, vol. 10322, file 27-10-2-2 pt.1. Originally classified as "Confidential."

around each island of the archipelago, with the consequence that large areas of most of the channels (and all of the main channel through the Northwest Passage) would constitute high seas open to unfettered access by ships of all countries, without any legal basis for Canadian control over their activities. Abandonment of the Canadian claim to the channels as internal waters would be inadvisable, particularly in light of the controversy engendered by the "Manhattan" project, the recent instance of oil pollution in the Northwest Passage, and the strongly adverse reaction which could be expected from parliament, the press and the public.

Course (B) – Continuing Present Policy

4. Canada could attempt to continue its past policy of maintaining its claim to the Arctic channels as internal waters by every means possible short of publicly asserting the claim in unequivocal terms (by legislation or proclamation) in such a manner as to provoke a confrontation with the USA over this question. Consistent with this policy the Government has treated the "Manhattan" project as a cooperative venture in which Canada has concurred; has emphasized the consultations held between the Canadian and US authorities in the planning of the project, as well as Canada's full participation in its execution; and has stressed the economic and scientific aspects of the project and stated that the issue of sovereignty does not arise in this connection. The objective has been to support a project which is in the Canadian interest and to avoid provoking US protests which could damage the Canadian position respecting the waters of the archipelago. It has been recognized throughout, however, that the policy of safeguarding Canada's claim without asserting it unequivocally will probably be no longer possible in the light of the "Manhattan" project. Prior to the "Manhattan's" voyage it could not reasonably be argued that the Northwest Passage was an established international shipping lane, although the USA appears to have maintained this view. However, this position could alter radically if the "Manhattan" project is successful and leads to numerous such voyages through the Northwest Passage. Moreover, heightened interest in commercial navigation through the Northwest Passage may require that the status of these waters be clarified. In any event, the extensive

and often confused and controversial press coverage of the "Manhattan's" voyage and the high level of public interest in this matter, also combine to make it appear that it will not be feasible to continue the policy followed so far.

Course (C) – Implementation of Straight Baseline System

5. Canada's claim that the waters of the Arctic archipelago are Canadian internal waters rests in part upon the straight baseline system, whereby the territorial sea may be measured from straight baselines linking fringes of islands and coastal headlands, rather than being measured from and parallel to the sinuosities of the coast. The straight baseline system is well established in international law on the basis of the Anglo-Norwegian Fisheries case of 1951 (in which the International Court of Justice upheld the application of the system by Norway) an the similar principle embodied in the 1958 Geneva Convention on the Territorial Sea. The application of the system to any particular area, however, must be justified on the basis of a number of complex legal, economic and geographical considerations. The Canadian Arctic lends itself admirably well in theory to the application of the system, but the distances involved in closing off the various channels are in many case so great that there is considerable doubt that such application could be justified in international law. There are, however, other legal bases for Canada's claim to the waters of the Arctic archipelago (discussed briefly below); it is therefore presumed for the purposes of this paper that the application of the straight baseline system to the Arctic archipelago is the long-term objective of the Canadian Government although this course of action has never been implemented by Canada, due chiefly to strong opposition expressed by the USA.

6. The straight baseline system could be applied to the waters of the Arctic archipelago either: (i) without a mandatory right of innocent passage, or (ii) with a mandatory right of innocent passage.

(i) Baseline system without innocent passage

The existence or non-existence of the right of innocent passage for foreign ships in the waters of the Arctic archipelago, after implementation of the straight baseline system, would depend on the grounds for Canada's claim that the waters in question are internal. If Canada were able to maintain successfully that the waters are and always have been internal on the basis of a historic claim, or a historic claim combined with the sector theory, or on the basis of the argument that the waters are more assimilable to land then to water because of their frozen state, there would then be no right of innocent passage for foreign ships (although such passage would no doubt be permitted as a matter of policy as is the custom of most states). In these circumstances, the straight baseline system would be used only to give precise definition to the limits of Canada's claim rather than to create a new legal status for the waters of the Arctic archipelago. (The straight baseline system was applied in this way to the "historic bays" of Newfoundland in 1967, and this would also be the case with respect to Hudson's Bay[sic], for example, where Canada's historic claim is well-established).

(ii) Baseline system with innocent passage

If Canada's claim that the channels of the Arctic archipelago are internal waters were, because of the weakness of Canada's historic claims to these water as a whole, to be established mainly in reliance upon the straight baseline system, there would then be, in accordance with the 1958 Geneva Convention on the Territorial Sea, a right of innocent passage for all foreign ships in those waters of the archipelago which has previously been considered either territorial sea or high seas. (This provision of the Convention applies whether or not the waters in question were previously used as international shipping lanes.)

Difficulties in Implementing Baseline System

7. Further study has been made of the legal basis for claiming that the waters of the Arctic archipelago are internal Canadian waters, both with or without the right of innocent passage as discussed above. The major legal difficulty is that the Canadian claim considerably surpasses in scope and scale any generally accepted claim by any other country. It has been concluded that Canada would have no more than a 50-50 chance of succeeding with such a claim. International acquiescence may be very hard to obtain. The USA, for example, opposes the Canadian claim on strategic grounds out of concern for World-wide freedom of navigation for its naval vessels. The US has threatened litigation if Canada attempts

to implement its claim to these and other "special bodies" of water (such as the Gulf of St. Lawrence). The US government has also warned that it would instruct its ships and aircraft to disregard such a claim by Canada. Canada would, of course, be in an extremely difficult position if the USA were to send a warship through the Northwest Passage in an open challenge to Canada's action. The possibility of economic retaliation against Canada has also been mentioned by the US side in US-Canadian talks on this subject; such action could, of course, take the form of a simple refusal to grant special concessions requested by Canada in such matters as the US oil import policy.

8. Although there is considerable domestic pressure for Canada to assert and establish its claim that the waters are internal, it is assumed, in the light of the foregoing considerations, that the Government would not wish to proceed immediately with the application of the straight baseline system to the Arctic archipelago unless it were to appear that Canada's position vis-à-vis these waters would otherwise be gravely prejudiced. In the circumstances, and in view of the danger of Canada's claim being defeated in the International Court or by other types of opposition, it is necessary to consider an immediate course of action, short of application of the baseline system, which would protect Canada's essential interests in relation to the waters of the Arctic archipelago.

Course (D) – Adoption of 12-Mile Territorial Sea

9. At present the breadth of Canada's territorial sea is fixed at three mile by the Territorial Sea and Fishing Zones Act (which further established a nine-mile limit for Canada's contiguous exclusive fishing zones.) By amendment of this legislation, Canada could extend its sovereignty (as opposed to fisheries jurisdiction) from three to twelve miles along its Atlantic, Pacific and Arctic coasts. By so doing, Canada would create a belt of territorial sea cutting across Barrow Strait at approximately the mid-point of the Northwest Passage. This would have the effect of establishing Canadian sovereignty, subject only to the right of innocent passage, over the entire width of the Northwest Passage at three of its most strategic points, since Prince of Wales Strait at the western

entrance and Pond Inlet at the eastern entrance already have the status of territorial waters by application of the present three-mile limit.

10. The right of innocent passage would not be in any way inconsistent with the aim of opening up the Northwest Passage to commercial shipping. Canada would have the right, however, in accordance with the 1958 Geneva Convention, to regulate the exercises of the right of innocent passage, to determine whether or not a particular passage is innocent (that is, whether or not it is prejudicial to the "peace, good order and security" of the coastal state), and to take steps to prevent passage which is not innocent. The convention provides that submarines are required to navigate on the surface and to show their flag for their passage to be deemed innocent. Moreover, the right of innocent passage in the territorial sea may be temporarily suspended by the coastal state if the suspension is essential for the protection of its security. (This right of suspension does not apply to established international navigation between one part of the high seas and another part of the high seas or the territorial sea of another state, but the Canadian position is that the Northwest Passage has not attained this status, since it has not thus far been possible to use the Passage for international navigation. This situation could soon change radically, which is the more reason for urgent action by Canada.)

Advantages of 12-Mile Territorial Sea

11. Canada's essential coastal interests, both in general and with particular respect to the Arctic archipelago and the Northwest Passage, relate to security, pollution, navigation, fisheries, and the continental shelf. If Canada could successfully claim the waters of the Arctic archipelago as internal, this would undoubtedly provide the greatest possible protection for the Canadian interests involved. Such a claim may accordingly be viewed as the ideal solution. As already indicated, however, there are serious legal and international difficulties in the way of this course of action. In the circumstances, adoption of a 12-mile territorial sea is an immediate alternative measure which, without suffering from the same drawbacks as the claim to internal waters, can afford very substantial protection to the interests concerned. The

advantages of a 12-mile territorial sea, from the legal point of view and in relation to safeguarding Canadian interests, are as follows:

(i) Legal

The most important advantage of a 12-mile territorial sea, as compared to a claim that the Arctic archipelago waters are internal, is that there is a much stronger legal basis for the establishment of the 12-mile limit. While a number of Western states, including in particular the USA, do not accept the legality of a 12-mile territorial sea, the fact remains that many states now successfully maintain such a claim and it is most unlikely that the International Court of Justice would find that a 12-mile territorial sea is contrary to existing international law. (The legal basis for the 12-mile territorial limit is discussed in detail further below). The same cannot be said of Canada's claim that the Arctic waters are internal. While historic claims are accepted in international law and the principle of the straight baseline system is firmly established, the application of these concepts to the waters of the Arctic archipelago is very much open to dispute. For these reasons it would be much more difficult for any state to successfully oppose a 12-mile territorial sea claim than would be the case with the claim that the waters are internal. It should be noted also that if Canada were to establish a 12-mile territorial sea the area of the waters of the Arctic archipelago not then subject to Canadian sovereignty would be considerably reduced and subsequent action by Canada to establish the claim that they are internal would seem less extreme.

(ii) Security

In view of the special situation which pertains in the Arctic, including its proximity to the USSR, security considerations would appear to be particularly relevant to the waters of the region. With the establishment of a 12-mile territorial sea, Canada would be able to exercise effective control over the passage of foreign ships through the Northwest Passage and deny entry to those posing a security threat. With respect to other areas of Canada's coasts, the security and other factors which make it desirable to exercise sovereignty over a marginal belt of three miles make it that much more desirable to exercise such sovereignty over a belt of 12 miles, subject only to the right of innocent passage.

(iii) Pollution

As a result of its effective control over the passage of foreign ships within the Northwest Passage by virtue of it sovereignty over the waters of Pond Inlet, Prince of Wales Strait and Barrow Strait, Canada would be able to enforce regulations to minimize the pollution threat posed by any future operation of foreign super-tankers in the Northwest Passage.

(iv) Navigation

The adoption of a 12-mile territorial sea would not represent an impediment to commercial navigation in the Northwest Passage, and indeed would provide Canada with the jurisdiction basis to provide the required aids to navigation in this area (and effectively restrict the provision of such aids by other countries). Thus, the claim to a 12-mile territorial sea would provide less grounds for opposition either by Canadian or US oil interests.

(v) Continental Shelf

According to the Geneva Convention on the Continental Shelf, the outer limit of the territorial sea represents the inner limit of the juridical continental shelf. Accordingly, the adoption of a 12-mile territorial sea would push the inner limit of Canada's continental shelf seaward by nine miles. In view of current international discussions which suggest that attempts may be made by certain developing countries in particular, and perhaps by the USA as well, to curtail severely the physical limits of the continental shelf as defined by the Geneva Convention, the extension of the shelf in this manner would be desirable.

(vi) Fisheries

If Canada claimed a 12-mile territorial sea, it would be much easier to settle finally and neatly a number of questions outstanding between Canada and the European countries which have so far been permitted to continue their traditional fishing practices in Canada's three to 12-mile fishing zones. (The Order-in-Council permitting the continuation of the traditional fishing practices of these countries would have to be terminated with the adoption of a 12-mile territorial sea, since the fishing zones in which these practices are permitted would disappear by virtue of being incorporated into the extended territorial sea.) As there is no precedent for the granting of a phasing-out period for traditional fishing practices in the territorial sea, Canada's bargaining position would be much stronger vis-à-vis these countries, and any further phasing-out period could be represented as a major concession. Special arrangements could nonetheless be made with the USA along the lines of the present reciprocal fishing rights granted by the two countries in their respective fishing zones. Although these benefits of a 12-mile territorial sea, as opposed to a three-mile territorial sea and a nine-mile fishing zone, are not of major significance, the wider territorial sea would undoubtedly strengthen Canada's bargaining position with other countries and would presumably be welcomed by the Canadian fishing industry.

Legal Basis for 12-Mile Territorial Sea

12. It can no longer be said that a 12-mile territorial sea is contrary to international law. Since the failure of the 1958 and 1960 Geneva Conferences on the Law of the Sea to fix an agreed breadth for the limit of the territorial sea, state practice has developed in such a way that, at present, about 70 countries claim a territorial sea greater than three miles. Of this number at least 40 countries (including the USSR) have successfully established a 12-mile limit and at least seven others claim still wider limits. Only about 30 countries hold to the once-traditional three-mile limit, and many of these (including the USA) have extended their fisheries jurisdiction out to 12 miles.

13. This new international trend has also been reflected in the seabed disarmament negotiations now under way in the Conference of the Committee on Disarmament at Geneva. A major issue in these negotiations has been the extent of the "coastal band" (so-called to avoid prejudicing various national positions as to the breadth of the territorial sea) which would be exempted from the arms control measures proposed be applied to the seabed. In general, the consensus has been in favour of fixing the extent of this band at 12-miles. Although the United States had advocated a coastal band extending only three miles, it appears that this position has been adopted mainly for bargaining purposes, and American officials have privately indicated that they would accept a 12-mile band in exchange for concessions from the USSR with respect to the scope of the arms prohibition under negotiation (which concessions have recently been made). More important, however, as evidence of

contemporary state practice, are the crucial test cases of the "Peublo" incident and the sinking of the Israeli destroyer "Eilath". In these cases the USA focused attention on whether or not the incidents in question occurred within or just outside the 12-mile belt; at no time did it appear that the USA questioned the 12-mile limit as such.

14. A further and very significant indication of the development of the law on this matter is the inclusion of the 12-mile limit in the draft US-USSR convention on the breadth of the territorial sea which is intended (and this is of paramount importance) to form the basis of a general multilateral agreement. It should be noted, of course, that this draft convention also provides for the establishment of a "high-seas corridor" or some analogous principle guaranteeing unfettered freedom of navigation (as opposed to innocent passage) in international straits which would otherwise fall entirely under national sovereignty by application of the 12-mile limit. Canada has been careful to safeguard its position (in international discussion on this matter) that the Northwest Passage is not an international strait to which the "high seas corridor" would apply.

Disadvantages of Unilaterally Claiming a 12-Mile Territorial Sea

15. Although the unilateral adoption of a 12-mile territorial sea could be reasonably justified under existing international law, the legal basis for the wider limit undoubtedly would be stronger if it were sanctioned by an international convention as proposed by the USA and USSR. More important than this, however, is the fact that the USA might accuse Canada of breaking faith with its friends by acting unilaterally at a time when the two great powers were attempting to produce a rule of law on this question. Moreover, the US views international agreement on the 12-mile territorial sea as a "package deal" involving similar agreement on the establishment of some principle guaranteeing absolute freedom of navigation in international straits. Thus, in unilaterally adopting a 12-mile territorial sea without awaiting the outcome of the law of the sea conference proposed by the USA and USSR, Canada would in effect be implementing one part of the package independently of that part relating to international straits and accordingly could expect opposition

from the USA and other NATO allies. In NATO discussions of this matter, however, Canada has made clear that while it accepts in principle the concept of "high seas corridors" in international straits, it reserves its position concerning the application of the principle to particular Canadian straits.

16. It should be noted that any possible objections by the USA could not effectively be based on grounds of international law (although, of course, an unfavourable US reaction could have adverse effects on Canadian interests regardless of the grounds on which it was based). In reply to such objections Canada could make the point that the immediate unilateral adoption by Canada of a 12-mile territorial sea was not inconsistent with the rule of law proposed in the US-USSR draft convention in view of the fact that the Northwest Passage (potentially the most important strait affected by Canada's adoption of a 12-mile territorial sea) could not reasonably be considered to be an established international shipping lane in the strict legal sense of the term and should not therefore in any event be subject to the proposed provision for a high seas corridor. Canada could also stress the fact that establishment of such a corridor in the Northwest Passage would defeat the legitimate interests which Canada wished to protect in this area. (At the same time Canada could attempt to allay US objection by offering to grant, on a bilateral basis in the interests of continental defence, unfettered freedom of naval as well as commercial navigation for the USA in the Northwest Passage, if this were considered necessary and desirable.)

17. Finally in considering possible US objections to Canada's unilateral adoption of a 12-mile territorial sea, it is relevant to note that the USA has so far found little support among its friends and allies for the draft convention it has negotiated with the USSR. The fisheries provisions of the draft agreement in particular have pleased neither the distant-water nor the coastal fishing states, and indeed it has become obvious that even the Soviet Union is reluctant to accept these provisions. Recent discussions with the US officials give grounds to believe that the USA foresees the possibility that it may eventually have to abandon this initiative for fear of failure of the proposed conference. Whatever the

outcome, however, it can be argued that Canada ought to be free to pursue its own independent foreign policy on such matters as the law of the sea, provided that in so doing it does not jeopardize the vital security interests of the Western alliance.

Conclusions and Recommendations

18. The adoption of a 12-mile territorial sea need not be viewed as an alternative or an impediment to eventual implementation of the straight baseline system in the Arctic archipelago. It is, rather, an immediate step which could protect vital Canadian interests without incurring the disadvantages of other approaches. While theoretically inconsistent with the claim that the Arctic waters are internal, this course need not imply the abandonment of Canada's claim to the channels of the archipelago as internal waters nor prejudice Canada's position on this matter. (Indeed, as already indicated, a 12-mile territorial sea would make subsequent assertion of the internal waters claim seem less extreme.) The claim to a 12-mile territorial sea would be advanced without prejudice to Canada's position that the whole of the waters of the Arctic archipelago are internal, and justified, if need be, as an interim measure aimed at immediate problems. (To protect this position it would be inadvisable to publish maps illustrating the 12-mile limit in the Arctic archipelago or in the other "special bodies" of water as to do so might imply abandonment of Canada's claims to these areas as internal waters.) Nor should the 12-mile limit be considered as a substitution for claiming other "special bodies of water" as exclusive Canadian fishing zones by means of the establishment of fisheries closing lines. The adoption of a 12-mile territorial sea would not prejudice Canada's long standing jurisdictional claims, since it is quite open to Canada to establish its claims one step at a time; similarly such action would not affect the possibility of eventually claiming additional fishing zones contiguous to the extended territorial sea if and when the development of international law might permit such a step.

19. In the light of all the forgoing consideration it is recommended:

(i) That Cabinet authorize the preparation of an amendment to the Territorial Sea and Fishing Zones Act incorporating a 12-mile limit for the territorial sea in substitution for the present limit of three-miles, without prejudice to the amendment already authorized in respect of the establishment of fisheries closing lines in the "special bodies" of water, and also without prejudice to the possibility of extending Canadian fisheries jurisdiction beyond the proposed 12-mile territorial sea.

(ii) That the require amendment be introduced in Parliament at its next session, with the precise timing to be decided in consultation between the Secretary of State for External Affairs and other ministers concerned.

(iii) That in introducing the proposed amendment in Parliament, or in announcing the Government's intention of doing so, it be made clear that the 12-mile limit for the territorial sea applies to the whole of Canada's Atlantic, Pacific and Arctic coasts.

(iv) That, within a brief period prior to the announcement of this amendment or its introduction in Parliament, the Government give notice to the USA of its intention to proceed in this manner.

2-7. Cabinet Conclusions, "Canadian Sovereignty Over the Waters of the Arctic Archipelago," 15 October 1969.[14]

The Secretary of State for External Affairs pointed out that after a long and difficult meeting, the Cabinet Committee on External Policy and Defence had recommended that the government introduce legislation adopting a twelve mile territorial sea for Canada.

During the discussion, the following points emerged:

a. No country had ever questioned Canadian sovereignty over the land or the continental shelf in the Arctic.

[(b) and (c) classified]

d. The Interdepartmental Committee of Officials had examined the problem extensively and recommended the adoption of a twelve mile territorial sea so that Canada could exert control in the waters through the consequent closing of the channels.

[(e) and (f) classified]

g. Any legislation dealing with a twelve mile territorial sea should also include legislation dealing with fisheries closing lines.
h. The Minister of Fisheries said that by selectively drawing four fisheries closing lines the government could close the whole Arctic Archipelago which would then make the Fisheries Act apply including its anti-pollution provisions.

[(i) and (j) classified]

k. The Secretary of State for External Affairs pointed out that since the strongest statement by the United States there had been a steady increase in claims by various countries to a twelve mile territorial

14 LAC, RG 2, vol. 6340. Available online at http://www.collectionscanada.gc.ca/archivianet/conclusions/001039-100.01-e.php.

sea and the United States had tacitly accepted a twelve mile limit in both the "Pueblo" and the "Elait" incidents.

l. Some ministers felt that Canada had generally followed the trend in international law in advancing its claims over territorial seas and, even disregarding the Arctic altogether, it would be useful for Canada to claim twelve miles. Such a stand would not preclude, nor should it preclude, more extensive action in the Arctic.

[(m) classified]

n. The Minister of Transport said that Canada and the USSR were probably the only countries which could successfully navigate the northwest passage.

[(o) classified)

p. The Prime Minister suggested that in the Throne Speech, in his own speech, and in the Minister's speeches, the government could develop the two themes of pollution control and economic development in the Arctic without mentioning the twelve mile limit and Canada could then go to the United States Government and advise it that Canada wanted to control pollution. The government could then assess the United States reaction and in the meantime wait until more countries had declared a twelve mile limit.

q. Some ministers felt that ownership of Northern Canada was a very real force in the spirit of many Canadians, and these strong feelings should not be dismissed by calling them jingoism.

The Cabinet agreed to defer the matter for further consideration the following week.[15]

15 The minutes of the 21 October Cabinet meeting are still classified.

2-8. Colonel K.W. Macdonald, Director Continental Policy (DConP), "Arctic Policy," 18 November 1969.[16]

ARCTIC POLICY
Reference: V3440-2 (DConP) November, 1969

1. There have been some interesting reactions from Washington and Moscow to the Prime Minister's statement of 24 October, during the Throne Speech debate, on the government's policy on the Arctic. The portion of the statement relating to the Arctic is quoted in Annex A; the passage referred to in the following paragraphs has been sidelined.

2. The U.S. Department of State has responded to the Prime Minister's invitation to the international community to join with Canada in supporting an international legal regime in the waters of the Arctic by proposing bilateral consultations. The U.S.S.R., it has been reported from discussions between a Soviet diplomat and a Norwegian official, may be considering a proposal to "neutralize" arctic waters; further details are being sought from our ambassador in Moscow.

3. Following is the text of an Aide Memoire handed to our ambassador in Washington on 6 November on the subject "International Protection of the Arctic Environment":

> The Department of State refers to the statement of the Prime Minister of Canada in the House of Commons on October 24, and in particular to the Prime Minister's invitation to the international community to join with Canada and support its initiative for a new concept, an international legal regime in arctic waters designed to ensure to human beings the right to live in a wholesome natural environment. The Department notes the concern expressed by the Prime Minister in his statement for adequate protection of the ecological balance in the Arctic, in interest in controlling water pollution and marine destruction, and his intention to propose a

16 Sutherland Papers, DHH 79/527 folder 2B. Originally classified as "Confidential."

> policy of use of arctic waters designed for environmental preservation.

The United States Government welcomes these views and this new initiative in international cooperation and is prepared to support steps toward an international agreement regarding the Arctic and the protection of its peculiar environment. Matters such as the preservation of the arctic ecology, pollution control, scientific cooperation, and the uses (navigational and otherwise) of arctic waters within and beyond the limits of national jurisdiction might be included among the subjects for examination and consultation. In this regard, the United States is mindful of the success of the Antarctic Treaty in promoting international cooperation and protecting the natural environment in that area and of the fact that interested arctic states have contributed to this success.

The Department refers to its Note to the Embassy dated September 18, suggesting consultation on Arctic matters between United States and Canadian experts and would welcome bilateral talks at the convenience of the Government of Canada on the general subject of arctic waters and the Prime Minster's new initiative in this regard in particular.

4. It was intended, the Deputy Assistant Secretary of State indicated in presenting the Aide Memoire, that:

a. it be seen by the Prime Minister before his scheduled meeting in New York with the Secretary General of the United Nations;
b. the U.S. would give no publicity to it;
c. it would indicate that the U.S. is in agreement with the views expressed in the Prime Minister's statement as they understand them; and
d. it would draw an analogy with international cooperation in the Antarctic.

5. In his reply [Canadian] Ambassador [to the US Charles] Ritchie pointed out that the Prime Minister did not indicate what he has in mind regarding the implementation of the objectives set out, and said that he was not in a position to amplify the Prime Minister's statement. He added, however, that without going too deeply into the matter, he

thought the presence of many competing claims in the Antarctic created a different situation from that existing in the Arctic.

6. According to the Legal Division of External Affairs, this "new initiative" has apparently supplanted immediate consideration by the government of a declaration by Canada of a 12-mile territorial sea; details on this question were given in the reference.

7. Paragraphs 1 to 5 summarize three messages repeated by External Affairs to the member of the Interdepartmental Committee on Territorial Waters for information.

Further information will be forwarded as it becomes available.

2-9. Extract from Prime Minister's statement in the Throne Speech, House of Commons Debates, 24 October 1969.

"Membership in a community, Mr. Speaker, imposes – and properly – certain limitations on the activities of all members. For this reason, while not lowering our guard or abandoning our proper interests, Canada must not appear to live by double standards. We cannot, at the same time that we are urging other countries to adhere to regimes designed for the orderly conduct of international activities, pursue policies inconsistent with that order simply because to do so in a given instance appears to be our brief advantage. Law, be it municipal or international, is composed of restraints. If wisely constructed they contribute to the freedom and the well-being of individuals and of states; neither states nor individuals should feel free to pick and choose, however, to accept or reject, the laws that may for the moment be attractive to them.

"It is in this mood that the government is studying its claim to the waters off the islands of the Arctic Archipelago. To close off those waters and to deny passage to all foreign vessels in the name of Canadian sovereignty, as some commentators have suggested, would be as senseless as placing barriers across the entrances to Halifax and Vancouver harbours. We would certainly prove by those acts that we were masters in our own house, but at immense cost economically by denying shipping of importance to Canada. On the other hand if we were to act in some misguided spirit of international philanthropy by declaring that all comers were welcome without let or hindrance, we would be acting in default of Canada's obligations not just to Canadians but to all the world.

"In the Canadian Arctic are found the breeding grounds, sometimes the only breeding grounds, of many species of migratory birds. Bylot Island is the nesting ground of the total population of the Greater Snow Goose. It is the site as well of the nesting colonies of some six million sea birds. Along 12 miles of the coast of Somerset Island are the nesting grounds of four million birds. Large numbers of air throughout the Canadian archipelago. The existence of these and other animals and birds is dependent upon an uncontaminated environment; an environment which only Canada can take the lead in protecting. The beneficiaries of this natural life are not only Canadians; they are the people of the world.

"For those reasons, I say in this place, Mr. Speaker, that Canada regards herself as responsible to all mankind of the peculiar ecological balance that now exists so precariously in the water, ice and land areas of the Arctic Archipelago. We do not doubt for a moment that the rest of the world would find us at fault, and hold us liable, should we fail to ensure adequate protection of that environment from pollution or artificial deterioration. Canada will not permit this to happen, Mr. Speaker. It will not permit this to happen either in the name of freedom of the seas, or in the interests of economic development. We have viewed with dismay the abuse elsewhere of both these laudable principles and are determined not to bow in the Arctic to the pressures of any state. In saying this, we are aware of the difficulties faced in the past by other countries in controlling water pollution and marine destruction with their own jurisdiction.

"Part of the heritage of this country, a part that is of increasing importance and value to us, is the purity of our water, the freshness of our air, and the extent of our living resources. For ourselves and for the world we must jealously guard these benefits. To do so is not chauvinism; it is an act of sanity in an increasingly irresponsible world. Canada will propose a policy of use of the Arctic waters which will be designed for environmental preservation. This will not be an intolerable interference with the activities of others; it will not be a restriction upon progress. This legislation we regard, and invite the world to regard, as a contribution to the long term and sustained development of resources for economic and social progress.

"We also invite the international community to join with us and support our initiative for a new concept, an international legal regime designed to ensure to human beings the right to live in a wholesome natural environment. In pursuit of this concept I shall be holding discussions shortly about this and other matters with the Secretary General of the United Nations. A combination of an international authority in the Canadian Arctic will go some considerable distance to ensure that irreparable harm will not occur as a result of the negligent or intentional conduct.

"Canadian activities in the northern reaches of this continent have been far-flung but pronounced for many years, to the exclusion of activities of any other government. The Royal Canadian Mounted Police patrols and administers justice in these regions on land and ice, in the air and in the water. The Canadian Armed Forces carry out continuous surveillance activities, Canadian postal services, health services, and communication networks criss-cross these territories to serve those who live and work there. Among these persons are the Canadian Eskimos, who pursue their food and conduct their activities over the icy wastes without heed to whether that ice is supported by land or by water. In all these activities, and in others, ranging from geophysical explorations to the distribution of family allowance cheques, Arctic North America has, for 450 years, progressively become the Canadian Arctic.

"Honourable members know that there is not now nor is it conceivable that there will ever be, from any source, challenges to Canadian sovereignty on the mainland, in the islands, in the minerals lying in the continental shelf below the arctic waters, or in our territorial seas. This happy situation is the result of the quiet, consistent policies in the past on the part of all Canadian governments. The present government pledges to be equally consistent. Those policies will reflect Canada's proper interest not only in the preservation of the ecological balance which I have already mentioned, but as well in the economic development of the north, the security of Canada, and in our statue and reputation in the world community."

2-10. DEXAF, Notes for Discussion: "What is Necessary to Maintain National Sovereignty? What is the Role of the Canadian Armed Forces?" 29 January 1970.[17]

U.B.C. Seminar

WHAT IS NECESSARY TO MAINTAIN NATIONAL SOVERIGNTY?
WHAT IS THE ROLE OF THE CANADIAN ARMED FORCES?

1. Canadians are preoccupied by pressures on sovereignty in a variety of fields: political, legal, economic, social and cultural. Defence planners are also involved with the question of maintaining sovereignty. The Prime Minister's defence policy statement of April 3 stressed the role of the forces in the "surveillance of our own territory and coastlines, i.e. the protection of our sovereignty". In his Calgary speech of April 12 the Prime Minister stated: "our first priority in our defence policy is the protection of Canadian sovereignty in all the dimensions that it means."

2. What is the relationship between defence and sovereignty and, in particular, what contribution do armed forces make to Canadian sovereignty? How can this contribution be enhanced in the development of Canadian defence policy for the seventies? The purpose of this paper is to suggest, in outline form and as possible framework for discussion, a check-list of some of the major "dimensions" of this concept for Canada, and of their possible implications for future defence planning. No attempt is made here to anticipate policy decisions on particular future roles for the forces.

Some Basic Concepts:

3.

a. Sovereignty is independence. Its chief characteristic is the element of "exclusiveness" or autonomous freedom of action, independent of the will of other states, i.e., the right to "do our own thing". In

17 LAC, RG 25, vol. 10322, file 27-10-2-2 pt.1. Marginalia suggests that these notes were written by E.B. Wang.

this sense any assertion or exercise of authority by a government, independently of the authority of any other government, could be called an expression of sovereignty.

b. Sovereignty may be legal or political. When the UN Charter speaks of "the principle of sovereign equality of all its members" (Article 2) it is upholding a legal notion rather than describing the distribution of political power amongst member states. Sovereignty can thus be broadly defined to mean two things: the right to exercise the functions of a state, independently of any other state; and, secondly, the power to exercise the functions of a state, independently of any other state. The first is a question of legal title under international law and the second relates to the manner in which the legal rights which flow from this title are exercised and enforced as a matter of national policy, in a highly interdependent world.

c. Sovereignty, as legal title under international law, is determined principally by three criteria: discovery, acquisition by treaty and effective occupation. In respect of remote areas, international courts have ruled (e.g. Clipperton Island case, East Greenland case) that the display of state activities required to establish "effective occupation" and sovereign title need not be continuous but may be intermittent.

Problem Areas

4. Questions of sovereignty of particular relevance to defence planning can be grouped under one or more of the three following areas: (a) collective security, (b) territorial integrity and (c) territorial jurisdiction. Some of the problems under these headings may be more theoretical than substantive. Similarly, defence activities may help strengthen in some areas, but may be inappropriate or irrelevant in other areas.

Collective Security

5. Security against the threat of armed attack lies at the core of sovereignty for Canada, as for any other nation. Without security, Canadians would be unable to pursue effectively the other goals which we may wish, as a sovereign nation, to set for ourselves.

6. Canada has chosen to protect its own security, and in this respect its sovereignty, through collective security, i.e. through co-operative military arrangements. Because the threat is that of nuclear war, these arrangements are aimed at helping to prevent such a war by protecting the U.S. deterrent and helping to contain conflicts which could break out in troubled areas. These arrangements, in order to be effective, require a measure of political solidarity and military integration, or in other words they require us and our allies to forego a measure of freedom in our policies and activities. Our dilemma is that in order to safeguard our sovereignty in one sense, we may derogate from it in another.

7. In the military sphere, for example, Canada, under the 1958 Canada-US NORAD Agreement, has conferred upon the NORAD Commander, (normally a US officer unless his Canadian deputy is acting for him) the power of operational control over Canadian forces assigned to him, within overall plans for air defence approved by the two governments. In the political sphere, Canada and its NATO partners have implicitly undertaken (although not as a legally binding commitment) to consult on and try to co-ordinate, arms control, etc., in the interests of the cohesion and effective functioning of the Alliance.

8. The following are some questions involving sovereignty which arise:

(i) Do such arrangements seriously increase the existing risk that we might be involved in hostilities against our will? Do they leave us with sufficient scope for independent judgment and initiative in efforts to maintain the peace, promote détente and arms control, etc.? If we had more scope as a result of a loosening of our political and military ties with our allies, would this increase our capacity to act effectively in the international arena?

(ii) Does our co-operation with the United State in the defence of North America make it easier or more difficult for us to deal with non-military (e.g. economic or cultural) pressures on our sovereignty emanating from south of the border?

(iii) Forces maintained primarily to respond to a threat of armed attack in concert with allied forces may also perform useful peacetime tasks in the protection of other, purely national interests (e.g. search and rescue, aid to the civil power). Are the Canadian forces which are committed to collective security tasks sufficiently flexible so that they can respond to national contingencies?

(iv) If more emphasis were placed on developing multi-purpose forces and if greater peacetime responsibilities were assigned to these forces (e.g. law enforcement, national development), would this jeopardize their effectiveness in their primary role of defence (or deterrence) against armed attack?

(v) Does the presence of US military personnel in Canada on joint defence activities pose problems with respect to Canadian sovereignty? If problems exist, are they related mainly to the numbers of such personnel (there are 3800 at present) or to other factors such as their location (e.g. DEW Line) or function (e.g. providing U.S. custody for nuclear weapons)?

(vi) How far can and should Canada go in attempting to ensure Canadian influence and control in Canada-USA joint defence programs? Are there any guidelines as to what is feasible or adequate in (a) manning by Canadian personnel, (b) Canadian participation in command and (c) cost-sharing arrangements? Are present NORAD arrangements satisfactory?

Territorial Integrity

9. It is usually held that because of our unique geographical position Canada does not face the classic military problem of a threat of limited armed attack across territorial borders, and that instead we are concerned primarily with the risk of all-out nuclear war which could, by design or accident, bring large-scale destruction on Canada. In this respect the following questions arise:

Even if the risk of limited military incursion, occupation or lodgment is considered remote, is there nevertheless a need for Canada to maintain, as a form of "insurance", a military capability adequate to deal with such contingencies, independent of any support we might expect from allies?

If so, are Canadian forces presently stationed in Canada and available for response to purely national tasks less than adequate or more than

A CH-135 Twin Huey from 427 Tactical Helicopter Squadron lands on Ellesmere Island, May 1978. (LAC)

adequate to respond effectively to such unforeseen military contingencies in our territories, airspace and coastlines?

As regards the risk of peacetime violation of Canadian laws and regulations (e.g. fisheries protection, anti-pollution, resource exploitation) by private trespassers, is there any advantage in assigning greater law-enforcement responsibilities to Canadian armed forces in addition to the civilian and police agencies (Fisheries Protection Service, Canadian Coastguard, RCMP, etc.) which have hitherto borne primary responsibility for enforcement in their respective areas?

In order to counter a military threat it is necessary to have a capability of (a) detection, (b) identification and (c) destruction. In respect of peacetime encroachments by private trespassers, is it necessary for Canada to have all three capabilities or is it sufficient, in order to maintain territorial integrity in peacetime, to have a surveillance capability (detection and identification) backed up by police forces (or military forces in police roles) and judicial sanctions?

Territorial Jurisdiction

10. Canada's claim to sovereignty over its Arctic territories and its exclusive sovereign right with respect to continental shelf resources

have not been challenged by any other state and are not in doubt under international law. Even though large tracts of territory are uninhabited and rarely visited, a multitude of Canadian Government activities in the north – civil and military – contribute to establish a pattern of effective occupation, in addition to the historical and treaty background.

Is there nevertheless a need for an increased level of activity (e.g. surveillance) by Canadian forces over remote areas to reinforce Canada's legal title against any conceivable future challenge by any other state by supplementing activities (e.g. law enforcement of national development) of other government agencies such as Indian Affairs and Northern Development, Transport, National Health and Welfare, RCMP, etc…?

The Prime Minister cited in the House on May 15, 1969 a statement made in 1958 by the then Minister of Northern Affairs, as follows

> "The area to the north of Canada, including the islands and waters between the islands and areas beyond, are looked upon as our own, and there is no doubt in the minds of this government, nor do I think was there in the minds of former governments of Canada, that this is national terrain.

The Prime Minister added that differences of opinion may nevertheless arise as to whether arctic archipelago waters constitute internal Canadian waters, or whether Canadian territorial jurisdiction may be limited to the traditional three-mile belt surrounding each island. From a legal viewpoint, can Canadian rights and claims in these waters be strengthened by increased Canadian Government activity? By increased Canadian military activity such as air or marine surveillance? Has the voyage of the S.S. Manhattan created new needs for such activity?

2-11. House of Commons Debates, 16 February 1970.

Mr. Stanley Knowles (Winnipeg North Centre): Mr. Speaker, may I direct a question to the Minister of External Affairs. In view of a report from Houston, Texas, that there is now a 50 per cent chance that the *Manhattan* will make another voyage through the northern waters of Canada in April, can the minister say whether the government has now received any requests, communications or intimations in connection with this proposed trip?

Hon. Mitchell Sharp (Secretary of State for External Affairs): Mr. Speaker, the information we have is rather the same as the report that has been referred to by the hon. Member. We have heard that there may be a chance that the *Manhattan* will travel through our northern waters again but we have not yet had a definite request; we understand that Humble Oil Company has not yet made up its mind whether the ship will make the voyage.

Mr. Knowles (Winnipeg North Centre): A supplementary question, Mr. Speaker. Is the government taking any action in the meantime by way of strengthening the regulations to make sure that if there is such a voyage there will not be a tragedy involving the pollution of our northern waters?

Mr. Sharp: Mr. Speaker, I believe that experimental voyages of the kind undertaken by the *Manhattan* are very much in Canada's interest. The ship will carry no oil cargo but only that oil it will need for itself. It is very important for us to find out the conditions under which these waters can be used safely. That is why the government welcomed the first voyage of the *Manhattan*. If the company wishes to undertake a second voyage, we would cooperate and welcome the effort because we believe that as the result of such voyages we will find out the conditions under which it will be safe to traverse these waters.

Mr. Diefenbaker: What price Canadian sovereignty! Heaven help us!

Mr. G.W Baldwin (Peace River): A supplementary question, Mr. Speaker. Since the minister used the words "our northern waters," is it the position of the government that the *Manhattan* or any other oil tanker must seek permission from the Canadian government in order to make a voyage through the Northwest Passage?

Mr. Sharp: Mr. Speaker, in the past they have sought our cooperation, which I am sure is the best evidence that they understand our position in the north.

Some hon. Members: Oh, oh!

Mr. Baldwin: A further supplementary question, Mr. Speaker. Is it the position of the government that the *Manhattan* or other similar vessels must seek the permission of the Canadian government before going through what the minister described as "our northern waters"?

Mr. Sharp: There seems to be some misunderstanding about this.

Mr. Baldwin: Not at all.

Mr. Sharp: When ships pass through our waters, wherever these are, they do not seek the specific approval of the Canadian government. They are assumed to be on innocent passage and we do not question them. We assume that the *Manhattan*, if it is to go again, will undertake an innocent passage. Indeed the purpose of the voyage would be to find out, by way of this experiment, what conditions are like in the north. That is why we welcome it and have cooperated and given our permission in the past.

Some hon. Members: Hear, hear.

Mr. Diefenbaker: What price Canadian sovereignty!

Mr. W.B Nesbitt (Oxford): A supplementary question, Mr. Speaker. Will the Secretary of State communicate with this colleague, the Minister of

Transport, to make sure that if the *Manhattan* does make the voyage she will fly the Canadian flag when in our waters, something that did not happen in the last trip?

Mr. Speaker: Order, please. I suggest that the hon. member is making a representation rather than asking a question.

Hon. Marcel Lambert (Edmonton West): A supplementary question, Mr. Speaker. Will the minister ascertain whether the Department of Transport or the government has received a direct request for the use of Canadian icebreakers in the event this voyage takes place?

Mr. Sharp: Mr. Speaker, as I explained in answer to the initial question, we have not been told whether the *Manhattan* will undertake a second voyage. There is uncertainty about it because I do not think Humble Oil Company has yet made up its mind. It is clear that if the ship were to undertake the voyage it would have to have the co-operation of Canadian icebreakers. These, of course, would be available.

Mr. Erik Nielsen (Yukon): Mr. Speaker, I have a supplementary questions concerning sovereignty over the Arctic waters. Is the government considering the reinstitution of the policy of the Mackenzie King government of issuing licences to ships and aircraft going through or traversing the Canadian Arctic sector? I refer to licences such as those issued by the Canadian government under Mackenzie King to the MacMillan-Byrd expedition.[18]

Mr. Sharp: I shall take the question as notice, Mr. Speaker.

18 Editors' Note: In 1925, American explorers Lieutenant Commander Richard E. Bird and Donald B. MacMillan mounted an aviation expedition to search for undiscovered lands in the Polar Sea which could be used for air bases and perhaps fly over the North Pole. Their incursion into Canadian territory generated sovereignty concerns and led Ottawa to insist that the Americans apply for permission and adhere to Canadian regulations. MacMillan complied with Canadian licensing requirements on subsequent expeditions. See D.H. Dinwoodie, "Arctic Controversy: The 1925 Byrd-MacMillan Expedition Example," *Canadian Historical Review* 53/1 (March 1972): 51-65.

Mr. S. Perry (Spadina): A supplementary question to the Acting Prime Minister. Has the government prepared base lines for the Arctic islands area? If so, when will the government be proclaiming them?

Mr. Sharp: No, Mr. Speaker. There are a number of areas where the government has not drawn base lines. It is not the intention to complete the map at the present time.

An hon. Member: Why not?

Mr. Sharp: To do so in some areas would be to take action that might compromise the position of the Canadian government in future declarations.

2-12. House of Commons Debates, 25 February 1970.

Mr. Robert Simpson (Churchill): Mr. Speaker, I have a question for the Minister of National Defence which I thought was supplementary to questions previously asked with respect to the defence of the North American continent. In view of reports to the effect that plans are under way to establish Canadian Armed Forces on several of our Arctic islands, is the minister in a position to enlighten the House or will he be making a statement on motions in the near future?

Hon. Léo Cadieux (Minister of National Defence): Mr. Speaker, these reports in my view are premature.

An hon. Member: But accurate.

Mr. Simpson: Mr. Speaker, may I direct a supplementary question to the Prime Minister. Although the Minister of National Defence said that the reports I alluded to are premature, is it not true that the Prime Minister made a statement last night to the effect that these units would be set up, as reported on this morning's radio.

...

Mr. Harold E. Winch (Vancouver East): A supplementary question, Mr. Speaker. Will it be possible for the Minister of National Defence in the near future to make an announcement as to the planning for two exercises by the Canadian Armed Forces in the Arctic this year.

Hon. Leo Cadieux (Minister of National Defence): Mr. Speaker, it is common practice whenever we do an exercise in the north, to advertise it.

Mr. Donald MacInnis (Cape Breton/East Richmond): I have a supplementary question for the Minister of Transport. Will the minister take this opportunity to explain to the House his own remarks with respect to a combined operation between the defence department and his own department with regard to protecting Canadian sovereignty in the north?

2-13. House of Commons Debates, 19 March 1970.

Mr. Gordon Ritchie (Dauphin): …This government's refusal to disassociate itself from academic abstractions and get down to the realities of Canada's problems has placed this country in posture of non-nation…. More and more policies laid down at Ottawa are reducing this country to the status of a non-nation. The Americans kindly take us aside and tell us which parts of the Canadian north they intend to take over. They produce reports saying Canadians want to sell water to the United States. Nothing could be further from the truth. Not one responsible Canadian has gone on record in favour of selling one drop to the United States. The solution in respect to the Canadian Arctic is simple. The Canadian Arctic is Canadian. The sooner this government so informs the people of the United States, the better. The Canadian Arctic is as much Canadian territory whether it be land, ice or water, as New York harbour is United States territory.

The United States has as much claim to Canadian territorial waters in the Arctic as it has to territorial waters in the Soviet Arctic, and I do not see them advancing that argument. There must be a reason. Somebody had better point out to the United States authorities in Washington - apparently this government cannot do it – that United States territory stops at the Canadian border and does not leap-frog the Canadian nation and come down again in the Arctic islands. A Canadian presence must be established in the Arctic and it must take the form of an immediate doubling of the number of Canadian military bases in the Arctic. That should not be hard; there are only two there now.

2-14. Cabinet Conclusions, "Legislation to Prevent Pollution of the Arctic Seas," 5 February 1970.[19]

LEGISLATION TO PREVENT POLLUTION
OF THE ARCTIC SEA

The Cabinet had for consideration the memorandum of the Prime Minister on "Legislation to Prevent Pollution of the Arctic Seas" (Cab. Doc. 62-70)…

[confidential]

The Cabinet agreed that:

1. Legislation be drafted, for introduction during the current session, to prevent pollution in the Arctic Sea, the legislation to be in accord with the following principles"

(a) the outer limit of the waters to which the Act applies be defined as 100 miles from Canadian land except where the lines of equidistance between Greenland and the Canadian Arctic islands is less than 100 miles from shore, in which case the line of equidistance would apply;

(b) the provisions setting forth the precise legal regime that is to apply within the defined area to be of three separate kinds, namely:
   (i) prohibitions (with penalties sufficient to provide an effective deterrent or negligent acts of pollution);
   (ii) preventive requirements (designed to prevent pollution before it happens); and
   (iii) financial responsibility and liability provisions;

(c) prohibition to be directed against anyone who knowingly or negligently deposits or permits the deposit of "waste" (basically as that term is defined in the Canadian Water Bill) in any waters within the area to which the Act applies or on adjacent land areas where such waste threatens to pollute said waters;

19 LAC, RG 2, vol. 6359. Available online at http://www.collectionscanada.gc.ca/archivianet/conclusions/001039-100.01-e.php.

(d) appropriate penalties be directed against any person engaged in exploitation of the resources of the continental shelf or land areas adjacent to Arctic waters and against the owner or operator of a ship whose master or crew contravenes the prohibition. Such a provision not to come into play where the incident resulting in pollution occurred otherwise than as a result of some blameworthy act or omission, e.g. not where the incident was the result of an accident;

(e) insofar as the prohibitions relate to shipping, the usual international approach of relying on prosecution in the flex state be reversed by providing for violations to be prosecuted in Canada, and the legislation empower the enforcement agency to arrest and detain a ship involved in a violation of the Act;

(f) a power in the Governor in Council to make regulations for "regulating and preventing" the pollution of any waters to which the Act applies;

(g) to authorize the designation (or subsequent change) of special "shipping safety control zones" by order of the Governor in Council, within which preventive provisions of the Act related to shipping would apply as appropriate in relation to each situation; such zones to be established anywhere within the area to which the Act applies; a requirement to be included in the legislation whereby proposals for the establishment of such zones would published in advance of formal action, this permitting the Governor in Council to receive and consider representations, including representations from other countries, before formally committing itself by legal action; such Orders when made should not be subject to parliamentary review before taking affect;

(h) to give power to the Governor in Council to make regulations prohibiting the entry of any ship into any waters within a shipping safety control zone except upon such conditions as might be prescribed by the regulations; the prescribed conditions to be basically concerned with whether or not a ship has complied with certain technical requirements, such as the ability of its hull to stand up to heavy ice conditions, whether its cargo is adequately protected, whether it carries the proper equipment, eg. radio and navigational aids, required in northern latitudes, and whether it must be escorted by an icebreaker;

(i) to confer a right on the federal government to recover, as a debt, any costs reasonably incurred by it in mitigating damage caused by an incident resulting in pollution. Such claims of the federal government to rank pari-passu[20] with claims of other persons arising out of the same incident and all such claims to be subject to the limit of liability to be prescribed by regulation;

2. the Minister of Indian Affairs and Northern Development in consultation with other ministers concerned prepares such detailed drafting instructions with respect to the proposed legislation as may be necessary and make recommendations to Cabinet concerning the administration of the Act;

3. at this time Canada make no claim to a 12 mile territorial sea;

4. the question of submitting a new reservation to Canada's acceptance of the compulsory jurisdiction of the International Court of Justice, and the timing aspects of such a measure, be referred to the Cabinet Committee on External Policy and Defence for consideration and report to the Cabinet. The draft bill to amend the Territorial Sea and Fishing Zones Act, 1964, dealing with exclusive fishing zones to be considered by the Committee in the same context.

20 *Editors' note*: pari-passu is Latin for "without partiality" and means, in legal terms, that creditors are equal and distribution of assets will occur proportionality but without preference between them. See L. West and F. Neave, Mozley and Whiteley's Law Dictionary, 3rd Ed. (London: Butterworth & Co., 1908), 236.

2-15. Director General Policy Control and Review, DND, Memorandum Exclusive to the Office of the Chief of the Defence Staff, 13 April 1970.[21]

BILL C-202 - An Act to prevent pollution in areas of the Arctic Waters.
BILL C-203 - An Act to amend the Territorial Sea and Fishing Zones Act.

1. Attached are copies of the two bills that were introduced into the House of Commons this past week.

2. In introducing these bills, the Government made the point that, with regard to the aspect of the authority of the Government of Canada, Bill C-203, being the act to amend the Territorial Sea and Fishing Zones from three to twelve miles, was one of full sovereignty; while the act to prevent pollution of areas of the Arctic Waters adjacent to the mainland and islands of the Canadian Arctic was for jurisdiction only. Because this distinction will have a significant impact on the enforcement aspect of carrying out these two laws when and if they come into being, I have requested JAG [the Judge Advocate General] to study the bills and send a memorandum to the CDS, pointing out the difference between "jurisdiction" and "sovereignty" from the enforcement aspect. This is being done in the event that the government wishes to charge the Department of National Defence with the enforcement responsibility, alone or in conjunction with DOT, or only for specific incidents.

3. It should also be pointed out that the immediate reaction of the USA is one of disappointment that the Canadian Government would attempt to take these two acts unilaterally. They also state that they will not recognize Canada's proposed claim of jurisdiction in the Northwest Passage for the purposes of pollution control; nor will they recognize Canada's proposed assertion of absolute territorial sovereignty out to

21 Raymont collection, DHH 73/1223/988, box 216. Originally classified as "Confidential" with the note that "This memo must not leave the Office of the Chief of the Defence Staff nor be placed on any Branch file."

12 miles instead of the present 3-mile limit. The following text was included in a statement issued by the State Department:

> "The United States is prepared promptly to seek bilateral and multilateral solutions to these problems within the framework of international law.
>
> The United States does not recognize any exercise of coastal jurisdiction over our vessels on the high seas and thus does not recognize the right of any state unilaterally to establish a territorial sea of more than three miles or exercise of more limited jurisdiction in any area beyond 12 miles."

In attempting to understand why the United States would take this attitude, it might be that what the States is really concerned with is that they may not have confidence in Canada's ability to enforce such acts. Therefore if, for example, a Soviet ship or submarine entered the 100-mile area adjacent to the mainland or the islands of the Arctic, or came within 12 miles of our waters, what action would the Canadian Government be prepared to take? If the United States feels that Canada would not take enough positive action to ensure that the Soviets would get out of the area, the US Government may feel that as long as they do not recognize Canada's jurisdiction or sovereignty up to 12 miles, it leaves them free to send their own ships to confront Soviet ships or submarines if they feel that the defence of North America is being jeopardized. Of course this is all speculative, but the U.S. reaction does throw up some interesting and difficult aspects of these two bills and how Canada will enforce them if they become law.

2-16. House of Commons Debates, 16 April 1970.

Mr. Stanfield (Leader of the Opposition): Having accepted the responsibility of controlling pollution in this area, and I agree that we should accept the responsibility, we must now make certain that we discharge this responsibility. I and the hon. members of this house will expect this government to prepare itself to discharge its responsibilities and, incidentally, to tell us how it intends to enforce these measures it proposes.

An hon. Member: Through flower power.

Another hon. Member: Through Jamieson's navy.

Mr. Stanfield: …The Secretary of State for External Affairs and the government owe this House and the people of Canada an explanation as to how Canada proposes to enforce these regulations which apply to areas beyond our territorial control. This is what this government is asking Parliament to define. If we accept that responsibility, than we must carry it out. We must not fail, not only because we do not want to look silly but because we have accepted a heavy responsibility.

I believe the Canadian people will support these measures if they are enforced. However, they want to know how the government hopes to enforce them. Without taking any more time of the House this afternoon, while there will be many questions of detail with regard to the bill that can be examined in committee, I say without any reservation that my party supports Bill C-202 in principle. We very earnestly support it as a measure to control the pollution of the North. However, we would like some information as to why this limit of 100 miles was chosen and we would like to know how the government proposes to enforce these regulations. While this party very heartily endorses the purpose of this bill, we and the people of Canada regret very much that in the process of placing these two bills before the House the government is redefining our territorial waters in such a way as to, in effect, abandon the Canadian claim of sovereignty of waters between the islands as well as some of the waters surrounding the islands. The abandonment of this claim will likely haunt governments for many years to some.

...

Mr. Thomas C. Douglas (Nanaimo-Cowichan-The Islands): I think this House should seize an early opportunity to make clear to our friends south of the border that we will not tolerate anyone pushing this government around. This is a privilege which we reserve for the opposition!

...

Mr. Nesbitt: Mr. Speaker, I wonder if the hon. member who has just spoken will permit a question. Just before the hon. member concluded his remarks he said he was going to deal with the question of how the government would enforce the new pollution regulations inasmuch as we have declared ourselves as sort of outlaws, outside the field of international law in this regard. I was listening attentively to what the hon. member had to say, but he dealt with another subject. I wonder whether he forgot to continue his remarks as to how we would deal with a country or a ship that would not obey our regulations...

Mr. St. Pierre (Coast Chilcotin): As the hon. member undoubtedly knows, Canada is not a signatory to the convention which requires us to provide free Decca service. We can charge ships for providing icebreaker services. Without it, ships may be left stuck, such as was the case with the *Manhattan* yesterday or the day before. It had to be broken free by the *John A. Macdonald*.

An hon. Member: The *St. Laurent*.

Mr. Paul St. Pierre: I am sorry, the *St. Laurent*. This is a part of the exercise of sovereignty.

Mr. Nesbitt: A supplementary question, Mr. Speaker. What does the government plan to do if a ship of one of the major powers of the world, such as the Soviet Union or the United States, said it would not pay any attention if one of our pollution officers wished to go aboard? What will we do? Will we shoot at the ship? That is a very practical question, and I should like to know the answer.

Mr. St. Pierre: What would the hon. member suggest we do if American troops marched into Saskatchewan? That question is about as sensible as the hon. member's.

Mr. Thomas S. Barnett (Comox-Alberni): …I overheard a suggestion that we have had a little bit of experience in the matter of enforcement of our authority on the sea with respect to our fisheries legislation. If the hypothetical situation which the member is trying to provoke in his line of questioning does develop, undoubtedly this Parliament will be convened. If such a major emergency as the member is trying to conjure up does develop, we will debate the situation when it ceases to be hypothetical….

2-17. House of Commons Debates, 17 April 1970.

Mr. Frank Howard (Skeena):…In the minister's introductory remarks, right at the start, he indicated that there were four primary interests in the Arctic. Presumably, these are the four primary reasons for the introduction of the bill. He mentioned the security of Canada, the economic development of the North, the preservation of the ecological balance, and the continued high stature of Canada in the international community. I think the continued high stature of Canada in the international community is more window dressing than a real reason for doing something. We should be doing something in this field, and I am sure the minister would agree, not because of any attempt to maintain public relations with the rest of the world but because of our concern about matters affecting the Canadian nation.

The security of Canada is a different matter. It is rather an unknown term. It could be given many interpretation or connotations. I would like to think of it in terms of political security, political integrity and economic security. These are the ones we are talking about. Today the Minister of National Defence issued a press release with respect

The Minnah runs aground off Resolute Bay during Exercise NORPLOY 1974, 23 August 1974. Concerns of a maritime accident were a pretext for the federal government's "functional approach" in the Arctic during the 1970s. (LAC)

to placing a national defence unit at Yellowknife. I think this would probably indicate that if need be, and if the tests came right down to it, we intend to preserve the security of the nation by military means, although that really is an extension of the security concept beyond that which we normally accept. We do no want to get involved in military engagements in order to preserve our own unity and integrity but the fact that military personnel are there and that we look north gives some substance to the ideas about security. Sovereignty is something which we have to declare for ourselves. It comes from the establishment of straight baselines and the declaration of everything within them as inland waters, from a declaration that anybody who moves in there does so through our grace and decision. It is not a matter of open right as is the case with respect to international waters. Sovereignty must first be declared and then secured if the need arises.

...

Mr. Neilsen:...I should like to hear the Secretary of State for External Affairs speak up in asserting Canadian sovereignty in the North, and I would urge upon him to convince the Prime Minister to do the same thing. After all, the work of one of Canada's finest sons from the province of Quebec was largely responsible for securing a great deal of our Arctic land and waters. Are we now to listen to, much less tolerate, another famous son of Quebec in the form of a Prime Minister say we are not asserting this valuable work of Joseph Bernier? It would appear so.

We have heard the hon. member for Notre-Dame-de-Grace (Mr. William Allmand) go through a list of the ways in which Canada is asserting her sovereignty in the Arctic. He says it is not necessary to legislate sovereignty. He says we have asserted sovereignty as a result of the establishment of weather stations.[22] I ask him to look at the composition of those weather stations; they are not all Canadian. He says we establish our sovereignty in the Arctic by establishing military stations and detachments. I ask him, where are these?

The Minister of National Defence (Mr. Cadieux) has released an announcement to the press that he intends to take this gigantic step of

22 On the Joint Arctic Weather Stations, see Gordon W. Smith, "Weather Stations in the Canadian North and Sovereignty," *Journal of Military and Strategic Studies* 11/3 (2009), 1-63. Smith's reading supports that of Mr. Allmand.

establishing military bases in the north, and will patrol some 1,750,000 square miles of Canada with 50 soldiers. This action has been taken after they destroyed the military installations at Whitehorse which comprised 250 air force personnel and a similar number of army personnel. I understand there is now a re-awakening of interest in the north and the Minister is putting in 50 soldiers.

Mr. Cadieux (Labelle): Mr. Speaker, if I may be allowed to correct the hon. member, there are now 400 men permanently stationed in the north. What we are planning to do is increase this activity. For instance, I am announcing an early exercise by the air arm regiment with a strength of a thousand. You are talking about 35 people, but I am talking about the headquarters.

Mr. Nielsen: We are going to have a headquarters staff of 50 people. As far as military exercises are concerned, we have had these over the years – exercise Beaver and goodness knows how many more in the north. What is the minister of defence asking the people of Canada to believe? This is obviously an effort to gain publicity at a time when the Prime Minister has raised grave doubts about the sovereignty of Canada over her northern regions. We are rushing forth with our fists in our pockets and saying we are establishing sovereignty now. We are going to send another 50 soldiers north. It is a simple exercise of mathematics, to divide 450 soldiers into 1,750,000 square miles to discover how effective that sort of assertion is going to be in connection with Canada's sovereignty in the north.

Much more has been accomplished since the days of [Joseph-Elzéar] Bernier when he assisted in the setting up the first mounted police post on Ellesmere Island. He was responsible largely for setting up subsequent mounted police posts. The same situation applies to our establishment in connection with the activities of our geologists, health facilities and our weather facilities in the north. Basically the people of Canada believe that the sending of 50 soldiers to Yellowknife to set up a headquarters to manage 400 men, which in itself is -

Mr. Cadieux: You are distorting the facts.

Mr. Nielsen: …I am using the minister's own explanation. The setting up of a headquarters in Yellowknife comprising 50 soldiers to manage 400 men is questionable management, but no one can ask the Canadian public to believe that this is somehow reasserting sovereignty over Canada's Arctic regions. The fact remains that our Arctic extends from the 60th degree of longitude to the 141st and up to the North Pole. The fact remains that this was the position adopted by Sir Wilfrid Laurier, by Sir Robert Borden, by Mr. Arthur Meighen, by Mackenzie King, and by the former Conservative Prime Minister, Mr. Diefenbaker. Yet, all of a sudden, it is negated by this Prime Minister when he says we are not asserting our sovereignty over the Canadian Arctic….

There is another point I would like to make. I heard the leader of the New Democratic Party say that there are three historical precedents for the action that the government is taking now and justifying it on that basis. As one hon. member opposite put it, we in Canada have a right to take the action we are taking now in this Parliament as a matter of self-defence, on the basis that we had to combat pollution effectively. This brought to mind the U.S action taken with respect to the missile emergency that occurred in Cuba, when Russia was supplying the material and the missiles to establish offensive bases in Cuba. The United States took unilateral action on the high seas to stop those ships, and theoretically if for not other reason, one might conclude that it was to present the polluting of Cuba with missiles. The fact is that they acted unilaterally, and if they can do so with respect to a situation like that, I suggest that Canada has a similar right. Whether we have the means to enforce it is quite another matter, because no one in all reason will advance the proposition that we should either be rattling the saber or preventing the intrusion of foreign vessels in our Arctic waters by any offensive unilateral action.

Mr. Gordon Aiken (Parry Sound-Muskoka): That is all we have left.

Mr. Nielsen: …What the Canadian government should do – and I advance this as one who lives in the north and sees the many errors of past Canadian governments of all political stripes – is to take up the torch where Bernier laid it down, to his great credit, and where the government of the day took it up and asserted in no uncertain fashion that Canada owns the Arctic land. They went to the extent of requiring anyone sailing the waters between the islands in our Arctic and overflying the land and waters in our Arctic to be licensed. This government has not the courage to even require vessels like the Manhattan to obtain permission. This is wrong. This is pussyfooting so far as sovereignty in the Arctic is concerned, and it is selling our heritage down the river, a heritage which Bernier worked so effectively and ambitiously to secure for Canada…We own the Arctic Islands and that is all there is to it. We own the whole of the area between the 60th meridian and the 141st meridian and up to the North Pole. That was the policy and that should continue to be the policy, and the Prime Minister should say so.

Mr. F.J Biggs (Pembina): ...I do not think that we should be bogged down in semantics. I do not think the problem is whether, in fact, we have the necessary armed forces to go up to Canada's Arctic Islands and maintain the old style physical control over all those islands. I should have thought that by now we were becoming mature in world affairs. I do not refer to Canada alone, but hopefully the whole world is becoming more mature in this day of trips to the moon and international cooperation… It seems to me we are not taking a big enough view individually, as political parties, as a nation, and certainly not as international brothers.

With respect to the problem of pollution and the handling of it from a very high level, it is obviously out of Canada's control. The problem may well become nothing but an international political football in the big power game. I have in my hand a letter I received from the U.S Information Service. I presume it has all the validity of the U.S State Department behind it. I have no reason to believe it is not an official document. It is datelined Washington, April 15, so is not ancient history…They lump the two bills together, C-202 and C-203, and it is very hard to discuss one without thinking about the other. I am certainly not anti-American. On the contrary, I look to the United States very strongly and sensibly for assistance, not only in the preservation of our identity as an independent nation but in continuing to develop what has been loosely called the western way of life. Whether the Prime Minister

(Mr. Trudeau) or the Minster of National Defence (Mr. Cadieux), the government in general, or Parliament itself states that these islands are ours, I am not sure is important. The important thing is to discuss the matter openly and in a friendly manner, not only with the Americans, but with the international people the Americans themselves suggest should be consulted.

The Eskimo people are willing Canadians. I have heard no statement from the Eskimo people that they would like to secede. If you took a proper empirical approach to the matter and you whine about people having a right to earn a living on their own land, and about the self-expression of peoples, which are some of the prime theories behind the formation of the United Nations organization, then I wonder what the Eskimo people would say if all the emphasis were placed on the land masses and it was stated that sovereignty over the waters that lie between the islands was not a meaningful thing?

Up until the recent development of oil resources in the north country, the Eskimo people relied entirely on the marine and animal life which lived on the ice and in the water between the islands. These waters between the islands were of vital importance to the Eskimo way of life. Who cared about the Eskimo people? The Canadian people cared. The Canadian taxpayers sent mounted police up there to occupy each and every one of the major islands under our flag. We gave those people our assistance through law and order, through medical attention, and in every other way in which we could cooperate with them. We gave them the security which they occasionally did not have among themselves. We maintained decent order in the north. Apparently, we gave them that which they appreciated because never, as far as I know, have they indicated that they wanted to leave the Dominion of Canada.

Unless the Americans are willing to sit down with us, as we are willing to sit down with them, and discuss this matter openly, friendly and consistently, in terms of the free determination of the rights of peoples – in this case the Eskimos – I think it would be an exercise in futility. But I am not cynical about it. The Americans have stated their position. They may sound inflexible, but I think we are in a good bargaining position…

Collectively and individually Americas want to be understood and admired, instead of being the target of an awful lot of rotten propaganda coming from every corner of the world, with 90 per cent of which I do not agree. Nobody loves them except us. Little Canada is the only real friend they have in international affairs. One of the reasons is that, by and large, we have been treated pretty well by them. By and large, we are happy to have their money here to develop our almost unlimited resources. But I do not think this means we have to be soft or subservient. On the contrary, I think it is time that our government stated in explicit terms to the Americans just what our hopes are in the area over which we have jurisdiction. I do not think we should get bogged down in semantics. The Canadian archipelago islands of the north are an economic unit. The ice between the islands is essential to the native people who have the greatest interest and the right to sovereignty over those islands.

Mr. Neilsen: Judge [William] Morrow decided that.[23]

Mr. Biggs: Yes, the courts decide things but from time to time their decisions are reversed. I am appealing on the principle of humanity....

I find it strange, Mr. Speaker, that the people who shouted the loudest about these principles of peacekeeping, understanding and world co-operation rather than shaking an empty fist in mock fury should be the first ones to delay a plan for consultation. One of the most important things is to go to the bargaining table with a clear idea of your requirements. In order to achieve our ends our best brains should be selected for the negotiations, particularly with the United States, because that country is in a position to help us maintain our sovereignty. At the present time we are militarily incapable of enforcing sovereignty.

We know only too well that the moral support of the world, if we were to rely on that, breaks down in the face of military strength. In this regard I only have to mention the fate of some of the small nations.... There is only one thing that will bring us any kind of lasting peace in the world Mr. Speaker. This will be when each nation is willing to give up some of its sovereignty to well co-ordinated League of Nations, a United Nations, with a peacekeeping force capable of maintaining law

23 *Editors' Note:* In 1969, Mr Justice W.H. Morrow decided in the case of *Regina v. Tootalik, E4-321* that the term "territories" included the sea ice. Donat Pharand, *Canada's Arctic Waters in International Law* (Cambridge: Cambridge University Press, 1988), 59. See also W.H. Morrow, *Northern Justice: The Memoirs of Mr. Justice William G. Morrow* (Toronto: Osgoode Society, 1995).

and order. International affairs are not so much different from human affairs. A policeman on duty on a Saturday night will not be able to maintain law and order if he is not given the authority. An International Court of Justice decision on Canadian sovereign rights in the Arctic would be without force if nations like the United States and the Soviet Union choose to ignore it.

And so, Mr. Speaker, I welcome the text of this note from the United States. I understand that the President of the United States has spoken to the Prime Minister by telephone and I hope they agree to endeavour to solve this problem in good faith. I hope it will not come to any sort of a show of strength. Sending our troops into the Arctic is not going to achieve a great deal at this stage – indeed it amounts almost to a comic opera.

This government should come out with a clear statement that for the last 5 years Canada has laid claim to the whole archipelago of the north, maintaining responsibility for the native population and the ecology of the land and sea. It would not be a sign of weakness to if we put our emphasis on the council table, as long as we have a plan for full cooperation in the development of our western way of life as well as the protection from pollution of the whole of the Arctic. We are already respected as world citizens and as we develop we should put emphasis in the right places.

Mr. Howard: I should like to ask the hon. member, as he has made a number of references to the bargaining table and to negotiations, if he would mind telling us who is going to be on the other side of the bargaining table and what it is we have to negotiate?

Mr. Biggs: Mr. Speaker, I think every nation in the world has an interest in the pollution of the seas. Perhaps there is an argument, as mentioned in this text, in favour of sharing sovereignty so that the international seaways of the world could be open for commerce and for peaceful purposes. I should like to think that people who are asking for that right would be willing to tax themselves and to co-operate with us in every way possible to avoid marine disasters in the north. If they want to share our sovereignty they should be willing to share the cost.

Incidentally, the Northwest Passage route was pioneered by the same mounted police who maintained law and order in that part of the country and made friends with people who lived there. If it had not been for the pioneering work of the of ships like *St. Roch*, and Sergeant Larsen of the mounted police, perhaps the *Manhattan* might not have gotten as far as he did. We did that at our own expense. Now, it is patently ridiculous for anyone to say that we have no vested interest in the Arctic. Whether or not our interest is exclusive is a matter for the bargaining table. I think the mere fact that Canada is willing to sit at the bargaining table and seek the advice and cooperation of others, and the fact that we have faith that other nations of the world are willing to do something in this area with us, in itself is an exercise of our sovereignty. On the other hand, the mere shaking of the sword at the present time would probably be ridiculous and not bring us closer to answering the question of how we are to assert the sovereignty of our country.

Mr. C. Terrence Murphy (Sault Ste. Marie): …From the newspapers and from information we have obtained from the Secretary of State for External Affairs (Mr. Sharp) we have learned that our good neighbour to the south is taking some exception to the provisions of this bill. I think it is interesting to note, Mr. Speaker, that as long ago as 1954 nations got together in an attempt to arrive at some agreement which would prevent pollution of the high seas. An agreement was reached in 1954 by some 22 nations. That agreement simply set out that the countries that were party to it, the 22 nations, would have the right to impose fines on ship owners of the other signatory nations when the ships involved discharged oil within 50 miles of the shoreline of any participating nation. That was the first step in this area, and it was a very mild one. It is significant to note that Canada was a party to the agreement, as were the governments of the United Kingdom and Japan. The United States government was not. For the United States government now to come forward and say that we, Canada, ought not to take this action without first trying to solve this problem by way of international meetings and agreements I think is a little far fetched….

Then, again, in November of last year the nations of the world met in Brussels and attempted to hammer out some sort of international agreement to meet this problem; unfortunately no agreement was reached. So, today, we are introducing this legislation at time when we are very, very vulnerable. As yet we have no law to protect us from these large super-tankers which are sailing the seas just off our coasts…If we do not act now, but wait until a disaster occurs, I think we shall be derelict in our duty as a nation….

I think, also, that the announcement made yesterday in the United States is very significant. The President of the United States has doubled the amount of money which is ordinarily made available for the purposes of naval research. He has doubled the amount of money to be spent on Arctic research. This money is to be used, as I understand it, to develop some sort of skimmer or surface craft, similar to a hovercraft, which is to be used for research in the Arctic. This step was announced only yesterday. We too must move, I submit; we must move now and show no timidity in asserting our rights. Our duty is to protect the people of our country and the people of the continent. Their rights and the rights of all Canadians will be upheld if we support this bill with everything we have.

Hon. W.G Dinsdale (Brandon – Souris): …As I hear hon. Members beating their breasts with patriotic fervour and saying that we must resist any intrusion on Canada's fundamental rights in the Arctic – the Minister of National Defence said just a moment ago that we are reinforcing our military defences in the Arctic to the tune of some 50 personnel – I received an impression similar to that which Don Quixote created when he was tilting at windmills.

2-18. House of Commons Debates, 10 June 1970.

Northwest Passage – Policy of Control

Question No. 1236 – Mr. [William Kenneth] Robinson (Lakeshore):
1. Does the federal government have a policy of control of the Northwest Passage and, if so, does the policy include the co-operation of any other government?
2. To what extent does the federal government intend to police the Northwest Passage?
3. Will the Canadian Forces be involved in the security of Canada's north, and in asserting sovereignty in the north and, if so, to what extent?

Hon. Mitchell Sharp (Secretary of State for External Affairs): 1. The Government intends to open the Northwest Passage as a waterway for passage by ships of all states subject to necessary conditions required for preservation of the Arctic environment. That policy is reflected in the Arctic Waters Pollution Prevention Bill and the Bill to Amend the Territorial Sea and Fishing Zones Act. The Arctic Waters Pollution Prevention Bill would provide for cooperation with other countries by empowering the Government to exempt from regulations the public and naval vessels of other states which substantially comply with Canadian standards; the Government has also indicated its intention to consult with other countries regarding the safety regulations to be adopted under the Arctic Waters Pollution Prevention Bill.
2. The Government intends to police Canada's coastal waters, including the Northwest Passage, in a manner which will achieve the purposes of existing and proposed legislation with respect to those waters.
3. The Canadian Armed Forces will be involved, along with other agencies of the Government of Canada, in protecting the security of Canada's North, and in promoting Canada's sovereign interests in the area.

3 Preparing a Plan for the Canadian Forces

3-1. Colonel R.M. Withers for CDS to Director Continental Plans (DC Plans), DND, 16 April 1969, re: Canadian Forces Plan for the Arctic.[24]

1. It is understood that the CDS has already spoken to you about the requirement to prepare an outline plan for Canadian Forces involvement in the Arctic. The purpose of this memorandum is to record additional guidance which CDS has given.

2. He requests that you develop, within your office and without further dissemination, an outline plan for the activities which could be undertaken over the next ten years. This study is to proceed independently of the work being done in accordance with Reference A. Although fiscal limits cannot be set at this time, you should consider that the budget will be very restricted. Additional items which should be included are:

a. proposals to assemble a planning staff;
b. requirements for a headquarters, perhaps at Yellowknife;
c. mobility needs such as hovercraft and aircraft;
d. requirements for ships, e.g. ice-breaker;
e. training of Eskimos and Indians and the use of indigenous personnel to man units and bases; and
f. language training requirements so that Regular Officers and NCOs can train indigenous personnel.

3. The CDS would like you to report on this matter at your earliest convenience.

24 Raymont Collection, DHH 73/1223/987 box 52. Originally classified as "Secret (Canadian Eyes Only)."

3-2. Report of the Steering Committee on the Canadian North, "Canadian Forces Policies Objectives and Activities in the Canadian North," 5 December 1969.[25]

CANADIAN FORCES POLICIES, OBJECTIVES AND ACTIVITIES IN THE CANADIAN NORTH

References: A. V 3120-13 over V 3010-36 TD 8324 (DConP) dated
B. CDS Directive D40/69 dated 31 Oct 69

General

1. Reference A provided guidelines for the examination of DND policies, objectives and activities in the Canadian North. A Steering Committee on the Canadian North was formed in January, 1969, under the chairmanship of the Director of Continental Plans and with representation from CFHQ branches, [the Defence Research Board] and the [Deputy Minister]'s office.

2. The Committee detailed a number of studies to sub-committees which were conducted throughout the year. For the most part, the work of these sub-committees has been completed. Some of the reports, however cannot be completed as they are related to the interdepartmental studies referred to in paragraph 6, which are expected to be completed by the end of the year, and which may have a decided influence upon DND policies for the Canadian North.

Aim

3. The aim of this report is to make recommendations, resulting from the studies conducted by the Steering Committee on the Canadian North, covering the Canadian Forces policies, objectives and activities in the Canadian North.

National Policies

...

25 Raymont Collection, DHH 73/1223/987 box 52. Originally classified as "Confidential (Canadian Eyes Only)."

6. The Cabinet agreed, on 12 June 1969, on the recommendation of the Cabinet Committee of External Policy and Defence, that, with regard to the capacities of the Canadian Forces to contribute to the national development of the country and to assist the civil authorities, a number of studies, to be co-oriented by Treasury Board, be undertaken and reported to the Cabinet as expeditiously as possible and, in any event, by the end of December, 1969. The studies, with implications for future military activities in the North, are as follows:

a. civil maritime patrol activities; (Task Force on Consolidation of Government Owned Ships and Vessels)
b. aviation support for VIP passengers and government freight;
c. extension of communications services to other federal government agencies;
d. engineering development project; and
e. provision of government supply services by the Canadian Forces.

Defence Responsibilities

7. Canadian defence interests are global in nature. It is essential that the policies and objectives of DND be in harmony with the broad national policies and objectives. Within this context, defence responsibilities in respect of the Canadian North are considered to be as follows:

a. Support of Canada's national policies by contributing to the maintenance of Canadian sovereignty.
b. All aspects of maritime, land and air defence. In some areas, these tasks are done in co-operation, or shared with the USA and other allies under international agreements.
c. Provision of search and rescue services.
d. Assisting other government and commercial agencies.

Defence Objectives

8. In the light of current national policies and the DND responsibilities considered above, the following defence objectives are identified:

a. Contributing to the maintenance of Canadian sovereignty in the North by:
   (1) providing a military presence,

(2) surveillance and reconnaissance of Canadian territory, airspace and territorial waters as well as the air and sea approached thereto.

b. Maintaining operationally ready maritime, lend and air forces capable of defeating illegal and forcible entry into the Canadian North.
c. Providing effective search and rescue services in Canadian territory and ranking co-operative contributions in international areas adjacent to Canada.
d. Assisting other government and commercial activities which enhance the economic development of the Canadian North which are not readily available from other sources.

The Threat

9. The direct military threat to Canada (North America) via the Arctic and the Canadian northland approach is significant only in the context of a general nuclear war. Although the possibility cannot be totally ignored, it is unlikely that incursions of Canadian northland territory, air space, and waters (including sub surface) would be deliberately attempted by Soviet armed forces prior to the onset of a general nuclear war. Not even Soviet ballistic missile submarines are likely to conduct regular patrols in the North American side of the Arctic basin, particularly to planned missile launch-stations for at least some years in the future. Under ice operations by Soviet submarines may increase but are likely to be concerned primarily with research, hydrographic survey, transit and possibly ASW operations in waters contiguous to the Soviet Union, and in Arctic sea areas beyond those of immediate Canadian concern. Polar flights by Soviet aircraft are likely to continue for crew training, intelligence gathering, surveillance, submarine cooperation and possibly ASW activities.

10. The indirect threat is related to the question of national sovereignty and it is more difficult to be precise about the absolute nature of this aspect. In law, Canadian sovereignty over the land areas claimed by Canada including established internal waters and territorial waters associated with these land areas, is not likely to be overtly contested.

The Canadian Government position concerning jurisdiction over the other waters of the Canadian Archipelago has not yet been stated and is therefore not discussed further in this report.

11. Sovereignty implies the right, and indeed the responsibility, of being "master of our own affairs", in those areas which are clearly established, in law, as Canadian. Mutual defence arrangements which involve the stationing of foreign forces on Canadian soil do not, in themselves, detract from these rights and responsibilities. In fact, in many cases, they serve to confirm them. If, however, foreign persons or unattended installations were allowed to operate in Canadian territory with impunity or if foreign commercial ventures were allowed to exploit Canadian resources to the detriment of national interests, pollute the environment or otherwise operate without police or other administrative supervision, such actions would seriously impair Canadian claims to sovereignty.

Military Activities in Support of Defence Objective

12. Consideration of the defence objectives has resulted in the identification of a number of military activities which would support those objectives. Some of these activities are being conducted now, some are feasible but are not being conducted, and some are ideas subject to further study. It is appreciated that any increase in activity in the Canadian North will require establishment of priorities and allocation of resources. However, it would be premature to make recommendations in this field until at least a general policy for the Forces role in the Canadian North is agreed in principle.

13. These activities, for the purposes of discussion, can be divided into roughly three categories:

a. Activities being conducted at present, and which divide into two sub-categories:
   (1) Those being conducted at a suitable level to meet the defence objectives.
   (2) Those being conducted below a suitable level to meet the defence objectives.

b. Activities which appear necessary and feasible, and which could be conducted if allocated priorities and resources.
c. Activities which appear desirable, but further study in required.

14. The following military activities are now being performed in the Canadian North either unilaterally or in co-operation with allies and are considered to be performed at levels compatible with defence objectives:
a. Air space surveillance (DEWLine)
b. Electronic surveillance
c. Search and Rescue (but see paragraph 16 b. below)
d. Cadet training. Perhaps more than anywhere else in Canada, this training is beneficial to the development of character and national unity. It. should be encouraged and expanded where facilities permit.

15. The following activities are being conducted, but at levels which are considered to be below a suitable level to meet the stated defence objectives:
a. Surveillance and reconnaissance of the land mass and waters of the Canadian North by air and surface means to:
(1) ensure a capability- to detect, identify and analyze (sic) alien activity;
(2) monitor the movement of transit shipping;
(3) demonstrate Canada's determination to exercise control over the area.
b. Training exercises and maneuvers to ensure the development and maintenance of military expertise for operations in the Canadian North. This activity has declined in recent years. Training plans of some commands recently place more emphasis on Northern operations and this should be encouraged.
c. Assistance to other agencies. The Canadian Forces possess a level of capability and expertise which can be used to advantage in furthering government objectives in the North. While the Nation is at peace, this should be exploited. Although Canadian Forces do assist other agencies in a number of important ways, the level and scope of these activities could be increased. This should be

done in concert with government policy and must not prejudice operational commitments. DND assistance must not be, or seem to be, in competition with civilian entrepreneurs.

d. Canadian Rangers. For various reasons, primarily through lack of support, this organization has lost cohesiveness. It still exists, however, and could perform a useful military function and, at the same time, make a direct and positive contribution to Canadian society. The possibility of associating the Rangers and Militia more closely should be examined. If appropriately organized it could:
   (1) assist in the surveillance and reconnaissance of remote areas and the air and sea approaches;
   (2) provide experienced guides for operations and manoeuvres;
   (3) assist in search and rescue operations.
e. Command and control of Canadian Forces activity in the North is exercised, at present, through a multiplicity of command agencies. Co-ordination is lacking. The whole system of command, control and co-ordination should be improved. The recent decision to station liaison detachments at Whitehorse, Y.T. and Yellowknife, N.W.T. should contribute to the improvement of liaison and coordination with local authorities. However, the formation of a small headquarters for this purpose is indicated and is discussed below.

16. The following activities would contribute substantially to the fulfillment of defence objectives and could be undertaken with current resources providing enough time for planning and co-ordination is allowed:

a. The establishment of adequate arrangements for the command, control and co-ordination of military activities in the North. As an initial step, planning should begin, with a view to the organization of a small, all-environment headquarters which would be responsible for the direction of military activity in the Canadian North which does not fall within the purview of responsibility of functional commands and which would be responsible for the co-ordination of all other military activity in the North;

b. Search and rescue activities are being conducted now, and, in many respects, may be considered to be adequate. However, expanding commercial activity in the North, and the expanding development of Northern air and sea routes for global transportation purposes is rapidly diminishing the relative effectiveness of the Canadian Forces SAR [Search and Rescue] organization. In particular, the rescue or recovery function lends itself to improvements. Functional commands are directed to be responsive to the requirements of SAR "Searchmasters" but are not otherwise specifically tasked. All commands with a rescue/recovery capability should be assigned responsibilities in this role and should maintain disaster plans and appropriate stores for this role. In addition, the fact that all Canadian Forces SAR units are located in Southern Canada limits effectiveness in terms of response time. To relocate SAR detachments in the North for this purpose alone would probably not be feasible from a cost effective point of view. However, the possibility of including this function in multi-purpose air element located in the North should not be overlooked and is discussed later in this report.
c. Assistance in ice reconnaissance. This function falls within the category of assistance to other agencies. With appropriate training, it could probably be performed in conjunction with surveillance and reconnaissance patrols and would be an important contribution to maritime operations in the Canadian North.
d. Northern orientation training. In the past, Canadian Forces officers and men possessed extensive expertise in Northern operations, but now this expertise has diminished. There is a need for a continuing program of orientation training for staff officers and planners as well as for personnel actively engaged in Northern activities. This program could be developed and some ideas are:
   (1) the utilization of scheduled and operational Canadian Forces aircraft flights in the North;
   (2) participation in research programs by DRB and other federal agencies;
   (3) familiarization programs at training schools and staff courses.

e. Research activities. Consideration of defence objectives and possible activities has indicated a number of areas which require additional research support to confirm feasibility. To cite one example, further research is needed in the field of under-ice detection of submarine activity. DRB research activities in support of defence requirements in the Canadian North should be given increased emphasis. This implies the need for specific guidance on which research programs may be formulated.

17. There are several other activities which would contribute to the fulfillment of the defence objectives and which, in the opinion of the Steering Committee, are feasible. However, they will require longer-term study and likely the allocation of additional resources. Several of these activities which would be in the category of supporting Federal Government and commercial activities must await the results of the interdepartmental studies referred to previously. The following list of possible activities, which is not exhaustive, may be considered as a basis for further study:

a. The permanent stationing in the North of a small Regional Headquarters. This would imply the provision of accommodation, including married quarters, and communications facilities, perhaps in conjunction with other government departments.
b. The stationing of a composite multi-purpose air element in the North. This element could provide immediate response to a search and rescue operation, could contribute to the military surveillance and reconnaissance activities as well as ice reconnaissance, and might also perform transport and liaison functions. Its presence would contribute to the credibility of Canada's determination to maintain its Territorial integrity.
c. Consideration of establishing a base for year-round marine operations, if such operations prove feasible, for both naval and civilian vessels. This facility could serve as a base for icebreaking, salvage and repair activities and also might be a convenient-location for a submarine detection centre.
d. Consideration of the requirement for a sub-surface surveillance system.

e. The provision in the North of support facilities either by contract or by other arrangements for Canadian Forces aircraft operating there. At present Canadian Forces aircraft rely heavily upon the US [Air Force] facilities at Thule, Greenland for these.
f. The assumption of responsibility for the operation of certain DEW Line airfields by Canadian agencies. This is now being examined by a sub-committee of the Advisory Committee on Northern Development.
g. Assisting in the provision of vital services in the event of the phase-out of the DEW Line as a Joint Defence installation in the surveillance role. The DEW Line now provides communications, navigation aids, and logistic services which are considered vital to military and commercial air operations in the Canadian North.
h. Assistance in the provision of navigational aids including sea navigational aids and the possible take over by a Canadian agency, of the US Coast Guard operated LORAN [long-range navigation] Station at Cape Christian, Baffin Island, N.W.T.
j. Increased levels of assistance to other government and commercial agencies. DND assistance must not be, or seem to be, in competition with civilian entrepreneurs and should not be under-taken to the prejudice of assigned operational commitments.

A Hercules is unloaded after making the long trip to the Arctic, May 1978. (LAC)

Conclusion

18. In view of the foregoing it is considered that:
   a. Large scale military activity in the Canadian North would not be justified on the basis of the direct military threat alone, nor would it be valid to permanently station large military establishments in the North. Nevertheless, it is imperative that the capability to conduct operations against a hostile enemy in the Canadian North be developed and maintained. By so doing the Canadian Forces would substantially contribute to the defence against the indirect threat to Canadian sovereignty in the Canadian North.
   b. As an effective segment of Canadian society, and in order to make its contribution both to economic and social development, and the maintenance of sovereignty, the Canadian Forces must establish a presence in the Canadian North. This presence can be established largely by operational and exercise activity, however, some permanent presence is considered essential.
   c. Major decisions for changes in defence policies for the Canadian North should await the results of the inter-departmental studies referred to in paragraph 6 above.

<u>**Recommendations**</u>

19. It is recommended that:
   a. The defence responsibilities as outlined in paragraph 7 above be accepted.
   b. The defence objectives identified in paragraph 8 above be approved.
   c. The military activities which are now being performed in the Canadian North at adequate levels (paragraph 14 above) continue.
   d. Immediate steps be taken to increase the tempo of the following military activities:
      (1) Surveillance and reconnaissance by air and surface means.
      (2) Training exercises and maneuvers.
   e. Planning begin immediately for implementation of the following activities:
      (1) Improved command and control arrangements including the organization of a small regional headquarters.
      (2) Search and rescue responsibilities to be assigned all commands.

(3) Assistance in the provision of ice reconnaissance.
(4) Northern orientation training for staff officers and staff planners.
(5) The provision of more detailed guidance for research activities.

f. Qualitative studies be initiated, to examine the desirability and feasibility of the following activities:
(1) The stationing in the North of a small regional headquarters.
(2) The stationing in the North of a composite air element.
(3) The establishment of a year-round base for marine operations in the North.
(4) The possible requirement for a sub-surface detection system.
(5) The provision of support facilities for Canadian Forces aircraft.

g. That DND participate in the following feasibility studies in co-operation with other government departments:
(1) The assumption of responsibility for the operation of certain DEW Line airfields (now under examination).
(2) The provision of vital services now performed by the DEW Line when the DEW Line is eventually phased out.
(3) The provision of navigational aids as needed including the take over by a Canadian agency of the Cape Christian LORAN Station.
(4) Increased assistance to other agencies (now under examination).

h. A series of CDS Directives be issued on a timely basis to implement those DND policies which are approved as a result of this paper as well as those which will subsequently be approved as a result of the interdepartmental studies referred to in paragraph 6 above.

3-3. Summary Record, CDS Advisory Committee Meeting 4/70, 18 February 1970.[26]

SUMMARY RECORD
CDS ADVISORY COMMITTEE MEETING 4/70
HELD IN THE CDS CONFERENCE ROOM
AT 09 00 HRS WEDNESDAY 18 FEBRUARY 1970

I Intelligence Briefing

1. [An intelligence officer with the Director Intelligence Production] briefed the meeting on items of current interest to the CF.

II Operations Briefing

2. [The Director of Operations] briefed the meeting on current operational activities of the CF.

III DG INFO Briefing

3. [The Director General Information] briefed members on current news items and editorials of interest to DND.

IV Canadian Forces Policies, Objectives and Activities in the Canadian North

4. DC Plans introduced this item. He referred the members to the Report of the Steering Committee on the Canadian North (dated 5 December, 1969), which had been distributed as supporting data for this item. Then, with the assistance of slides, DC Plans reviewed the more important factors discussed in the Report. A transcript of the DC Plans presentation is attached at Annex A.

5. Following discussion of several minor factors incidental to the presentation VCDS noted that the purpose of the briefing had been to

26 Raymont Collection, DHH 73/1223/987 box 52. Originally classified as "Secret."

obtain CDSAC [the Chief of the Defence Staff's Advisory Committee's] advice on subsequent staff action. He pointed out that the Minister had stated that a Northern HQ would be established in the near future, but important decisions relative to the purpose, location, composition, etc, of the HQ had yet to be decided. VCDS added that specific direction is also required to resolve the present conflict of interest among the functional commands which have northern responsibilities. Similarly, the activities of the CF in Northern Canada should complement other government interests and programmes in the area.

6. The [Combat Training School] and [Deputy Comptroller General] questioned whether the primary purpose of CF participation in northern affairs is in the interest of sovereignty or to assist other government departments in the development and protection of the North. They suggested that this matter must be resolved before related decisions such as type of operations, size and composition of forces and location of headquarters or bases can be made. Other members agreed and added that without a rational, long term policy the effectiveness of DND, and the Canadian Forces in particular, will be suspect.

7. The CDS noted the comments of the members and proposed that the recommendations of the Report be considered by the members to determine their validity and to establish guidelines for further staff action. The consensus by item follows.

a. <u>Defence responsibilities;</u>
   (1) contributing to Canadian sovereignty,
   (2) maritime, land and air defence,
   (3) search and rescue services, and
   (4) assisting other agencies.

b. <u>Defence objectives;</u>
   (1) contributing to sovereignty by,
      (a) military presence resulting from new CF activities, and
      (b) surveillance and reconnaissance,
   (2) military capabilities,
   (3) search and rescue services, and

(4) assisting other agencies with economic development.

c. Continuation of current military activities;
   (1) DEW Line surveillance,
   (2) electronic surveillance,
   (3) search and rescue, and
   (4) Cadet training.

d. Increased military activity;
   (1) surveillance and reconnaissance to be increased through better co-ordination of current military operations in the area and through increased military activity generally, (interest is to be developed in the Northern Islands and under-ice detection),
   (2) training exercises and maneuvers,
   (3) assistance to other agencies, and
   (4) Canadian Ranger programmes.

e. Implementation Planning which is to begin immediately;
   (1) command and control to be co-ordinated by CFHQ,
   (2) improved search and rescue capabilities,
   (3) ice reconnaissance assistance,
   (4) orientation training, and,
   (5) guidance for research activities in co-operation with DRB and other government departments and agencies.

f. Further DND studies to be co-ordinated by VCDS;
   (1) tactical headquarters - organization, functions and location,
   (2) composite air element,
   (3) base for maritime operations,
   (4) under-ice detection system, and
   (5) support facilities for CF aircraft.

g. Feasibility studies to be initiated with other government departments;
   (1) assumption of responsibility for the operation of DEW Line airfields,
   (2) replacement of DEW Line support service when DEW Line is phased out,
   (3) provision of navigational aids, and
   (4) DND assistance to other agencies.

8. Concluding discussion of this item the CDS stated in summary that the continuing studies should identify requirements, define tasks and recommend a suitable command and control structure. The results are to be presented to CDSAC as soon as completed. In the interim Mobile and Maritime Command Headquarters are to be advised of the CDSAC proposal concerning the relationship of the Northern Headquarters and CFHQ.

9. The CDS authorized presentation of an updated briefing, based on the "Report of the Steering Committee on the Canadian North," to Defence Council prior to the Minister's tour of Northern Canada in April.

Annex A

DC PLANS PRESENTATION TO CDSAC ON CANADIAN FORCES POLICIES OBJECTIVES AND ACTIVITIES IN THE CANADIAN NORTH

INTRODUCTION

1. General Sharp and Gentlemen. My purpose this morning is to brief you on our proposals for the future objectives and activities of the Canadian Forces in our North.

BACKGROUND

2. To set the stage for this presentation, perhaps you would permit me to take a few moments to review the background of Canadian Forces activity in the North.

3. Pre-World War II activity involved communications and aerial survey. In 1923, in order to help develop the Canadian North, the first radio-telegraph stations of the Northwest Territories and Yukon Radio System were established by the Canadian Army. The system provided an invaluable service including the directing of ships in the Arctic and at

some stations a soldier acted as postmaster, airport superintendent and justice of the peace.

4. RCAF [Royal Canadian Air Force] flying activity in the North began in 1927 when a small air detachment played a prominent role in the Hudson Strait expedition by the Department of Marine and Fisheries. This paved the way for subsequent aerial survey activities which resulted in the mapping of the Canadian North.

5. The wartime requirement for a military highway to Alaska, and an air route to Europe for short range aircraft accelerated military activity in both the eastern and western Arctic. This was followed in the post-war period by several military activities including extensive aerial survey by the RCAF; ground control surveys by military engineers; the establishment of a winter warfare school at Fort Churchill, and the introduction of the icebreaker Labrador into the fleet. In addition, post-war exercise activity strived to build up and maintain a high degree of expertise for the conduct of air supported land operations in the North. Exercises, for example Exercise Muskox, went a long way towards the development of this expertise.

6. Our gradual withdrawal from activities in the North was highlighted by the transfer of the [Royal Canadian Navy] Icebreaker Labrador to DOT in 1958, the handover of the North West Territories and Yukon Territory communications system in 1959, the ceasing of military activity at Churchill in 1963 and the phase-out of responsibility for the Alaska Highway in 1964-65. At the same time the RCAF Photo Survey activity was phased-out and in recent years only a small proportion of ground control survey activity had been carried out in the North.

7. This gradual run-down of military activity was in keeping with the recommendations of the [Glassco] Royal Commission. In 1968 the emphasis of Canadian Foreign and Defence Policy commenced to shift away from NATO Europe and it was coincidental with an awakening of government interest in Northern Canada. It was then timely and

appropriate for us to re-examine the matter of military activity in our North.

8. Our present level of activity and military presence in the North is very limited. The largest activity of a permanent nature is the communications research stations at Inuvik and Alert. We also have five Canadian military personnel at each of the four DEW Line main stations, Cape Dyer, Hall Beach, Cambridge Bay and Cape Parry, and two small liaison detachments are now being established at Yellowknife and at Whitehorse.

A DEW Line Station keeping its quiet vigil over the Far North. (LAC)

9. However, military presence can be achieved by activities other than those which are permanently stationed in the North. Maritime patrol aircraft carry out periodic surveillance and there are plans under review for increasing the frequency of these flights. Also, Mobile Command, in conjunction with Air Transport Command, are planning an increase in northern exercises.

10. Nevertheless, it seems apparent that our military activity has fallen below an acceptable level by our loss of expertise for northern operations.

Although the direct military threat is negligible, we must certainly maintain a capability to operate anywhere in our country.

PRELIMINARY STUDIES

11. With the approval of the CDS our studies at CFHQ began during the summer of 1968. This resulted in the formation of a steering committee charged with the responsibility of examining and reporting upon Canadian Forces activity in the Canadian North.

12. The committee divided its work into eight studies covering the subjects of this chart.

13. During the period January-October 1969, the committee coordinated the studies and several members participated in tours of the North. Throughout the studies, contact was maintained with other government departments through the Advisory Committee on Northern Development (ACND) on which I represent you as the Canadian Forces member.

PREPARATION OF THE REPORT

14. The final report was prepared and staffed within CFHQ during the period October-December 1969, and now has the support of all members.

15. At the same time [Colonel] R. Berube, who was assigned to my staff temporarily from Mobile Command, carried out a further tour of the North. He was able to monitor the preparation of the committee's report and subsequently submitted a report on his findings separately. His report supports in detail the recommendations contained in the committee's report, and in addition provides a basis for certain follow-up actions.

ASSOCIATED STUDIES

16. As a result of a Cabinet decision in June 69 a number of interdepartmental studies were undertaken to consider the capacities of the Canadian Forces to contribute to the development of the country.

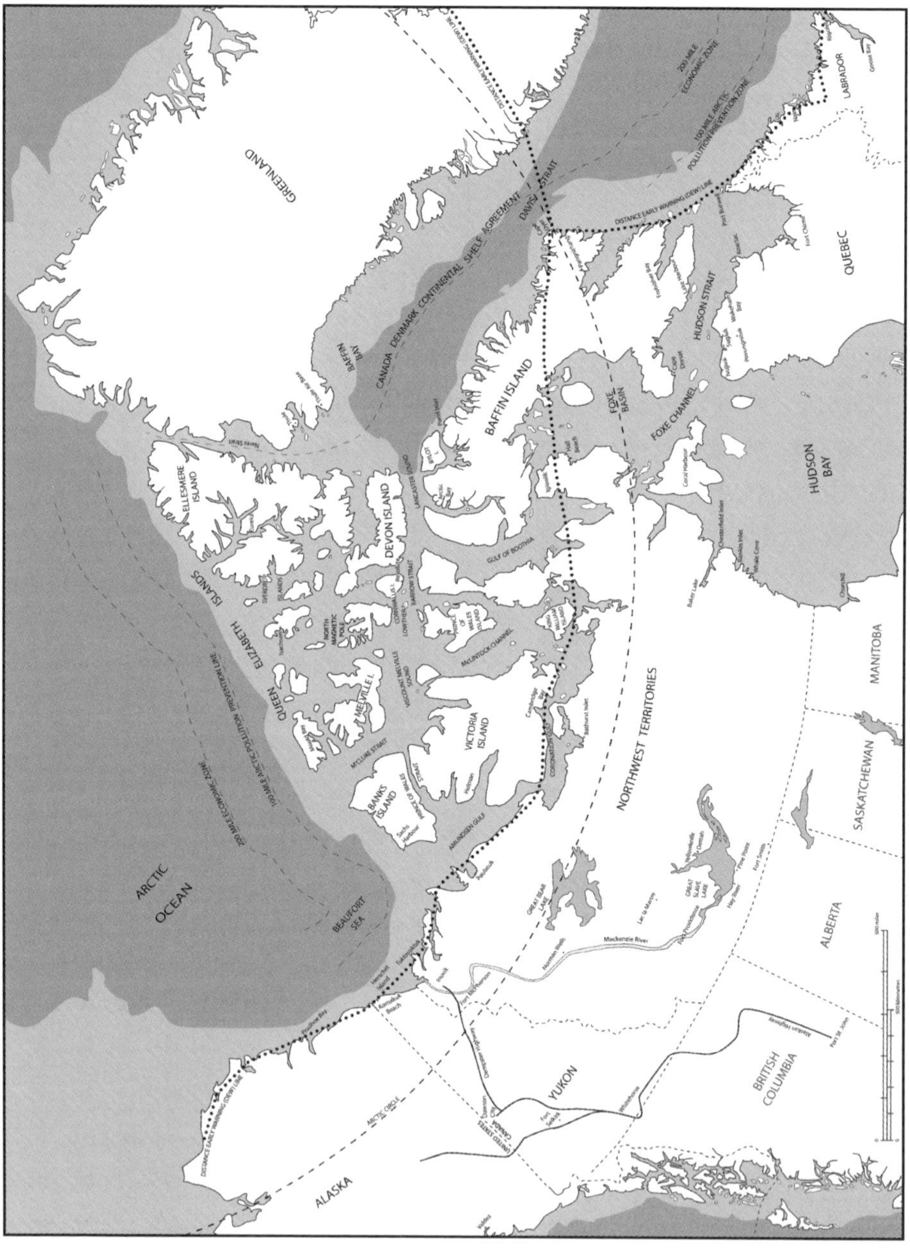

For a larger version of this map, visit www.wlu.ca/lcmsds/arctic_sovereignty_security

STEERING COMMITTEE ON THE CANADIAN NORTH

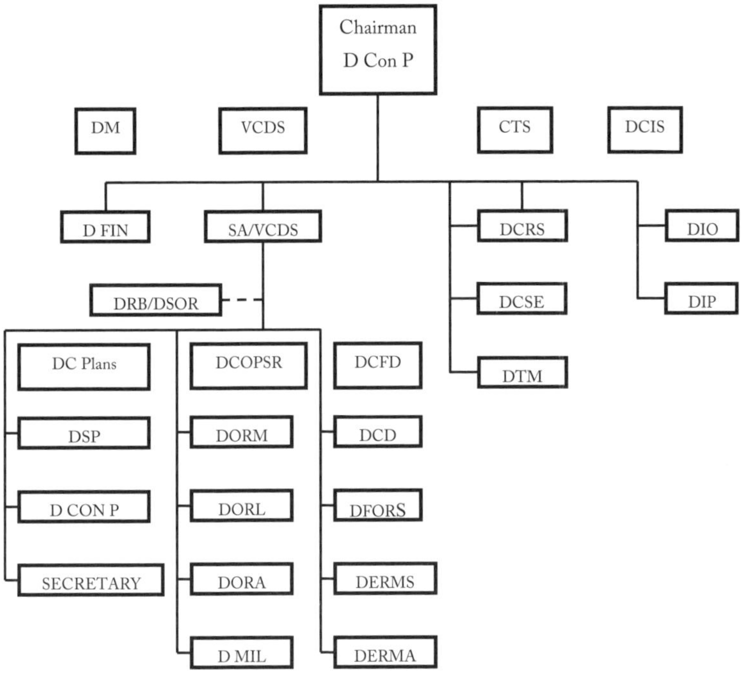

These studies are being co-ordinated by the Treasury Board and the results have not yet been made known. Those which have implications for future military activities in the North are shown below:

a. civil maritime patrol activities; (task force on consolidation of government owned ships and vessels)
b. aviation support for VIP passengers and government freight;
c. extension of communications services to other federal government agencies;
d. engineering development project; and
e. provision of government supply services by the Canadian Forces.

CONCLUSIONS

17. The conclusions of the report are summarized as follows:

1. Military activity in the Canadian North is not justified on the basis of the direct military threat alone, but:
    a. military activity will contribute to defence against the indirect threat to Canadian sovereignty; and

   b. a capability to conduct military operations must be developed and maintained.
2. The Canadian Forces must establish a presence:
   a. primarily by operations and exercise activity; and
   b. by small permanent establishments.
3. DND policy in the Canadian North must be thoroughly co-ordinated with other government departments.

A word of caution is necessary.

We must be careful not to allow ourselves to be drawn into programs which might be short-lived as this would bring into question the credibility of military activity and would have a disruptive effect on local economy.

RECOMMENDATIONS

18. The report makes eight recommendations covering 22 activities...[27]

19. And finally, Sir, I recommend that the report be approved as submitted.

27 The recommendations were adopted by the CDS Advisory Committee as listed in the summary record.

3-4. Defence Council, Minute of the 287th Meeting and Briefing by BGen H. Tellier, Director General Plans, 23 March 1970.[28]

II. Canadian Forces Policies, Objectives and Activities in the Canadian North

7. Introducing this item, the VCDS called upon BGen H. Tellier, Director General Plans, who briefed the members on the Report of the Steering Committee on the Canadian North. Employing the medium of slides, BGen Tellier reviewed the background of Canadian Forces activities in the North, preliminary studies and preparation of the Report, the conclusions and recommendations of the Steering Committee and the action taken to establish a Northern Command Headquarters. The details of this presentation are reproduced at Annex "B" to the minutes.

8. Opening the discussion, the Minister wondered about participation by the native population and inquired if they were included in the Cadet training activities. BGen Teller called on LCol J.A. Cameron of the Directorate of Continental Plans for the figures on Cadets and LCol Cameron stated that approximately 80% of the Cadets in the North were natives.

9. The Minister then inquired if Resolute Bay was an interim base only and not necessarily the permanent location of the Northern Command Headquarters. In reply, BGen Tellier confirmed that a permanent Headquarters location would not be established until further studies were completed.

10. Replying to an inquiry from the Minister concerning planned facilities at Frobisher Bay, the VCDS stated that present plans call for a Staging Base for Argus aircraft engaged in surveillance operations. The immediate objective was to establish a military presence and further studies will be carried out in order to fully assess the scope of future military activities in the North. The VCDS then went on to say that,

28 Raymont Collection, DHH 73/1223/987 box 52. Originally classified as "Restricted."

following analysis, surveillance may be achieved by other means such as employment of less sophisticated aircraft than the Argus which would not be put to its best use in the North.

11. Following further discussion, the Minister expressed his appreciation for the presentation.

Annex "B"

Briefing to Defence Council …
by BGen H. Tellier, Director General Plans

INTRODUCTION

Mr. Minister and Gentlemen. As the Defence Council members are aware, this presentation was given by [Rear-Admiral Robert W. Timbrell] to CDSAC on the 18th of February [1970], in a slightly different form *[see doc. 3-3]*. I trust that this will be useful to you in view of your forthcoming trip in the North.

AIM

1. My aim is to bring you up-to-date on our proposals for military planning and activities of the Canadian Forces in our North.

BACKGROUND

…

9. … A series of platoon-sized environmental exercises (New Viking) will begin in April [1970] and will continue twice per month throughout the year. In addition, two larger exercises will be held during the year:

Exercise Nemesis North - [Commando Group] - May

Exercise Northern Lancer - [Airborne Regimental Group] - December

…

17. As I mentioned previously we have already taken action to set up a Northern Command Headquarters (NCHQ). A CDS directive was issued last week, authorizing its formation.

18. The Northern Command Headquarters shall be established in three stages:

Stage I - Assemble at CFHQ by 15 May to review Canadian Forces activities in the North and establish a presence at Resolute Bay by 1 July.

Stage II - The Commander NCHQ shall present recommendations to the CDS for approval followed by preparation and finalization of detailed plans for the establishment of NCHQ at a permanent location.

Stage III - NCHQ shall be established at a permanent location in Northern Canada, and shall assume the responsibilities for CFHQ-assigned tasks. The timing of this stage will depend upon the recommendations resulting from Stage II; however, the target date for planning purposes is 1 March 1971.

Terms of Reference

19. NCHQ shall function directly under CFHQ and shall be responsive to VCDS/DC Plans during Stages I and II.

20. Direct liaison with commands and CFHQ staff branches is authorized.

21. The Commander NCHQ shall be prepared to present his recommendations to the CDS by 15 October, 1970. Recommendations are to include consideration of the following:

a. The roles of NCHQ
b. Tasks
c. Terms of reference including:
   (1) Command and control
   (2) Geographical areas of responsibility/interest
   (3) Relationships with commands.
d. Establishment requirements
e. Location
f. Communications requirements
g. Logistic support
h. Other pertinent considerations (other government departments).

22. Terms of reference for NCHQ will be issued by CFHQ after consideration of the Stage II recommendations, and prior to commencement of Stage III.

23. And that, Sir, is the approach we intend to take as a basis for military planning and activities in the North.

3-5. DND Press Release, Announcement by the Hon. Leo Cadieux, Minister of National Defence, 17 April 1970.[29]

The Canadian Forces will establish a permanent headquarters at Yellowknife, NWT, this year to coordinate increasing military activities in Canada's northern regions.

The headquarters will be organized during the spring and summer in Ottawa and move to Yellowknife in the fall. *The decision to establish a headquarters in the North was announced last Sept 19 in the statement outlining the restructuring of the Canadian Forces.*

Activities of the Department of National Defence in the north are being carried out in cooperation with the Hon. Jean Chretien, Minister of Indian Affairs and Northern Development. The selection of Yellowknife as the headquarters was made in conjunction with the Department of Indian Affairs and the government of the Northwest Territories.

Establishment of the headquarters is one of several steps being taken to strengthen Canada's military presence north of the 60th parallel, including the setting up of a small aircraft servicing detachment at Frobisher, increased air surveillance coverage and year-round land and tactical air operational exercises.

The headquarters, officially designated Headquarters Northern Region, will be commanded by Colonel Ramsey Withers, 39, Ottawa, who will be promoted to brigadier-general on taking up his appointment later this spring. He will be responsible for co-coordinating military activities in the north including liaison with the Territorial Government. The headquarters staff will reach a strength of approximately 35 personnel by late 1971. Married personnel on the staff will be accompanied to Yellowknife by their families.

Small regional military liaison detachments were formed in February at Yellowknife and at Whitehorse in the Yukon to carry out liaison with territorial authorities and civilian agencies in these areas. The Yellowknife detachment will be absorbed by Headquarters, Northern Region when the latter is established in the fall.

A small detachment of air personnel from Maritime Command will be located beginning next month at Frobisher Bay airport. Facilities

29 LAC, RG 25, vol. 10322, file 27-10-2-2 pt.1.

provided by the detachment will permit Argus aircraft to operate from the airfield, extending the surveillance coverage of the Canadian Arctic Archipelago. Air hours on surveillance flights are being increased by 25 per cent over last year.

Arrangements will also be made to operate Tracker aircraft on coastal patrol from Goose Bay, Labrador and Fort Chimo near Ungava Bay. These aircraft, which will continue to be based at Shearwater, N.S., have been deployed successfully to northern Canada on previous occasions.

Earlier this month the Canadian Forces began a series of ground exercises in the Arctic which will continue on a year-round basis. The exercises are designed to familiarize troops with winter and summer operations in northern areas. Next month the Canadian Airborne Regiment, based at Edmonton, will carry out a full scale exercise in the Coral Harbour area.

Approximately 400 Canadian servicemen are now serving in the north, most at the communications research station at Alert and Inuvik. Others serve at DEW Line Establishments.

3-6. DEXAF, North American Defence and NATO Division (OMD) to Legal Division (FLE), re: Department of National Defence – Paper on Sovereignty, 24 March 1970.[30]

The Chief of the Defence Staff, General F.R. Sharp, has passed to us for comment the attached paper on sovereignty. The aim of the paper is to examine the concept of sovereignty in so far as it relates to defence planning. Your comments are requested on the legal issues raised in the paper.

2. Under the section on "territorial sovereignty" the paper makes the point that the only real problem for Canada is the legal status of the archipelago waters. The paper suggests that this problem is a legal, political and economic problem (rather than a military one) and refers to Canada's commitment to peaceful settlement of disputes.

3. In our view, the paper overlooks one important question, i.e. whether an increased level of military surveillance or patrols in the area of the archipelago waters could help to strengthen Canada's legal claim to these waters, for example, if the dispute were ever referred to arbitration in the International Court. This notion has figured from time to time in public discussion of the issues, and some statements by the [Secretary of State for External Affairs] (e.g. his letter to the Globe and Mail) and by [the Minister of National Defence] and can be interpreted to suggest that this is the case. We would be grateful if you could address yourself to this question along with other legal aspects of the paper.

4. It would be greatly appreciated if we could receive your comments by April 1.

30 LAC, RG 25, vol. 10322, file 27-10-2-2 pt.1. Originally classified as "Confidential." Some of these points were raised by E.B. Wang in his memorandum to R.P. Cameron, 20 March 1970, on the same file.

3-7. DEXAF, North American Defence and NATO Division (OMD) to Legal Division (FLE), subject: Role of Canadian Armed Forces in the Protection of Sovereignty, 20 April 1970.[31]

We have been asked by the Chief of the Defence Staff to comment on a draft study "Canadian Defence Policy in the 1970's" dated March 24, 1970, which was prepared in the Department of National Defence for their use as a basic planning document. Since this document, when finally approved, is intended by DND to provide authoritative guidance to their planning staff and operational commanders in the years ahead, we are reviewing the text carefully in light of the foreign policy interests of this Department.

2. The study contains several sections on the role of the Canadian Armed Forces in the maintenance of sovereignty. We have some misgivings about the way in which this aspect is treated and we would appreciate your comments especially on the references to requirements of sovereignty under international law. We attach extracts of the main passage dealing with sovereignty.... There are also other brief references to sovereignty and should you wish to examine the complete document which runs to 31 pages, we would be glad to make a copy available.

3. Our misgivings relate mainly to para. 62. It may help to put the issues in clearer focus if we were to outline our tentative thoughts in this regard.

4. Para. 62 seems to us to confuse two different problems facing Canada:

(a) the need for an adequate regulatory/law enforcement capability (whether civilian, police or military or some combination of the three, as at present) in respect of foreign and domestic activities and commercial enterprises (the new anti-pollution legislation should be mentioned here); and

31 LAC, RG 25, vol. 10322, file 27-10-2-2 pt.1. Originally classified as "Confidential."

A Tracker aircraft on patrol in the Arctic flies past a large iceberg, 25 August 1971. (LAC)

(b) the need for Canada to establish or strengthen a legal basis for claims over archipelago waters and pollution control zones.

On the latter problem DND attaches some importance to "presence" or "persistent presence" (also referred to elsewhere in the document) as a requirement of Canada which could justify an increased level of military activity in the North, apart from any military or strategic rationale.

5. As regard the lands, islands and continental shelf of the Canadian Arctic, it is our understanding that there is no requirement for an increased level of activity by any government agency solely on grounds of an alleged need for more "presence", since there is no challenge to Canada's sovereignty in this respect. We note that the Advisory Committee on Northern Development recently reached an informal consensus to this effect and agreed that "programmes for northern development should be proposed on practical reasons and not always with "effective occupation" as the principle reason" (Minutes of ACND meeting of March 24, Document XND-13 of April 3, 1970 attached).

6. As regard contiguous waters, we question whether "persistent presence" has ever been a factor (much less an important factor, as DND

suggests) in establishing an accepted claim under international law. This appears to be a misapplication of the doctrine of "effective occupation" of land territories. It was also our understanding that international courts have interpreted this doctrine to include intermittent (and not "persistent") presence in remote areas. We would, however, appreciate your opinion as to whether DND have any basis for suggesting that some form of "presence" on water or ice in the archipelago region or in the 100-mile pollution control zone could be a factor for the future in the development of international law in this area.

7. We would also appreciate your judgment on whether "knowledge of what is going on" is "vital" to a legal case for jurisdiction over coastal waters. In a similar vein you will note that para. 87 asserts that there is a "need to be able to detect transits" not only for military reasons but also for reasons of establishing Canadian sovereignty. We were not aware of any requirement in these terms under international law. Similarly, we would question whether "some degree of enforcement capability" can be regarded as a requirement under international law.

8. Taken together with other evidence of thinking in the Department of National Defence it would appear that the Forces could be moving in the direction of a substantial shift in emphasis and activities, involving a substantial re-allocation of resources, without any clear rationale, whether legal (would it strengthen our claims?), regulatory (will the RCMP, Coast-guard, etc. need more support from the Forces), political (would Canadians somehow sleep better, or is it intended to serve as a signal to Washington of our national resolve?), military (are we, as a matter of joint defence, agreed with our allies about the threat of, for example, Soviet submarine transits in the North and about what response should be made to that threat?) or economic (should the Forces support DOT in ice reconnaissance and ice-breaking activities?). This tendency is illustrated in the recent briefing by Brigadier General Tellier to the Defence Council on plans for Forces' activities in the North (a copy of which we have already referred to you) where considerable stress is placed on an increased military "presence" in the North not for any

military or strategic reason but because of what are perceived to be Canadian requirements in relation to the maintenance of sovereignty.

9. We do not suggest that there is no rationale for an increased level of military activity in the North; we are merely suggesting that the basis for such activity should be more clearly formulated. A more realistic approach is reflected, in our view, in the DND draft paper on sovereignty (which we forwarded to you for comment with our Memorandum of March 24) where the emphasis is on roles for the military in specific areas where a useful job can be performed in support of other government agencies with operational responsibilities in the North. The extent to which roles can be identified and defined in specific terms will clearly have an important bearing on future decision on new and expensive equipment programs for the Forces.

3-8. Parliamentary Standing Committee on External Affairs and National Defence, Proceedings: Tenth Report to the House, 26 June 1970. Excerpts.

1. Canadian Maritime Interests

Canada has never been regarded as one of the great maritime nations. Such recognition has been traditionally accorded to great naval powers or to nations with a large merchant marine.... Canadians themselves, by and large, have taken the sea for granted and have not looked on Canada as having important maritime interests which need active protection. But this situation is very rapidly changing.

While Canada has no merchant marine of consequence, it is one of the great trading nations of the world with an interest in the free movement of commerce. Surrounded by oceans of strategic importance on three of four sides, it has had thrust upon it by geography an unwanted interest in the deployment of strategic weapons at sea and their effect on the balance of nuclear deterrence.

...Recent technological developments have also suddenly made possible the exploitation of the sea bottom. Canada, with its vast continental shelf, which international law recognizes as being open to exclusive Canadian exploitation, has suddenly become enormous underwater territories which require some form of policing. The tremendous increase in sea transport of oil has opened up new dangers of pollution to every littoral nation, against which effective protections is urgently required.

That Canada has great maritime interests and obligations now and in the foreseeable future there can remain no doubt. But whether Canada has the appropriate maritime forces to protect these interests and meet all obligations in the changing conditions of the times is another question. It is with respect to the latter that this Report of the Subcommittee on Maritime Forces is submitted.

...

3. Orientation and Capabilities of Existing Maritime Forces

Two predominant features of Canadian maritime forces are the division of maritime forces by department according to function, "police" type functions and military functions being almost completely separated, and the almost exclusive ASW specialization of Canada's armed maritime forces, particularly with respect to North Atlantic operations in a NATO Context.

3.1 Division of Maritime Forces by Department

In addition to the Department of National Defence, five other departments maintain maritime forces: The Department of Energy, Mines and Resources; the Department of Fisheries and Forestry, the Department of the Solicitor General; the Department of Transport; and the Department of Public Works.

A notable aspect of this division of maritime forces by function is the assignment of responsibility for police functions of a para-military nature to the maritime forces of departments other than the Department of National Defence. Specifically this includes: fisheries protection and regulations to the Department of Fisheries and Forestry; and enforcement of the Customs Act and associated regulations to the Royal Canadian Mounted Police. With the establishment of specific regulations for the S.S *Manhattan* during its second voyage in the Canadian Arctic, the Department of Transport will probably exercise some form of police responsibility in ensuring appropriate safety measures are maintained.

Responsibility for research and data collection relating to the oceanic environment is assigned to departments with direct interests: oceanography and hydrography to the Department of Energy, Mines and Resources; fisheries research and oceanography to the Department of Fisheries and Forestry...and weather and oceanographic data collection as well as ice reconnaissance to the Department of Transport.

In addition, all the departments maintaining maritime forces have some responsibility to carry out support functions either as a prime responsibility (such as ice breaking, Arctic resupply, maintenance of navigation aids and cable repair) or as ancillary responsibilities (such as transport of departmental personnel and search and rescue).

The responsibilities and capabilities of departments other than the Department of National Defence to carry out police functions, research and data collection functions and general support functions stand in contrast to the present almost exclusive ASW specialization of the maritime forces maintained by the Department of National Defence.

Insofar as the maritime forces of other departments have carried out, and are carrying out, these non-military and para-military roles, the Department of National Defence has to a large extent been relieved of any significant obligation in this respect (a notable exception being search and rescue). In consequence Canada has been able to assign its armed maritime forces purely military roles without having to accommodate necessary para-military and non-military roles often required of maritime forces.

...

3.4. Para-military and Non-military Capabilities

...

3.4.4 Icebreaking and Arctic Resupply

A major responsibility of the Canadian Coast Guard is to provide icebreaking services in the Gulf of St. Lawrence and the Arctic and to carry out Arctic resupply. Five major icebreakers and 19 other vessels with capability for operating in ice conditions are maintained for these purposes. In Arctic operations the same vessels (icebreakers) are used for icebreaking, Arctic resupply, marine traffic control and transport of scientific staff and equipment.

While the Subcommittee did not investigate the capabilities of the Canadian Coast Guard in detail, it is apparent that this service has developed a high level of expertise and a major capability in all non-military facets of Arctic operations.

...

5. Strategic Considerations for the 1970's

5.1 Maintenance of Canadian Sovereignty and Extra-territorial Jurisdiction

The fact that Canada has the longest coast line and as large an area of associated continental shelf as any country in the world is a strategic consideration of great importance.

Whereas defence against any military violation of Canadian sovereignty is assured by the over-arching U.S interest in world and continental security (and defence capability commensurate with this), the same support is not assured for violations of a non-military nature. With the sudden appreciation of the potential value of seabed resources and the need for new kinds of measures to protect fisheries resources, Canadian sovereignty and extraterritorial jurisdiction may be subjected to new challenges. An appropriate police capability is therefore increasingly necessary.

To date the responsibility for police functions required has been carried out by the maritime service of various federal departments which have no capability for underwater operations. However off-shore exploration for oil and other resources on the continental shelf and the possibility of submarine transportation of such resources in the Arctic archipelago (as outlined by General Dynamics Ltd. to the House of Commons Standing Committee on Indian Development and Northern Affairs on May 21, 1970) adds an underwater dimension to such police requirements. While Canadian maritime forces for the exercise of these police functions seem to have been adequate to date, the Subcommittee anticipate a need for further police capabilities both on account of greater surface activity and the development of underwater activity.

In essence the police function to be exercised is a manifestation of national sovereignty. Since the countries likely to challenge such assertions for commercial or other reasons include the USA and other NATO countries, the Subcommittee considers that Canadian maritime forces must be capable, unilaterally, of carrying out any increased police functions.

…

6. Discounted Strategic Considerations

…

6.4. Surface Operations of a Military Nature in the Arctic Archipelago

The Subcommittee sees a requirement for forces capable of carrying out surveillance and for investigating and identifying military and non-military activity in the Arctic archipelago. But the subcommittee does not anticipate a need for maritime surface operations of a military nature in Arctic waters because ice makes such operations virtually impossible. Any necessary challenge to individual surface vessels could be made by appropriate registration of political protest. If a demonstration of force were required, armed aircraft would be most effective.

...

9. Priorities and Criteria in Allocation of Roles for Canadian Maritime Forces

9.1 Maintenance of Sovereignty and Enforcement of Extra-territorial Jurisdiction

The Subcommittee considers that the first responsibility of Canadian maritime forces during the 1970's must be the maintenance of sovereignty and enforcement of extra-territorial jurisdiction.

As already noted (Section 5.1) Canadian maritime forces need an independent capability to carry our police functions – military and non-military- required to maintain sovereignty and enforce extra-territorial jurisdiction. This is a requirement which has recently taken on vast increased importance as a result, on the one hand, of rapidly growing exploitation of the continental shelf as defined and permitted by the Geneva Conference on the Law of the Sea, and on the other hand by the extension twice over the past six years of Canadian fishing zones and the recent extension of Canada's territorial sea from 3 to 12 miles. Moreover, the increased attention to the Arctic where Canada has longstanding claims to sovereignty over the waters between the islands (which have now been greatly strengthened by the extension of the territorial sea), as well as the establishment of an extensive pollution control zone, have created further requirements. However, because the Arctic waters are frozen or ice-covered most of the year, these latter requirements call for a special solution. (See Section 10.5)

The Subcommittee is of the opinion that effective maintenance of sovereignty requires a capability of extensive surface and subsurface surveillance and identification, as well as a limited capability to localize and track specific instances of exploitation or violation – whether these be of resource rights on the continental shelf, transport regulations, customs regulations or fisheries regulations to name obvious examples. There is a further requirement for some limited but effective capability

HMCS Margaree makes her way through some 'growlers' (small chunks of floating ice), 28 September 1971. (LAC)

to challenge any actual instance of illegal exploitation or other violation of Canadian laws.

In view of the increasing use of submarines with long endurance, already for military purposes and possibly soon for commercial purposes, the maintenance of sovereignty must be supported by some capability for subsurface surveillance and tracking.

...

10. Capabilities for Canadian Maritime Forces

...

10.5 Capabilities in the Arctic

The combination of oceanic conditions in the Canadian Arctic – year-round ice in some areas and seasonal ice in others, large areas of relatively shallow waters, and the archipelago itself consisting of numerous islands separated by relatively narrow bodies of water – provides a unique maritime problem, with respect both to maintenance of sovereignty and to defence against any threat to security originating in the Arctic.

Ice coverage limits the effectiveness of all maritime systems in more or less drastic ways. Surface vessels, other than heavy icebreakers, effectively cannot operate in the arctic. If they are strengthened to resist floating ice, they become to slow for open waters. Hovercraft provide a potential for such surface movement which is being explored, but their range will be, at best, limited. Maritime patrol aircraft can effectively detect surface activity, but movement of ships is virtually non-existent. Because of ice cover, such aircraft have no capability for underwater surveillance. The effectiveness of bottom-based detection systems is somewhat reduced by ice noise. The nuclear-powered submarine is the one vessel capable of relatively free movement in arctic waters. With hull strengthening it can even beak through ice pack and surface.

The large areas of shallow waters less than 20 fathoms in depth limits the area of feasible submarine operations. Areas of water of more than 20 fathoms in depth are of two types: 1) connecting channels from the Arctic Ocean (Northwest Passage and Nares Strait) to Baffin Bay as well as the Davis Strait form Baffin Bay to the Atlantic; and 2) cul de sacs and underwater bays from the perimeter of the archipelago, or from connecting channels, the largest and most significant being Hudson Strait and part of Hudson Bay.

The Subcommittee believes that the connecting channels have potential importance as transit routes through the Arctic archipelago for both military and non-military submarines. It sees some future possibility of exploitation of the channels and of the cul de sacs and underwater bays for strategic or commercial purposes. The Subcommittee does not consider military use of either the channels (other than for transit) or other areas is now taking place. But the unique character of Arctic waters and the unknown geography make it important that Canada develop further competence and experience in the Arctic environment so as to be able to meet a threat if it should develop in these waters.

The Subcommittee concludes that it would be desirable, if technically and economically feasible, for Canada to acquire subsurface perimeter surveillance and identification capability to cover the entrance to connecting channels (and possible cul de sacs) where submarines can operate. To make this perimeter surveillance and identification capability effective, it would have to be backed up by a limited localizing and tracking capability.

The Subcommittee was told that four additional large ice-breakers would be required by the Canadian Coast Guard, to keep open Arctic sea routes, if a decision were taken to ship arctic oil by surface tankers. The Subcommittee understands and agrees that some additional capability is needed only if maritime surface transportation of oil proves to be technically and commercially feasible or if the minerals in the central and eastern arctic become commercially attractive.

11. Recommended Equipment and Structure for Canadian Maritime Forces

In order to develop and maintain the capabilities recommended in Section 10 for the next decade, the Subcommittee envisages a large and continuing re-equipment programme. While some of the recommendations involve the replacement of existing equipment, the Subcommittee urges the Government seriously to consider the possibility of procuring new maritime systems to take account of new technological developments and new requirements, particularly in the Arctic.

In summary the Subcommittee recommends:

1) the continued maintenance of long range airborne maritime patrol forces to provide considerable surveillance and identification as well as limited localizing, tracking and challenge and/or destruct capabilities;
2) the maintenance of surface forces, with the emphasis on light and fast general purpose vessels to provide limited surveillance as well as limited localizing, tracking and challenge and/or destruct capabilities;
3) careful consideration of the possibility of developing and deploying in appropriate locations in Arctic regions bottom-based systems providing these are found to be capable of effective surveillance and identification under ice;
4) no acquisition of nuclear powered submarines, given the high estimated cost.

The Subcommittee was impressed by the evidence of the Department of National Defence that no single platform or detection system could provide the appropriate capabilities given the varied maritime activity and the varied oceanic environment to be covered. In the opinion of the Subcommittee the general types of equipment recommended are of a complementary nature and would provide a limited Canadian capability in all Canadian waters.

In addition the Subcommittee accepted that Canadian maritime forces will continue to require specialized equipment for icebreaking, to service navigation aids, and to provide facilities for research and data collection.

11.1 Airborne Maritime Patrol Forces

The Subcommittee understands that no final decision has been taken whether to replace the Argus with new maritime patrol aircraft in the near future or to modify the equipment in the Argus in order to extend its useful life.... It is, however, convinced that Canadian maritime forces must be equipped with an adequate number of effective maritime patrol aircraft....

Maritime patrol aircraft are also able to provide a considerable surface surveillance and detection capability in the Arctic, and the Subcommittee has been told that maritime patrol flights in the north have been sharply increased. However, in view of the large size of the area involved and the absence of shipping activity, the Subcommittee doubts whether the use of an aircraft with expensive specialized equipment is justified when visual observations are essentially involved. However, it does recognize a need for some training experience and a requirement for basic intelligence on the Arctic region to which such flights undoubtedly make some contribution.

The Subcommittee suggests that the possibility of using observation satellites to provide regular surveillance of the Arctic regions should be examined. It is aware of the high cost of such systems and recognizes that a specialized observation satellite programme is out of the question. However, it understands that the possibility of using satellites to conduct earth resources surveys over Canada's North is being carefully studied. The Subcommittee suggests that equipment capable of conducting such surveys might with minor adaptation offer some capacity for regular surveillance at slight extra cost. The definition would, however, be coarse so that activity on a small scale would not be detected. Nevertheless, if an adaptation could be made to a satellite program intended primarily for other purposes, the Subcommittee believes that the more extensive flights now being scheduled in the Arctic could be cut back. It would be necessary however, to complement the surveillance capability of a satellite with aircraft (probably operated by Canadian ground forces) which would be capable of inspecting any suspicious activity and perhaps even have some capability of landing on ice for close investigation. The Subcommittee believes such a system would provide for more effective coverage of Canada's Arctic regions at reasonable cost than the present maritime patrol flights now offer.

The Subcommittee has learned that arrangements have been made for maritime patrol aircraft to use facilities at the airport at Frobisher Bay. The Subcommittee considers this to be an important measure to extend the effective range of maritime patrol aircraft, both over the North Atlantic and over the Canadian Arctic. It received evidence regarding the feasibility of building a combined air and maritime base on Devon Island. While Frobisher provides a good air base, the harbour has bad ice conditions which prohibit its use during most of the year. Ice conditions on Devon Island are said to be superior. In view of the still uncertain future of surface maritime activity in the Arctic and the very large cost which would be incurred, the Subcommittee does not believe grounds exist at this time for developing a new base on Devon Island....

11.2 Surface Forces

The Subcommittee recommends that surface forces comprising light and fast general purpose vessels be maintained to provide a limited surface and subsurface localizing, tracking and challenge/destruct capability....

Now that the government has taken steps to extend Canada's territorial waters and to establish fisheries and pollution control zones, the Subcommittee believes that a distinction may appropriately be made between inshore and offshore police capabilities (i.e. law enforcement, fisheries protection, pollution control, seabed exploitation). Evidence given to the subcommittee suggests that inshore police type activities involved in the main local maritime activity required an intimate and personal knowledge of the area concerned. Offshore police capabilities necessitate enforcement over wider areas, in more varied weather conditions and with respect to both Canadian and non-Canadian maritime activity. With the extension of Canadian waters and jurisdiction and with increasing levels of exploitation of all sea resources, there is a need for more sophisticated maritime forces with more formally organized material and intelligence support. While the question of final responsibility for specific facets of such offshore policing may rest with departments other than the Department of National Defence, the Subcommittee considers it important that the Department of National Defence maritime forces should have a limited capability and authority to support this requirement.

11.3 Bottom-based surveillance systems

The Subcommittee understands that bottom-based systems for surveillance and identification provide and excellent capability for continuous surveillance and identification of surface and subsurface maritime activity over wide areas, particularly over the continental shelf and slope.

Their use in the Arctic is made difficult by ice damage to equipment and by background ice "noise". However, given Canada's need for subsurface surveillance capability in the Arctic, the Subcommittee recommends that research and development of bottom-based systems appropriate for Arctic operations be given high priority in order to determine whether effective operational systems could be established and at what cost.

11.4 Submarine forces

The Subcommittee closely examined the question whether Canada should acquire nuclear-powered submarines. It should be made clear that when referring to nuclear-powered submarines the Subcommittee is considering the submarines' propulsion system and not the nature of their armament. In the past, this possibility has been rejected because of the extremely high capital costs and the substantial support costs (maintaining two crews per submarine, special communications requirements and other facilities). Canadian shipyards probably lack the expertise, at this time, to build nuclear submarines which has undoubtedly been a further deterrent.

It may be possible to substantially reduce acquisition costs by means of buying or leasing used nuclear-powered submarines. No evidence, however, was received as to what these costs might be.

If purchase costs could be greatly reduced, then the Subcommittee could more readily attach importance to the following arguments for acquisition of the nuclear-powered submarine:

1) it is the only maritime vehicle capable of year round operation in Arctic waters. It would be an essential support system to a bottom-based detection system. If a bottom-based system for Arctic waters proves impossible to devise, the nuclear-powered submarine would give an initial detection capability as well.
2) it has proven to be the most effective subsurface surface surveillance method. If Canadian maritime forces were equipped with a small number of nuclear-powered submarines, they could effectively complement the existing surface and airborne forces and result in increased Canadian knowledge of the activities of other submarine forces.
3) it offers a platform for carrying out detailed hydrographic surveys of Arctic waters. Areas of these waters have been charted during periods when the waters are open by the Canadian Hydrographic Service and Department of Transport, but this is not feasible in seas which are covered with permanent ice. Evidence submitted by General Dynamics to the Commons Committee on Indian Affairs and Northern Development indicates that surveys to locate underwater pinnacles in the area of proposed submarine transport routes would have to be made by submarines prior to establishing any such routes.
4) it may become a commercially viable means of exploiting arctic oil. Given the extent of Canadian resources involved, the Subcommittee considers that Canada has an interest in developing knowledge and experience in this area of technology. There might even be important technological spin-off benefits to be gained. If the General Dynamics proposal – or one like it – to ship oil by submarine tanker should prove to be feasible, a trans shipment port with repair facilities might be established in Canada. If this were done the cost of maintaining Canadian submarines could be reduced.

Although evidence suggested that there are many potential advantages in terms of protection of sovereignty, exploration of Arctic waters and the development of a new technology of possible industrial importance, the Subcommittee does not consider that it should make a recommendation that Canada seek to acquire nuclear-powered submarines in the period 1973-1983, unless it can be shown that acquisition costs would be very much less than the figure given of $100,000,000 per submarine.

...

11.6 Organizational considerations

The Subcommittee has given considerable attention to the question of whether the Canadian maritime forces maintained by the various government departments should be integrated. The present divided structure appears to be somewhat unusual, with most nations consolidating their maritime forces under operational control of one or two agencies.

The primary argument for integration of maritime forces is to achieve greater coordination of operations and, particularly, more efficient use of equipment through multitasking. This would involve the delegation of appropriate authority for both military and non-military duties to officers commanding vessels...

Several arguments against total integration of Canada's maritime forces were presented to the Subcommittee. Of these four seemed particularly relevant:

First, total integration of all Canadian maritime forces under the Department of National Defence appeared inadvisable from an organizational point of view. It would be inconsistent with the reorganization of the Canadian Armed Forces as a unified military force; extend the scale of military operations into non-military areas and make civilian control over such operations more difficult; and might give the impression that Canada was increasing the size of and expenditures on its armed forces.

Secondly, the existence of separate maritime services has permitted innovation and development in non-military areas of expertise such as ice-breaking and oceanography that might well have not been given any priority in a single integrated service facing other more immediate demands.

Thirdly, the increasing potential use of maritime forces to enforce sovereignty and extra-territorial jurisdiction against non-military violation or exploitation, possibly by Canada's military allies as well as others, may make it desirable on occasion for non-military maritime forces to be able to carry out police type functions, thereby avoiding any military implications....

In conclusion, the Subcommittee recommends against the integration of all Canadian maritime forces as a single service. However, it does recommend that the Government consider:

1) the possible integration of non-military maritime forces having responsibility for day to day surface operations with respect to transport, fisheries protection and law enforcement at sea as an enlarged Canadian Coast Guard, the latter acting as an autonomous government agency, providing all non-military maritime services to other government departments on demand.
2) the integration of military and non-military maritime forces having responsibility for research and data collection as a specialized service, this not precluding the incidental use of Canadian Coast Guard or Department of National Defence vessels and aircraft for such activities when available.
3) the assignment of concurrent authority and responsibility to commanding officer of Department of National Defence submarines, surface vessels, or aircraft and to those of Canadian Coast Guard Vessels for the enforcement of Canadian sovereignty and extra-territorial jurisdiction against non-military violation or exploitation, particularly with respect to off-shore violations of the 12 mile territorial limit and the fisheries and pollution control zones beyond.
4) other measures to ensure that the greatest degree of co-ordination of maritime activities of the various services is maintained and that, where possible, equipment of these forces is multi-tasked for maximum efficiency. An example of this kind of special service might be emergency task forces trained and equipped for

immediate action to control oil pollution in the event of damage to tankers. Just as air-sea rescue is directed by the Department of National Defence, the Subcommittee believes the Department of National Defence might also be made responsible in this field.

3-9. DEXAF, M. Shenstone, OMD, to PSI – Security and Intelligence Division, re: Joint Intelligence Committee 1970-71 Work Programme, the Canadian Arctic, 10 June 1970.[32]

We would suggest that in addition to the proposed list of papers for the 1969-70 programme it might be timely for the JIC [Joint Intelligence Committee] to take a closer look at our own Canadian backyard. From our viewpoint, it would be useful to have an up-to-date intelligence study in some depth on the subject: "the military threat to the Canadian Arctic".

2. Increased Canadian military activity in the Canadian North is, as you know, a prominent feature of the Government's new defence policy. The first priority in roles for the Forces as formulated in the Prime Minister's statement of April 3, 1969, was: "the surveillance of our own territory and coastlines, i.e. the protection of our sovereignty". It has, however, to our knowledge never been made clear in any classified or published document whether the shift in emphasis and activities in this direction is based in part on a military or strategic rationale or whether it is based solely on non-military or peacetime consideration such as the need for an increased level of law enforcement in support of the RCMP, the Fisheries Protection Service and other civil agencies, or requirements of national development.

3. We are not aware of any current intelligence estimates forecasting a need for a greater level of military surveillance and capability in the North. CANUS '70, as you know, touches on this area only very briefly and in general terms which suggest that there is in fact no new military threat to the Arctic as distinct from the threat of a general nuclear war involving Canada and the United States.... Along the same lines, the Prime Minister stated in the House on April 23, 1969, "Not since Confederation has there existed a viable threat to our territorial integrity." We also have in mind the conclusion of Mr. R.J. Sutherland of the DRB in his published study: "The Strategic Significance of the

32 LAC, RG 25, vol. 10322, file 27-10-2-2 pt.1. Originally classified as "Secret."

Canadians Arctic" (1969)[33] when he argued that in the ICBM era the military importance of the North has diminished.

4. On the other hand, it is clear from recent announcements that the Canadian Armed Forces are moving in the direction of a significant reallocation of resources towards the North and away from other areas such as NATO Europe. We attached, for example, the text of an announcement by the Minister of National Defence on April 17, 1970, announcing the establishment of a permanent northern headquarters at Yellowknife and describing it as:

> "…one of several steps being taken to strengthen Canada's military presence north of the 60th parallel, including the setting up of a small aircraft servicing detachment at Frobisher, increased air surveillance coverage and year-round land and tactical air operational exercises."

5. Similarly, the Sub-Committee of the House of Commons on External Affairs and National Defence has heard testimony from expert witnesses such as Rear-Admiral [John] Charles and Dr. George Lindsey which has been interpreted in the press to suggest the need for an increased level of military surveillance against the risk of foreign military "encroachments" and Soviet [ballistic missile-carrying submarine] transits through Canadian Arctic waters.

6. We do not suggest that there is no rationale for an increased level of military activity in the North; we are merely suggesting that the basis for such activity should be more clearly formulated. A JIC paper on this subject would in our view help in the process of identifying in specific term useful role for the military in the North.

33 *Editors' Note:* "The Strategic Significance of the Canadian Arctic," in *The Arctic Frontier*, ed. R. St. J. MacDonald (Toronto: University of Toronto Press, 1966): 256-78.

3-10. Concept of Operations – Canadian Forces Northern Region, 14 July 1970.[34]

References: A. V 1150-110/S36 (DCOMP) over V 3120-13 of 5 December, 1969
B. S 3120-13 (CDS) of 17 April, 1970 (CDS Directive D 7/70)

BACKGROUND

1. As the result of the Government's new defence policy, announced by the Prime Minister on 3 April, 1969, Defence Objectives for the North were identified in reference A as follows:
   a. Contributing to the maintenance of Canadian sovereignty in the North by:
      (1) providing a military presence;
      (2) surveillance and reconnaissance of Canadian territory, airspace and territorial waters as well as the air and sea approaches thereto.
   b. Maintaining operationally ready maritime, land and air forces capable of defence illegal and forcible entry into the Canadian North.
   c. Providing effective search and rescue services in Canadian territory and making co-operative contribution in international areas adjacent to Canada.
   d. Assisting other Government and commercial activities which enhance the economic development of the Canadian North and which are not readily available from other sources.
2. Reference B authorized the establishment of Canadian Forces Northern Region Headquarters [NRHQ], effective 15 May 1970, and established the following objectives over the period 21 March 1971:
   a. to assemble NRHQ by 15 May 1970;
   b. to establish the presence of NRHQ in Yellowknife by 1 July 1970;
   c. to prepare recommendations for consideration by the CDS by 15 October 1970; and,
   d. to be prepared to implement detailed plans by 1 March 1971.

34 Northern Region file 3000-1 (COMD). Originally classified as "Secret, Canadian Eyes Only." Copy provided by Canadian Forces Northern Area (now Joint Task Force North).

3. Interim terms of reference for the Commander Canadian Forces Northern Region have been issued. While these terms of reference provide guidelines and establish parameters for the conduct of the studies and liaison which must take place to enable attainment of the objective specified in para. 2.c. (above), there is also a need to state a concept of operations on which proposals can be developed. Such is the purpose of this paper.

AIM

4. To postulate a concept of operations for Canadian Forces Northern Region.

GENERAL

5. NRHQ is the "agent" of CFHQ in the North. As directed by the CDS, Commander Northern Region is to co-ordinate Canadian Forces activities in the North and is to provide direct liaison with the Commissioners of the Northwest Territories and the Yukon Territory plus other government departments and civil agencies located in the North.

6. The objectives and goals of Northern Region will be established to contribute to the attainment of the Defence Objectives described in para. 1 (above). These same defence objectives determine the type of activity which will be undertaken by NRHQ.

CANADIAN SOVEREIGNTY – MILITARY PRESENCE AND SURVEILLANCE/RECONNAISSANCE

7. Surveillance and reconnaissance of Canadian airspace, territory and territorial waters will be performed by Mobile Command, Maritime Command, Air Defence Command and Northern Region. Northern Region's involvement would be as follows:

a. the making of local arrangements for assistance and support in the deployment of maritime units;
b. input to planning of areas to be covered;

An Inuk instructor leads a Canadian Forces contingent on a march across the tundra, March 1971. (LAC)

c. the receipt of the results of Air Defence and Maritime surveillance activities in order to make appropriate information available to the Commissioners and to federal agencies concerned; and,
d. the provision of surveillance within the region through reports of the Canadian Rangers, communications flying and the interrogation of indigenous people.

8. Dealing with para 7.c. (above), it goes without saying that the Commissioners must have a complete as possible picture of activities within their areas of responsibility to enable them to perform their tasks. Furthermore, specific information will be of value to several agencies and regulatory officers both to assist in resource studies and to broaden the effectiveness of application of Canadian law. As examples of the latter category, the following would be applicable:

a. Air Defence Surveillance. Assistance in identification of flights which might subvert Canadian Customs and Immigration Regulations (Note 1[35]).

35 Note 1 – On a recent visit to the [Defence Research Board] installation in Tanquary Fiord, DCIS was surprised to find that a group of American and Japanese scientists had visited that location without the knowledge of the Headquarters or any official in authority. There is wide-spread hearsay evidence that this is but one of a very large number of similar cases. It may well be that persons are entering

b. Surveillance of territorial waters. Identification of ships acting in contravention of Arctic Pollution Control Regulations.
c. Surveillance of the land mass. Identification of offences against Territorial Land Use Regulations.

9. Turning now to the requirement to provide a military presence in the Territories, it is clear that the attainment of this part of the objective will require demonstration of our capability over a very extensive area. High-flying surveillance aircraft only meet this requirement when they are on an airstrip in the North and/or can be seen by others. Both land units and ships of Mobile and Maritime Commands will contribute by their presence on exercises and visits. However, all such elements of the Canadian Forces will be known to be permanent residents of the South and, while their activities in the North demonstrate the capability of remote area operations, they will not represent the more permanent aspect of "presence" either to the Northerner or to the foreign "long term visitor". It will be necessary, therefore, for Commander Northern Region and his staff to engage in the personal contact type of reconnaissance and planning which demonstrate not only a military presence but also a long term interest and involvement.

10. An activity which assists in both surveillance and the establishment of a military presence is the Canadian Rangers Organization. Responsibility for the Rangers is being assigned to Northern Region and will carry with it requirements for planning, tasking of units and sub-units, training and administration. This activity ties in naturally with that described for NRHQ in para 9 (above). The question of Ranger contribution to the attainment of other objectives will be covered below.

11. In summary, the activities of Northern Region which will contribute to the sovereignty objective are as follows:

a. Assistance to other commands in arrangements for local support of their surveillance operations and Northern operational training.
b. Input to the planning of surveillance operations.

Canadian territory without the permission or knowledge of Canadian authorities and carrying out activities which may not necessarily be in the best interests of Canada.

c. Receipt, collation and passage of information to territorial and federal authorities in the North in support of their activities and operations concerned with the enforcement of Canadian law.
d. Direct contact involved with on-site reconnaissance for military activities and planning in conjunction with the civil authority for civil emergency operations.
e. Command, control and administration of the Canadian Rangers.

MAINTENANCE OF OPERATIONALLY READY FORCES

12. All regular operational and combat units are found within existing functional Commands of the Canadian Forces. The objective of the commanders of these Commands is to so equip and train their units as to be capable of operations in the Canadian North. Furthermore, it has been for some time the responsibility of these same Commands to conduct operations as directed by the CDS. In satisfaction of this requirement and in addition to the plans which have been prepared by commanders, agreements have been made for the defence of this part of North America in co-operation with the United States. All such arrangements will continue and Commander Northern Region will be in a position to assist, particularly in the case of Mobile Command. The responsibility of Commander Northern Region with regard to the conduct of operations will be as directed by the CDS.

13. Northern Region activities which would contribute to the attainment of the objective of maintaining operationally ready forces capable of defeating illegal entry and forcible entry into the Canadian North are as follows:

a. Information. Being located in the Capital of the Northwest Territories and with a detachment in Whitehorse, Northern Region Headquarters will be in an ideal position to establish an information bank on the North. This information bank will provide not only collateral for the evaluation of surveillance and intelligence reports but also will be invaluable in the planning and conduct of both operational training exercises and actual operations. CFHQ and all Commands must be able to call for information whenever required and must be confident of its accuracy.

b. Arrangements for facilities and local logistics support. As exemplified by the problems currently being encountered in the establishment of forward deployment facilities for Maritime Patrol aircraft, NRHQ will be required to make arrangements for the support of units and elements of other Commands with appropriate government and commercial agencies in the North.
c. Preservation of the ecological balance. In making arrangements for land use in connection with tactical exercises, NRHQ must ensure both that the requirements of operational commands are met and that Canadian Forces activities do not disturb the ecological balance to the detriment of not only territorial interests but also Canadian public opinion.
d. Liaison with United States Forces Alaska Command. NRHQ may be expected to establish liaison with U.S. Forces Alaska Command to ensure the profitable solution of mutual problems and to make arrangements for U.S. Forces authorized to pass through or operate in the Territories.

14. In addition to the relatively large scale operations which have been planned, particularly those under the ALCANUS [Alaska, Canada, United States] agreements, there may be a requirement for smaller operations to follow up surveillance reports. There is a very slight probability that these would be the result of suspicion of an enemy lodgment but rather that they would be in satisfaction of some aspect of enforcement of a Canadian law or the protection of Canadian sovereignty. Northern Region would expect to contribute to the contingency planning involved but would not expect to exercise tactical command of the task forces. On the other hand, there may well be cases in which investigation on the ground can be handled by a very small party (e.g. 2 or 3 people including an officer) which would be logical tasks for NRHQ to perform either within its own resources or with an extremely small temporary organization. Finally, it should be noted that Canadian Rangers can provide guides for large-scale operations and can be used for the minor surveillance follow-up tasks which would be performed by Northern Region.

15. Although not specifically covered in the objectives defined in Reference A, the statutory requirement exists for the Canadian Forces to act in Aid of the Civil Power and to assist the civil authority in emergency. In the same way as in all Commands which have regional responsibilities, Commander Northern Region will be expected to carry out such planning with appropriate civil authorities and to perform the duties required by regulations in all actual cases. Such operations will require planning for the use of troops from other commands, principally Mobile Command.

16. In summary, Northern Region activities with respect to the maintenance and employment of operational forces would be as follows:

a. establishment, maintenance and updating of an information bank on the North;
b. arrangements for support of training and operations in the Territories;
c. arranging land requirements for exercises with regard to both the requirements of the Canadian Forces and the protection of the ecological balance;
d. conduct of very small scale surveillance follow-up operations; and,
e. planning and execution of civil emergency operations.

SEARCH AND RESCUE

17. Although the question of Search and Rescue resources for the North is now under study, it is safe to forecast that the trend indicates the need for a greater effort in terms of response time if nothing else. At the very least, Northern Region can be expected to perform the same regional functions as exist in any other Command in Canada. This will require planning and careful co-ordination. Communications aircraft, which are essential to the day-to-day operation of NRHQ, can be given a secondary task of Search and Rescue.

18. Of particular concern is contingency planning for a large scale aircraft disaster in the Canadian area of responsibility. The ever increasing tempo of air movements, including the operation of large charter aircraft in the tourist trade (being flown by aircrew with little

Oqsuralik Ottokie receives pay from a Canadian Forces officer at Cape Dorset, 2 October 1976. (LAC)

Northern experience), raises the specter of 50 or more ill-equipped passengers fighting for survival in an extremely hostile environment. That this is entirely possible is proven by the recent case of a DC-8/707 type charter aircraft being lost over the MacKenzie District, picked up by the DEW Line and vectored into Norman Wells with almost no fuel left. If such an aircraft is lost during the long winter, there will be very little time to spare in providing life-sustaining first aid shelter, food and medical care if any are to survive. There is now a need for a contingency plan to be prepared and practiced to ensure that the Canadian Forces can discharge their statutory responsibilities in satisfaction of our international agreements. Furthermore, and in addition to the purely humanitarian aspects of such a case, failure by Canada could result in intervention by another power, with the right capability, to the detriment of Canadian sovereignty. NRHQ is most concerned that this aspect of contingency planning and preparation receives the attention it deserves.

19. Finally, NRHQ would be expected to play its part in the passive aspects (i.e. education) of Search and Rescue preventive programs.

NATIONAL DEVELOPMENT PROJECTS

20. To the extent possible and consistent with primary attention to the objective of ensuring the security of Canada, the Canadian Forces are to contribute to the attainment of regional development goals. Nowhere in Canada are such projects of greater value and importance than in the North. Examples of the type of project which may be expected are as follows:

a. Engineering projects. Current cases are the Ogilvie River Bridge and the Remote Airfield Construction Program;
b. Telecommunications. There may be pressure for a repeat performance of the NWT and [Yukon] Radio System farther North and centered on the general area of Viscount Melville Sound and the Parry Islands. Additionally, proposals might be forthcoming on a tropospheric scatter link, on the South to North axis, linking current assets to Resolute Bay;
c. Training of native people. For some years assistance has been provided for trades training at appropriate Canadian Forces schools. The indication is that such requirements will continue and increase;
d. Organization and management of task forces. Such projects would be in the nature of scientific expeditions, execution of a specific work project, or the national historical type project. This type of request is probable because of the wide-spread knowledge of Canadian Forces capability in organizing, transporting, providing logistical support and general management of task forces in difficult areas.
e. Aircraft support for the Territorial Governments and other government departments. (Dependent upon the outcome of the Treasury Board Study);
f. Exploration and information. In addition to the results of remote sensors and general surveillance flying, Canadian Forces parties involved in exploration to determine the resource inventory to

support military operations could fulfill requirements of civil agencies. The information bank, referred to earlier in this paper, could be of considerable value to other agencies.

21. Considering the very close links which will be developed by NRHQ in its work with the Territorial Governments and other agencies, it will be possible to identify the need for these types of projects at a very early stage. NRHQ would conduct the initial feasibility study, advise agencies concerned and provide early warning to CFHQ and Commands. During the planning and project formulation stages, NRHQ would be responsible for co-ordination. In most cases project execution would be the responsibility of the particular unit or specialist group from CFHQ or one of the Commands. NRHQ would support them in the same way as for any unit deployed in the North.

22. Information requests would be met directly by interrogation of the NRHQ information bank.

OTHER ACTIVITIES

23. Certain activities will contribute to the attainment of all four Defence Objectives. In addition some others will contribute to objectives in the forces as a whole. Examples of these two types are covered below.

24. NRHQ will be expected to provide regional support for the cadet movement and to encourage its growth.

25. The CDS is most concerned that native peoples have the same opportunity as other citizens to serve in the regular force. This matter is now under study by CFHQ. NRHQ can expect to play a part in the resultant program.

26. NRHQ will probably have a heavy load with respect to visits which are over and above those required in connection with operations to attain the four primary objectives. The current northern orientation program is a case in point. It would be reasonable for NRHQ to assume responsibility for such flights in the future. Tours such as that recently

completed by military attachés accredited to Canada help advertise Canadian military presence in the North and therefore are a logical charge to NRHQ. Such visits and tours may involve groups ranging in size from two or three individuals up to 100 (as would be the case with staff colleges…). De-briefing of appropriate visitors to Northern locations would be valuable in connection with the maintenance of the NRHQ information bank.

27. Mapping is an essential support function for all Northern activities and, in addition, makes a major contribution to national development. NRHQ will be involved as follows:

a. Input to the survey and mapping program to assist in the determination of priorities for large scale (1:50,000) maps.
b. Assistance to [the Mapping and Charting Establishment] in field survey work.

28. Although at the moment there are no militia units north of the 60th parallel, studies may well indicate the need and/or desirability for their establishment. Should such be the case, NRHQ would acquire additional responsibilities of the same type as now envisaged for the Rangers Organization.

3-11. DEXAF, Legal Division (FLE) to North American Defence and NATO Division (OMD, subject: DND Paper on Role of Canadian Armed Forces in the Protection of Sovereignty, 5 August 1970.[36]

Our comments on an earlier draft of the subject paper were provided in our memorandum to you of June 6, 1969; some of these comments are reflected in the revised draft forwarded with your memorandum under reference.

2. We agree with the paper's conclusion that "forces maintained primarily against a threat of armed attack, in concert with allied forces, can also make important contribution in the protection of other sovereign or national interests." In our view, however a fundamental weakness of the paper is that it scarcely recognizes the fact that some of the most important of these "other sovereign or national interests" are strongly opposed by Canada's major ally, namely Canada's various claims to sovereignty and/or fisheries or pollution control jurisdiction in such areas as Hudson Bay and Strait, the waters of the Arctic archipelago, the Gulf of St. Lawrence, Bay of Fundy, Dixon Entrance, Hecate Strait and Queen Charlotte Sound. The paper regrettably does not explore the legal, political, or economic implications of this opposition of interests between Canada and the USA, and in particular the possible difficulties to which it could give rise as between the "collective security role" and the "national role" of the Canadian Forces. In this connection it would seem important to bring out the fact that the USSR, while being the power against which Canada's "collective security" arrangement is primarily directed, is also the power which (for its own reasons, of course) most clearly supports Canada's position on the status of the waters of the Arctic archipelago. Without attempting to draw military conclusions from these facts, we would nevertheless urge that they are of major importance to any consideration of the role of the Canadian Forces in the protection of sovereignty.

36 LAC, RG 25, vol. 10322, file 27-10-2-2 pt.1. Originally classified as "Confidential."

3. We would also agree in principle with the conclusion that present CAF activities and capabilities appear to be generally adequate for the purpose of maintaining the legal basis for Canadian claims to territorial sovereignty, i.e., Canada's claims to sovereignty over its Arctic mainland and islands and Canada's claims to exclusive sovereign rights for the exploration and exploitation of the resources of its northern continental shelf. We would similarly agree in principle, but with an important qualification, that expansion of the present level of forces in the North would not of itself legally strengthen Canada's disputed claim to the waters of the Arctic archipelago. The qualification we wish to make in respect of this conclusion is that, to the extent that Canadian legislation has asserted specific types of jurisdiction in the Arctic waters (i.e. pollution control), Canada must be in a position to enforce that jurisdiction (not necessarily through military agencies however). It is of course Canada's position that its claim to pollution control jurisdiction in the Arctic waters is juridically valid; without effective enforcement, however, that position would be seriously weakened. Law which is not or cannot be enforced may eventually cease to be law at all. On the other hand, consistent and effective enforcement of a jurisdiction claim, despite protests from some other countries, can eventually lead to resignation, acceptance or perhaps even emulation on the part of the countries concerned; the changed status by Russia in 1909 is a case in point. (There are, of course, risks to be calculated in connection with the enforcement of disputed jurisdiction.)

4. As regards regulatory and law-enforcement functions, we agree with the conclusions that (a) the Canadian Forces could play more active roles in support of the civil agencies which have traditionally been responsible for these functions, especially in remote areas along Canada's coasts and in the north, and that (b) the possibilities for increased military surveillance should be examined constructively in relation to specific needs and interests of other government agencies.

5. As regards the conclusion that improvements in research and training for possible future military operations in the Arctic might be made to maintain at least a minimum level of military expertise

in this difficult environment, we believe that the DND paper might profitably bring out the fact that the USA has recently announced plans for increased Arctic military research, including in particular the development of a Hovercraft-type vessel by the US Navy. In the Annual Report of the President to the Congress on Marine Resources and Engineering Development (issued in April, 1970), particular stress is laid on the strategic importance of "the Arctic", its significance to US national security and the need for "Arctic operational capability" in the form of "fast, long range, high payload transportation over open water, pack ice and tundra". This US view of the strategic importance of Arctic areas and Arctic operational capability does not of itself give rise to legal questions as such; it is relevant, however, to the question whether the maintenance of Canadian sovereignty in the Arctic, in all its "dimensions", should be viewed as coming primarily under the "collective security role" or the "national role" of the Canadian Forces. We would suggest that the factors determining the most appropriate mix as between these roles are not entirely the same as those which apply in other areas. The dispute between Canada and the USA as regards the status of the Arctic waters and the exercise of pollution control jurisdiction is one special factor; the matter of effective occupation is another. While we agree that Canada-USA joint defence arrangements do not detract from Canadian sovereignty, and while we agree also that Canada's legal title to its Arctic lands is well established, the factual (and political) situation in the Arctic is nevertheless a special one; where there is so little "presence" of any kind, what presence is required for practical, functional purposes should, to the greatest possible extent, be that of the "proprietor".

6. In the light of the preceding general comments on matters of principle, we would offer the following observations on particular sections or points in the DND paper:

(a) Paragraph 8

We would suggest that it would be more accurate, in view of developments since the DND paper was drafted, to say that the status of the Arctic archipelago waters is a subject of dispute with the USA, particularly as regards the assertion of jurisdiction to prevent and control pollution in these waters. We would also suggest that the references to the legal effect of an expansion of the present level of forces in the Arctic might be modified to bring out the possibility of a contribution by the Canadian Forces to the effective enforcement of the Arctic Waters Pollution Prevention Act, while at the same time stressing the need to avoid a possible conflict between any such enforcement role and the inter-forces relationship required by collective security arrangements with the USA.

(b) Paragraph 28

In describing the ways in which other states may affect or trench upon Canada's sovereignty without resorting to armed attack, this paragraph should, in our view, refer to the opposition of the USA to Canada's various maritime claims.

(c) Paragraph 35

This paragraph might give a more balanced view of the international legal situation as regards continental shelf jurisdiction if it were to bring out the fact that some countries challenge the "exploitability test" under the Geneva Convention, and if it were to refer as well to President Nixon's proposal for the renunciation of national claims to seabed resources beyond the 200 metre isobath. This conflict of views with the USA on the extent of coastal state jurisdiction over offshore resources is relevant, of course, not only to the Arctic but to Canada's Atlantic and Pacific coasts as well. The reference to rights over offshore resource being "based" on the Continental Shelf Convention should be amended as follows: "These rights derive from Canada's sovereignty over the adjacent lands and are secured under established principles of international law as reflected in the Geneva Convention on the Continental Shelf".

(d) Paragraph 36-40

These paragraphs should be revised to take into account Canada's recent extension of its territorial sea to 12 miles, the introduction of the Arctic Waters Pollution Prevention Act, and the resulting controversy with the USA (including developments relating to the Arctic conference proposed by the USA in response to the Canadian legislation). In the reference to Hudson Bay in paragraph 36, the qualification "probably" should be deleted. In paragraph 37 line 3, the reference to "high seas" should be amended to read "and thus if high seas". In line 5 of the same paragraph the phrase "in accord with the international law" may appear tendentious and would best be deleted; in line 7, the reference to exclusive fisheries jurisdiction seems confusing and unnecessary. In the final sentence of paragraph 40, we believe that it is an over-simplification to suggest that the problem of sovereignty (or pollution jurisdiction) over the Arctic archipelago waters is purely legal, economic and political and has no military implications.

(e) Paragraph 41

The phrase "at first" in the reference to the application of the sector theory by the USSR is misleading and should be amplified to make clear that the Soviets have never in fact proclaimed the sector theory in respect of Arctic waters and ice. In the final sentence of this paragraph the words "can be" should be changed to "has been" to bring out more clearly that the Government's policy is to avoid prejudicing possible use of the sector theory.

(f) Paragraph 44

We wish to stress our agreement with the view that increased surveillance activities must be developed in response to specific needs and interests and not on the basis of some pious hope that aimless over flights somehow contribute to "sovereignty". This paragraph could usefully expand on the fact that there is no legal need for surveillance, for the sake of surveillance, in the Arctic, or, otherwise put, that the need for surveillance is functional rather than legal (although having legal implications).

(g) Paragraph 48

The reference to intrusions by foreign vessels should mention the problem of unauthorized research on Canada's continental shelf. Also we believe it may be somewhat an overstatement to describe such intrusions as being "very rare" in light of recent Soviet activities in particular.

(h) Paragraph 50

The reference to "circumstances where Canadian and US policies diverge" is, in our view, scarcely sufficient recognition of the difficulties which arise, in respect of Canada's defence policy, out of the growing opposition between Canadian and US interests as regards claims to maritime sovereignty or jurisdiction. This issue is one which we believe should be carefully and thoroughly reviewed in the DND paper.

7. We are providing in a separate memorandum our comments on a related DND paper entitled "Canadian Defence Policy in the 1970's" which you forwarded to us with your memorandum of April 20, 1970.

3-12. DEXAF, FLE to OMD, subject: DND Paper On "Canadian Defence Policy in the 1970's," 5 August 1970.[37]

This memorandum should be read in conjunction with our memorandum of even date concerning the DND paper on "The Role of Canadian Armed Forces in the Protection of Sovereignty."

2. We have reviewed the subject paper in the light of the thoughtful analysis and the observations made in your memorandum under reference. In general, we would agree with your view that the paper tends to confuse the problem of the legal basis for those claims. The distinction between these two problems, as we see it, is that a military "presence" in the Arctic waters will not of itself establish the legal validity of Canada's claims, whereas the enforcement of Canada's claims (whether by military or other agencies) is essential to their effectiveness. The legal validity of a claim is not necessarily destroyed if it is not or cannot be enforced, and similarly the legal validity of a claim is not necessarily established because it is effectively enforced. The dividing line between de facto and de jure, however, can be crossed; good claims can be lost and doubtful ones can be sanctioned by the force of fact.

3. Our comments on specific points made in the DND paper and questioned by you are as follows:

(a) Paragraph 28

We consider that the statement that "sovereignty depends to some extent upon demonstrated (or at least apparent) capabilities for surveillance and occupation" could be misleading. Does it refer to land, the continental shelf or water? Effective occupation is, of course, the most widely recognized means of establishing sovereignty over land territory, but Canada's sovereignty over its Arctic lands is already securely established on precisely this basis. As regards the continental shelf, the coastal states' exclusive sovereign rights (as expressly provided in the Continental Shelf Convention) do not depend on any form of occupation. As regards water (and, to a lesser extent, ice) "occupation" would at best be a relative concept and is not one which has been accepted under international law in this context. So far as "surveillance" is concerned, it may well be a necessary function of sovereignty but

37 LAC, RG 25, vol. 10322, file 27-10-2-2 pt.1. Originally classified as "Confidential."

could not be considered a basis for or sine qua non of sovereignty in legal terms.

(b) Paragraph 62

This paragraph appears to confuse sovereignty with jurisdiction (e.g. for fisheries or pollution purposes). We agree, of course, that it is necessary to protect Canadian territory against encroachments and to enforce Canadian jurisdiction. Like you, however, we question that "persistent pressure"[38] is "an important factor in establishing sovereignty over channels or coastal waters". Effective control of a sea area, on the other hand, may be the basis for a claim of sovereignty on historic grounds under international law; and effective enforcement may consolidate a claim to jurisdiction. (The relevance of "beneficial actions", from the legal point of view, rather escapes us). As regards "knowledge of what is going on", we would say rather that it is essential to effective control of an area, or effective enforcement of jurisdiction, or the protection of national security; similarly, surveillance is required for these purposes of control, enforcement and protection, but not on the grounds of "enforcement capability", we have already noted our view that while this is not necessarily a requirement for the validity of a claim under international law, a claim which cannot be enforced can be lost while a claim which can be enforced can be consolidated.

4. In summary, we consider that the DND paper requires careful review and re-thinking; its insistence on "presence" suggests some misunderstanding of both law and reality. While we agree with the paper's general thesis that developments in the Arctic will undoubtedly call for a new and expanded role for the Canadian Forces, we also agree with your assessment that the rationale and basis for this role should be more clearly formulated. "Sovereignty" is not a magic word which automatically requires or justifies a certain type of military set-piece. It is rather the political and territorial framework within which a state exists and functions. It is not made up of, or protected by symbols, tokens or gestures.

38 *Editors' note:* This phrase appears in the original, but the author may have intended to write "persistent presence."

3-13. DEXAF, E.B. Wang to Mr. [R.P.] Cameron, re: Canadian Forces Activities in the North: Sovereignty, 25 November 1970.[39]

At the meeting of the Coordinating Committee of the ACND on November 19 BGen [Ramsay] Withers presented a briefing on current planning for our Forces' activities in the North. So far as I could see the briefing was largely a rerun of the briefing Withers recently made to Defence Council. As part of the briefing he covered the "Statement of Defence Objectives for the Canadian North" which defines the 1st objective as follows:

> "1. Contributing to the maintenance of Canadian sovereignty in the North by: providing a military presence, and surveillance and reconnaissance of Canadian territory, airspace and territorial waters as well as the air and sea approaches thereto."

2. During the discussion period which followed the formal briefing, the Chairman (Digby Hunt) asked Withers about the results of inquiries which DND had put to individual departments concerning their surveillance needs in the North. Withers said that departments had been slow in responding and that further discussions would be necessary. In this context I raised a question as to what requirements had so far been identified in relation to "providing a military programme." I referred to the studies of the sovereignty question carried out by this department. Withers' reply will, I assume, appear eventually in the minutes of the meeting but it might be worthwhile noting here the gist of his response, together with some comments he made to me privately after the meeting. I understood him to say in effect that the question of any additional needs for military presence was still under study but that the tentative working approach they had adopted was to put the emphasis on the need for the Forces to have a capability to move and operate anywhere in the North, rather than establishing additional fixed military outposts. In a sense, Withers acknowledged, this objective tended to merge with the second defence objective – "maintaining operational ready...forces

39 LAC, RG 25, vol. 10322, file 27-10-2-2 pt.2. Originally classified as "Confidential."

capable…etc." During a coffee break Withers raised the subject with me again and asked about studies which we had done in our department.

3. I reiterated our departmental view that Canadian sovereign title to the northlands and islands was unassailable and undisputed under international law, and that although there might be other needs there was no need for increased presence of military forces in the North merely for the sake of presence in order to bolster our legal claim to the real estate. Ivan Head had done a good study of our claims in the 1963 McGill Law Journal, showing how strong these claims were. I recalled that the Prime Minister had on several occasions in the House asserted that Canadian territorial jurisdiction was not in question. I said it would be misleading and unfortunate if any public announcement by DND gave rise to an impression that the Government was concerned about a shaky title. Withers agreed that care would have to be taken to avoid any appearance of putting our sovereignty in question. He said there was, as far as he knew, no intention to announce publicly the "Defence Objectives" as presently defined. They were not cast in concrete and would be subject to further review in light of ongoing studies which would probably not be completed until after his command (North[ern] Region Headquarters) had been in the field for about a year.

4. Withers told me (to my surprise) that he had not yet seen the two papers prepared by Legal Division dated August 5, 1970, which we had passed informally to General [G.G.] Bell. He would track them down now that he was aware of their existence. I told Withers our Department had a direct interest and responsibility in relation to various aspects of the sovereignty question (e.g. territorial waters and pollution control zones) and that we would be glad to assist in further efforts to identify useful roles for the Forces in this area.

5. I said that the reference to "presence" in the Statement of Defence Objectives seemed to me to be misleading in another sense. It seemed to connote something static and symbolic, whereas the Government's approach to questions of sovereignty had been a functional approach, seeking to define and identify where Canadian interests lay (i.e. anti-

pollution and safety of navigation) and shaping policy and legislation to meet what needed to be done to protect those interests. It seemed to me that DND, in canvassing Government departments on their needs, had already launched its studies in the same direction. A pre-occupation with "presence" for the sake of "presence" would be inconstant with this approach. If DND had in mind Canada's recent claims to extended jurisdiction over Arctic waters for pollution control, different questions arose as to how this control can be best exercised and enforced.

6. Withers said that he had formally asked the Defence Research Analysis Establishment [DRAE] of the Defence Research Board (Dr. Joe Vigder) to pursue further studies on the role of the Forces in relation to the protection of sovereignty. He said he would be getting in touch with Vigder to suggest External Affairs be invited to participate in some way in these studies.

7. As a follow on to this conversation Major Stonehouse of DRAE called on me today. He seemed to have no clear idea of what form any further study would take. His main interest at this stage was to ensure that he was aware of the studies and reports already prepared by various people in DND and External. I went through our file and gave him references to several key documents which were already available to DND. I reiterated to Stonehouse that if there were questions or areas where DND would like to have further views by this Department, they should not hesitate to let us know.

8. It is depressing to think that after twenty months of studying what the Prime Minister meant in his reference to the role of the Forces in the protection of sovereignty (April 3 statement) DND are still at the stage of preparing a background bibliography.

4 The Canadian Armed Forces, Other Government Departments and the Functional Requirements of Sovereignty

4-1. DEXAF, M. Shenstone to E.B. Wang, re: "Report of the Working Group to clarify The Role of the Canadian Forces in Relation to Sovereignty" (undated), 23 September 1970.[40]

This is an important document which, as you said, is not altogether satisfactory from some points of view; nevertheless, it is a good deal better than it might have been.

2. The "assumptions" outlined in Paragraph 4, as expected, state that DND must consider and allocate resources to the four military roles in their order of relative priority; but it is encouraging that this is qualified by the statement that these roles are to be "mutually supporting" - - which seems to me to admit the principle of double-tasking under a less provocative name - - and by the statement that greater resources should not necessarily be allocated to the first role then to the second and subsequent roles. This should help to head off tendencies to starve international roles which are of concern to this Department, in order to flesh out the first role, although the problem will by no means be solved.

3. I agree with your observation that sub-objective No. 5 under the first role ("to provide assistance in the protection of the rights and property of Canadians citizens abroad") is a contentious new item which the Department will need to examine carefully and perhaps criticize when and if the paper reaches us officially for comment. I have not been able to locate anything of this kind in Arthur Kroeger's "Rationale for Canadian Defence Forces" paper of 1968 (CFP243), the 1969 Defence

40 LAC, RG 25, vol. 10322, file 27-10-2-2 pt.2. Originally classified as "Confidential."

Review paper, or the October 1969 Maritime Strategy Study; nor does it appear in the programme description for the 1970-71 DND estimates, although most of the other sub-objectives appear in the same or slightly different form under the Canadian security heading on p. 14-16 of these estimates.

4. Another change from the formulation in the 1970-71 estimates is that cooperation with the USA in North American defence is described in the paper as "to ensure the security of Canada..." whereas our NATO activities are described merely as "to enhance the security of Canada." The '70-'71 estimates described the purpose of both kinds of activity as "to enhance the security of Canada...." Moreover, the NATO activity is better described in the present estimates ("through cooperation with allies under the North Atlantic Treaty in collective defence activities in Europe and the North Atlantic area") than in the paper ("By cooperating in collective defence measures under the North Atlantic Treaty"). The older formulation, by localizing geographically the activity in question, avoids the complicated question as to whether our North American defence activity should be regarded as part of our cooperation with NATO. The new formulation, in contrast, implies gratuitously that our cooperation in "collective defence measures under the North Atlantic Treaty" is something separate from our cooperation with the USA.

5. Another innovation in the paper is that military assistance is included under the fourth role ("to promote international stability by contributing to peacekeeping activities in cooperation with other members of the international community and by providing military assistance to designated friendly nations"). In the '70-'71 estimates only the first half of this sentence (slightly amended) is used ...; it is true that there is a reference to military assistance on the following page (the Canadian military assistance team in Ghana) but I wonder whether the military assistance element in this role is sufficiently important to warrant its inclusion in the statement of major programme "sub-objectives" or "activity objectives." This might seem somewhat illogical as our own Department's estimates contain a military assistance item. You may want to discuss this with Colonel Newlands (who should

note that the paper in question has not yet been officially received by this Department and should accordingly not be mentioned to DND contacts as yet).

4-2. "Role of the Canadian Armed Forces in Relation to Sovereignty: Report on Consultations with Other Government Departments and Agencies," 26 January 1971 (Revised 11 May 1971).[41]

ROLE OF CANADIAN ARMED FORCES IN RELATION TO SOVEREIGNTY

REPORT ON CONSULTATIONS WITH OTHER GOVERNMENT DEPARTMENTS AND AGENCIES

I. INTRODUCTION

1. In its statement on Defence Policy issued on 3 April, 1969, the Government established as the first of four roles assigned to the Canadian Armed Forces, "the surveillance of our own territory and coastlines, i.e., the protection of our sovereignty". On 23 July, 1970, the Deputy Minister of National Defence, with the agreement of the Chief of the Defence Staff, the Secretary to the Cabinet and Clerk of the Privy Council, and the Secretary of the Treasury Board, established a Working Group to clarify the role of the Canadian Armed Forces in relation to sovereignty.

2. In its Report, which was submitted to the principals on 21 August, 1970 and subsequently accepted by them, the Working Group agreed that it was the intention of the 3 April, 1969 defence policy statement that the first role should comprise those military activities needed to ensure the maintenance of Canada's territorial integrity, jurisdictional authority and sovereign interests against challenges or threats other than those of armed attack by the forces of a foreign country. In addition, the Working Group concluded that, in order to meet the requirement of that first role, the Department of National Defence should, in its future planning and programming, maintain suitable military capabilities, inter alia, to enable the Canadian Armed Forces:

41 DHH Raymont Collection 87/253-11-8.2. Originally classified as "Confidential."

a. to support the civilian departments and agencies of government in the discharge of their responsibilities to carry out surveillance and to exercise supervision and control over Canadian territory, territorial waters and airspace and Canadian jurisdiction over the seabed, the continental shelf and in the sea areas adjacent to Canada within the limits established by international agreements or by government policy and Canadian legislation;
b. to carry out surveillance and to provide means to exercise supervision and control in those areas not covered by the civil departments and agencies of government or in which the capabilities provided by the latter in the discharge of their normal responsibilities are inadequate to provide full protection of Canadian interests.

3. Following acceptance by the principals of the Report of the Working Group and on the basis of the understandings therein agreed, the Deputy Minister of National Defence on 21 September, 1970 initiated a series of consultations with those federal departments and agencies charged with statutory responsibilities for surveillance and control of Canadian territory and the exercise of Canadian jurisdiction in relation to the activity of foreigners and of foreign interests. Separate consultations have taken place with the Departments of Fisheries and Forestry, Energy, Mines and Resources, Indian Affairs and Northern Development, and National Revenue (Customs and Excise Division), and with the Ministry of Transport and the Royal Canadian Mounted Police.

4. The principal objectives of these consultations, which have taken the form of one or more meetings between officers of the Department of National Defence and the Canadian Forces and the responsible officials of each of the other Departments or Agencies concerned have been, in relation to the maintenance of Canadian sovereignty:

a. to determine with precision the statutory and other responsibilities of each department or agency for surveillance and control of Canadian territory, territorial waters, airspace and other areas over which Canada exercises jurisdiction and for the regulation therein of activity by foreigners,

b. to determine the capabilities required and the means employed by each department or agency to discharge these responsibilities, and
c. to determine the extent and kinds of support, if any, required by each department or agency from the Canadian Armed Forces in the normal discharge of these responsibilities.

5. The information gained from the consultations relating to the above objectives is set out in Part II of this report. In the consultations with them, a number of departments manifested an interest in assistance from the Canadian Armed Forces in carrying out various responsibilities other than those relating directly to the maintenance of Canadian sovereignty. The information obtained relating to those interests is summarized in Part III of this report.

II. SURVEILLANCE AND CONTROL

GENERAL

6. Canada's geographical situation is such that, except across its two borders with US territory and, with almost prohibitive difficulty, across the polar regions, it can be approached or entered from foreign countries only by sea or by air and, with minor exceptions, only by travel over a relatively long distance and at relatively high cost. This relative inaccessibility means that foreigners, other than those coming from US territory, are unlikely to approach or enter Canada casually or for reasons other than those which are purposive and are likely to result in significant advantage to the foreign interests involved, whether these be political, military, commercial and economic, scientific, social or cultural.

7. It has been notable, in the consultations which have taken place with the departments and agencies concerned, that the laws under which Canada controls and regulates the use of its territory by foreigners, and exercises its jurisdiction over them, are specific and oriented to particular national interests rather than general, and that they are in the main regulatory rather than exclusionary. These characteristics of Canadian law appear to be attributable partly to Canada's relative inaccessibility to most foreigners as a consequence of its geographical situation, partly

to the closeness, the wide variety and the day by day frequency of its relationships with the USA, partly to the open and democratic character of Canadian society, and partly to Canada's status as a trader on the world's markets, Canadian policies, as expressed in the body of statute law and in Canadian regulations, manifest almost no xenophobia and little of the desire to exclude foreigners from the territory and economic activity of the nation that has been a classic characteristic of most nation states.

8. No major external challenge to Canada's national sovereignty currently exists or appears likely to arise in the foreseeable future. No other state covets or seeks to deprive Canada of any part of its territory or seeks to reduce or to deny to Canada its political independence. To the extent that Canada's national jurisdiction is disputed by other states, the disputes centre on areas into which that jurisdiction has recently been extended beyond the limits traditionally recognized in international law and are mainly with states with which Canada is allied or enjoys friendly relations and which consequently are unlikely to use physical force to impose their will upon Canada. It has been noteworthy that that the departments and agencies consulted believe that, within their specific areas of responsibility, Canadian laws and regulations and the means which they employ to enforce them are for the most part adequate to protect Canada's national interests. As will be evident from the following discussion, where they have been expressed, concern and an interest in support by the Canadian Armed Forces have focused on those areas where Canada's jurisdiction has been most recently extended and where Canada's right to exercise it is not fully defined and accepted internationally, and in those areas where newly perceived problems, such as those relating to pollution and quality of the physical environment, or new levels of interest and activity, such as in the mineral resources of the Arctic and the Continental Shelf, have come to the fore.

MARITIME SURVEILLANCE AND CONTROL

9. Because from most foreign countries the main avenues of approach to Canada lie on or over the sea, because there is increasing national and international interest in both the conservation and exploitation of the

resources found in and under the sea, because, largely in consequence, it is on and under the sea that the most recent extensions of national jurisdiction have taken place, and because, no doubt, maritime matters are almost exclusively a Federal responsibility, the marine environment and Canada's maritime interests have figured prominently in the consultations with other departments. The information obtained is as follows:

a. Interest Identified: Conservation of Fishing Resources and Prevention of Unlawful Foreign Fishing in Territorial Waters and Exclusive Fishing Zones.
Governing Legislation: Coastal Fisheries Protection Act; Territorial Seas and Fishing Zones Act.
Responsible Minister and Department: Fisheries and Forestry.
Nature and Source of Challenge: Some of the world's most important fishing grounds lie off the East and West Coasts of Canada both within and outside the limits of Canada's territorial seas and exclusive fishing zones. On the East Coast these fishing grounds annually attract commercial and state-owned fishing fleets from a large number of both Western and Eastern European countries. With the exception of US and French fishermen who enjoy longstanding treaty rights, foreign fishermen are forbidden by Canadian law from fishing within territorial waters and exclusive fishing zones. Similarly, off the West Coast, the fishing grounds annually attract foreign fishing fleets mainly from the Soviet Union, Japan, Korea and the USA. With the exception of US fishermen, who have treaty and reciprocal fishing rights, these foreign fishermen are forbidden by Canadian law to fish in Canada's territorial seas and exclusive fishing zones. While there is no evidence to suggest that, on either coast, foreign fishermen make any large scale and concerted attempts to breach Canadian law, they do at times both accidentally and deliberately seek to carry out fishing in waters from which they are excluded and would no doubt do so more often if no preventive measures were taken.

HMCS Preserver docks at Churchill, Manitoba during Exercise NORPLOY 1974, August 1974. (LAC)

Discussion: The Department of Fisheries and Forestry is responsible for the conservation of Canada's ocean fishing resources and for the control of fishing in Canada's territorial seas and exclusive zones, including both the regulations of operations by Canadian fishermen and the prevention of unlawful fishing in these waters by foreign fishermen. These responsibilities are discharged mainly by the Fisheries Protection Service, which maintains a fleet of patrol vessels, some of which are armed, operating off both the East and West Coasts of Canada. Off the East Coast, the capabilities of the Fisheries Protection Service are supplemented during the fishing season by charter of commercial aircraft to maintain surveillance of foreign fishing fleets fishing outside Canadian waters in order to obtain information on changes in their fishing patterns. The frequency of this surveillance varies from about once every week or two weeks to once every two or three days when the foreign fleets are reported as having moved closer to the boundaries of exclusive Canadian fishing waters. The Department of Fisheries and Forestry state that the locations and patterns of operation of the foreign fishing fleets are 75-80% predictable. At times, however, the fleets move from the predicted areas giving rise to a requirement for immediate short-term reconnaissance to locate them. The Department of Fisheries and Forestry have indicated that they would seek the support of Canadian naval vessels in turning back or arresting foreign fishing vessels in the event of a large scale and determined incursion into Canadian waters beyond the capabilities of the fisheries patrol vessels to deal with. Such incursions are stated to occur very rarely. In this regard, officers of the Canadian Forces have been authorized by Order-in-Council PC 1970/1512 to exercise the powers of Fisheries Protection Officers under the Coastal Fisheries Protection Act, at the request of the Department of Fisheries and Forestry.

Support Required from the Canadian Armed Forces: The Department of Fisheries and Forestry have indicated interests in the following support of their operations by the CAF:

(i) Area surveillance of foreign fishing fleets off the East and West Coasts during the fishing season at frequencies ranging from once every two weeks to once every two or three days to replace the capability now provided by charter of commercial aircraft. As the present operator has limited capability, he is often unable to respond

(ii) Reconnaissance on a quick response short-term basis to relocate these foreign fishing fleets when they move to new fishing areas.

(iii) On call support by naval vessels on both East and West Coasts to deal with large scale incursions into Canadian waters.

b. Interests Identified: Control and Regulation of Offshore Mineral Resources Exploration and Exploitation.
Governing Legislation: Oil and Gas Production and Conservation Act.

Responsible Minister and Department:

(i) Energy, Mines and Resources in respect of all areas south of a line of administrative convenience described in Order-in-Council PC 1965/2284.

(ii) Indian Affairs and Northern Development in respect of areas north of this line.

Nature and Source of Challenge: Canada has full sovereignty and exercises exclusive national jurisdiction over the sea-bed and subsoil within the boundaries of its territorial waters. In addition, under the terms of the Convention on the Continental Shelf concluded at Geneva in 1958, Canada, as the coastal state, exercises sovereign rights and exclusive jurisdiction over the continental shelf, as defined in the Convention, "for the purpose of exploring it and exploiting its natural resources." The Convention defines the term "continental shelf" as referring (a) to the sea-bed and subsoil of the submarine areas adjacent to the coast, but outside the area of the territorial sea, to a depth of 200 metres or, beyond that limit, to where the depth of the superadjacent waters admits of the exploitation of the natural resources of the said areas, (b) to the sea-bed and subsoil of similar submarine areas adjacent to the coasts of islands." On the basis of this definition, Canada asserts and exercises jurisdiction, for the purposes of exploration and exploitation, over the whole of the geological shelf out to the bottom of the slope. Canada's jurisdiction over part of this area is legally disputed, but has not been physically challenged, by some states party to the Convention who contend that the outer limits of the jurisdiction of the coastal state should be more restricted. Furthermore, Canada has not yet reached agreement with the USA regarding the boundary between the Canadian and American areas of the continental shelf on the East Coast nor with France as to the extent to which a portion of the continental shelf on the East Coast comes under French jurisdiction in respect of the Islands of St. Pierre and Miquelon. Extensive commercial exploration of the continental shelf areas off Canada's coasts for oil and natural gas is currently taking place with several projects nearing the point of exploitation or production. Foreign companies, mainly American, engaged in this activity have to date respected Canadian jurisdiction and complied with the applicable Canadian regulations, even in areas open to dispute. The reasons for this appear to lie in the fact that sea-bed exploration and exploitation activities involve high levels of investment which the investors are not prepared to put at risk of loss or seizure by acting contrary to the laws of a state exercising jurisdiction, even where its rights to do so may be somewhat in doubt.

Discussion: The Department of Energy, Mines and Resources is responsible for the administration and management of mineral resources off the East and West Coasts and in the Hudson Bay and Hudson Strait regions. The main elements of the system of offshore resource management are the following. At the outset, an individual or company planning to undertake offshore exploratory work must obtain an exploratory license. This allows the party concerned to undertake exploration work, short of drilling a well, anywhere on Canada lands subject to securing prior approval of the Department for each program proposed. The second element in the system is the exploratory permit which, in contrast to the license, involves a specific area. The permit conveys to the permittee two advantages over his competitors: first, the option of acquiring exploitation rights, i.e. leases, within the permit area; and, secondly, the privilege of being able to drill wells within the permit area. A permittee must obtain prior approval from the Department for each program (including each individual well). An applicant must pay a fee for each permit at the time it is taken out, and must at the same time make a guaranty deposit covering in full the first-period work requirements of the permit to ensure that this amount of work will be performed. Permit work obligations become increasingly stringent with time, and guaranty deposits must be made prior to each succeeding work period. These deposits are returned upon satisfactory evidence that appropriate work has been performed. The third element in the regulatory system is the exploitation lease. Commercial production may not be undertaken while acreage is in permit form; it must first be converted to lease, whereupon at least fifty percent is relinquished to the Crown. The Crown receives a rate of royalty on production. Each individual offshore program is subject to prior approval, and on site inspections by EMR engineers, with a geologist participating on occasion, are carried out as required, normally at the expense of the permittee.

Compliance of licensees, permittees and lessees with the above regulatory system is ensured by means of comprehensive requirements whereby they must provide information and appropriate materials on a current basis; assist in the carrying out of inspections by authorized officials; furnish comprehensive technical reports; and support claims for refunds of guaranty deposits with certified statements of expenditures. As regards the possibility of an unauthorized offshore program being initiated, the Department of Energy, Mines and Resources relies principally on commercial intelligence gained from both trade publications and more generally from the Department's contacts with the industry. Enforcement is obtained through the administrative action with the commercial enterprise concerned or, if necessary, in respect of foreign enterprises, through diplomatic action with the parent state. The responsible officials of the Department of Energy, Mines and Resources consider that the above means enable them to exercise adequate control over offshore oil and gas operations and doubt that a major offshore program could be carried out without coming to their attention.

These officials recognize, however, the possibility that a foreign company, perhaps with the support of its state, might test Canadian resolution especially in an area of dispute. They have, therefore, expressed interest in some surveillance of offshore waters to detect and report seismic or other underwater exploration, particularly in the areas off the Islands of St. Pierre and Miquelon disputed with France and in the Gulf of Maine region where the line of demarcation seaward from the Canada-US border is not yet agreed. In the former area, there is an informal agreement between the two states to refrain from authorizing exploration activity notwithstanding the issuance of permits by both for the same area, and the purpose of surveillance would be to verify that this agreement is being observed. In the latter area, the purpose of surveillance would be to determine whether exploration authorized by the USA is being carried out in areas claimed by Canada. The Department of Energy, Mines and Resources has, in addition, expressed interest in the use of submersibles operated by the Canadian Forces in underwater inspection or surveillance of sub-sea equipment or facilities such as well heads, storage facilities and pipelines.

Support Required from the Canadian Armed Forces: The Department of Energy, Mines and Resources have indicated interest in the following support for their operations:
(i) Area surveillance of offshore surface waters to detect and report seismic and other exploration activities particularly in areas where Canadian jurisdiction in disputed.
(ii) Sub-surface inspection and surveillance of underwater equipment, facilities and installations.
(iii)Air or sea.

c. Interest Identified: Safety of Shipping and Navigation in Canadian waters.
Governing Legislation: Canada Shipping Act, Navigable Waters Protection Act.
Responsible Minister and Department: Transport.
Nature and Source of Challenge: Strictly speaking, there is no specific challenge to Canada's sovereignty or jurisdiction in this area of interest. Canada is, however, highly dependent on the year round movement of shipping to and from its ports for the carriage of its international trade. In addition, during the summer months, Canadian communities and ports in the Eastern Arctic depend on shipping for annual resupply of the necessities of life. Ice, especially in the Gulf of St. Lawrence during the winter months and in the Eastern Arctic during the summer months, impedes navigation and creates a hazard to shipping.

Discussion: The Ministry of Transport is responsible for the provision of a wide variety of services to shipping and of aids to navigation in Canada's territorial waters and other navigable waters under Canadian jurisdiction. For the most part, the Ministry considers its capabilities entirely adequate to the discharge of these responsibilities. The responsibilities include ice-breaking services and the maintenance of safe passage for shipping in the Gulf of St. Lawrence and on the St. Lawrence river in winter and in Arctic waters in the summer. The acquisition of up-to-date information on ice conditions is important in both cases to the discharge of the Ministry's responsibilities and, in addition, is of considerable value for meteorological and other scientific purposes. The Ministry currently employs aircraft under commercial charter to carry out ice reconnaissance operations over the shipping routes in southern waters during the winter and in the Arctic during the spring and summer months. An assured and continuous service is required to meet the Ministry's needs. The current charter is shortly due to expire and the aircraft currently used are obsolete and in many respects unsatisfactory. The Ministry also takes advantage of the CAF arctic patrols by sending ice observers on a percentage of the flights. This is only partly satisfactory from their point of view because they are not consulted beforehand as to flight routes, and because staff limitations only permit the provision of observers on flights where a reasonable proportion of the route will be over Arctic waters as opposed to land. The Ministry, therefore, has under study a proposal to acquire its own aircraft for ice reconnaissance purposes. Even if this proposal is accepted, the Ministry of Transport would be interested in some support in ice reconnaissance from Canadian Forces aircraft engaged in other surveillance operations. If the proposal is not accepted, the Ministry would be interested in having the Canadian Forces assume full responsibility for ice reconnaissance provided that its need for an assured and continuous service were met and that the aircraft involved were not subject to withdrawal in the event of military contingencies.

<u>Support Required from the Canadian Armed Forces</u>: The Ministry of Transport has indicated an interest in the following support by the CAF:

(i) Support of the Ministry's Ice Reconnaissance Operations or, possibly, full conduct of these operations on behalf of the Ministry.

d. Interest Identified: Prevention and Control of Pollution of the Sea and Sea-shore by Shipping.
Governing Legislation: Canada Shipping Act: Arctic Waters Pollution Prevention Act.
Responsible Minister and Department: Transport.
Nature and Source of Challenge: The ever increasing use of petroleum as a source of energy and for industrial purposes, and the increasing carriage of petroleum by sea and use for this carriage of very large tankers, often operated with inadequate standards under flags of convenience, have combined with the large scale use of fuel oil for the propulsion of ships to very much increase the risks of discharge of pollutants from ships in the seas and the consequent risks of contamination of beaches and shorelines, of fishing grounds for oysters, lobster and other sedentary species, and of destruction of sea birds and other disturbances of the marine and littoral ecology.

Discussion: The Ministry of Transport has the responsibility under the Canada Shipping Act for shipping standards and for prevention, or when it occurs, control, of discharge of pollutants from ships in Canada's territorial sea and in other Canadian navigable waters, and expects to be assigned similar responsibilities in relation to the pollution control zones established under the Arctic Waters Pollution Prevention Act. The Ministry does not undertake regular surveillance of ships entering Canadian waters to watch for pollution. Some surveillance of ships in the Great Lakes is undertaken in the course of Coast Guard pollution patrols. At the present time, apart from certain prohibitions regarding the discharge of oil or oily waste over the side, there are no regulations concerning anti-pollution standards of ships. Such regulations are now being prepared for ships in Arctic waters and the Ministry officials think it reasonable to expect that, in due course, these will be followed by regulations for more southerly Canadian waters and by international agreement on standards of construction and operation to decrease the risk of oil pollution. In the meantime, it is customary to enforce the existing regulations prohibiting the discharge of oil or oily waste and to prosecute offenders in Court. The majority of the prosecutions follow offences in port because of the difficulty of obtaining the necessary proof in the case of ships at sea. If a ship leaves Canadian waters before a summons could be served on the Master, it is customary to await its return on the next voyage before instituting action, and there has been no case of attempting to arrest a ship at sea. In such a case, the Ministry would probably look to the Canadian Forces to take the necessary action.

The Ministry of Transport states a requirement for aerial surveillance of Canadian waters to detect pollution by ships, and while it employs one aircraft in the summer months on area surveillance and helicopters on local surveillance the Ministry considers that, as a subsidiary task, military aircraft should keep an eye out for pollution of this kind.

Support Required from the Canadian Armed Forces: The Ministry of Transport has indicated an interest in the following support by the CAF:

(i) Surveillance of Canadian waters by military aircraft, as a subsidiary task, to detect pollution by ships at sea.

(ii) Arrest, within territorial waters and on rare occasions, of foreign ships in breach of Canadian regulations respecting the discharge of pollutants.

c. Interest Identified: Customs Control of Shipping in Canadian Waters.

Governing Legislation: Customs Act.

Responsible Minister and Department: National Revenue (Customs and Excise Division). The RCMP act as the principal enforcement agency.

Nature and Source of Challenge: Some of the most important international shipping routes enter Canadian territorial waters or pass through or close to the limits of these waters off both the East and West Coasts of Canada. Canada, in addition, depends largely on shipping of foreign registry for the carriage of its international trade. While these factors do not in themselves give rise to any specific challenges to Canada's territorial integrity or to Canadian jurisdiction, they do heighten the possibility that foreign shipping will be used either for the illegal importation of foreign goods into Canada or for other purposes, such as coastal trade (limited under the regulations to ships of Commonwealth registry) which are contrary to Canadian law and may be inimical to Canadian interests.

Discussion: The Department of National Revenue (Customs and Excise Division) is responsible for the administration of the Customs Act and the Customs Regulations made under the Act. Enforcement action is the responsibility, under the Act, of the Royal Canadian Mounted Police. Customs control and enforcement of the Customs Regulations in respect of shipping is carried out principally in Canadian ports of destination. Both under international law and under the Customs Act, foreign shipping is accorded the right of innocent passage in Canadian territorial waters whether proceeding to a Canadian port or in transit through these waters. Regulations under the Customs Act prohibit foreign ships from anchoring or "hovering" (that is to say remaining stationary without anchoring or moving other than on proper course to their destination) in Canadian territorial waters, other than in recognized harbours or ports of entry. The regulations also prohibit foreign ships, other than those of Commonwealth registry, from engaging in coastal trade between Canadian ports. The Department of National Revenue consider that some surveillance of Canadian territorial waters to detect foreign vessels illegally at anchor or illegally "hovering" is desirable. Such surveillance was provided by sea-going patrol vessels operated by the RCMP. The RCMP, however, have concluded that in present day circumstances such patrol activity is not cost-beneficial and have recently disposed of the larger patrol vessels which they employed for this purpose.

Support Required from the Canadian Armed Forces: The Department of National Revenue (Customs and Excise Division) have expressed an interest in the following support from the CAF:

(i) Limited surveillance of Canadian territorial waters to detect and report foreign vessels illegally anchoring or hovering therein.

SURVEILLANCE AND CONTROL OF LAND AREAS

10. No foreign state currently poses a physical challenge to Canada's territorial integrity or disputes Canadian jurisdiction over any of its mainland or island territories. Nevertheless, the vast expanse of Canadian territory, the fact that much of it especially in the remote regions of the North is sparsely settled, the growing interest in the resource potential of these remote regions especially as a source of oil and natural gas and an increasing awareness of the dangers which the exploitation of resources may pose to finely balanced ecology of the Northern and Arctic territories, have combined in recent years to heighten governmental and public concern over the possibility that foreign enterprise might, either without proper authorization or under inadequate regulation, seek to exploit remote areas of Canada in ways and for purposes contrary to Canadian interest. As a consequence, a need has been recognized to strengthen Canadian presence and the means of exercising Canadian jurisdiction in Canada's Northern and Arctic regions, in order to ensure that the international community is fully aware of and will act in conformity with Canada's interests and jurisdictional authority.

a. Interest Identified: Control and Regulation of Land Use and of Mineral Exploration and Exploitation in the Territories, and in Canada Lands under the waters of the Beaufort Sea, Arctic Ocean, Arctic Archipelago, Foxe Basin, Foxe Strait, Baffin Bay and Baffin Strait.

Governing Legislation: Territorial Lands Act: Public Lands Grants Act: Oil and Gas Production and Conservation Act. Other related Acts.

Responsible Minister and Department: Indian Affairs and Northern Development.

Nature and Source of Challenge: The closing of the Suez Canal in 1967 and the state of political disturbances in the Middle East and in some other oil producing areas have led the countries of North America and of Western Europe to seek more reliable and strategically secure sources of oil and natural gas to meet their energy and industrial requirements. Especially since the discovery of a major oil field at Prudhoe Bay in Alaska, this search has resulted in tremendous growth of commercial interest in the oil and gas potential of Canada's Northern Territories and in a major increase in oil and gas exploration in the Territories and especially on the Arctic Islands. These activities, in which both Canadian and foreign companies are involved, have brought with them a need to ensure that exploitation of the resources is carried out and regulated in accordance with Canada's long-term national economic and social interests and a danger that increased human activity and oil or other pollution resulting therefrom could reduce the purity of the Northern environment and disturb the finely balanced ecology of the region.

Discussion: The Department of Indian Affairs and Northern Development has broad responsibilities to regulate the use of land in the Territories. Included in its responsibilities is that of regulating oil and gas exploration and exploitation of Canada Lands to the north of the line of administrative convenience mentioned in paragraph 9 b. above. The Department employs a regulatory system for oil and gas operations essentially the same as that employed by the Department of Energy, Mines and Resources in respect of offshore resources. Like the latter department and for the same reasons, the Department of Indian Affairs and Northern Development considers it unlikely that foreign commercial interests would seek to carry out exploration or exploitation activities in a manner contrary to Canadian regulations. The Department, nonetheless, foresees a requirement for aerial surveillance to verify the location and status of authorized projects and, unlike the case further south, for air transportation of its technical inspectors to project sites, in case of urgent need.

Support Required from the Canadian Armed Forces: The Department of Indian Affairs and Northern Development has expressed an interest in the following support from the CAF:

(i) Aerial surveillance and photography of sites of mineral exploration and exploitation projects to verify their location and status.

(ii) Area surveillance of offshore surface waters to detect and report seismic and other exploration activities, particularly in areas where Canadian jurisdiction may be disputed.

(iii) Sub-surface inspection and surveillance of underwater equipment facilities and installations.

b. Interest Identified: Prevention and Control of Pollution of Arctic Waters from Sources on Land.
Governing Legislation: Arctic Waters Pollution Prevention Act.
Responsible Minister and Department: Indian Affairs and Northern Development is expected to be responsible for implementation.
Nature and Source of Challenge: The increasing level of governmental and commercial activity in the Arctic and particularly the activity in oil exploration and exploitation heightens the potential risks of pollution of Arctic waters by discharge of oil or other pollutants from land-based installations including oil wells on land and on the sea-bed, pipelines, sewage and storage facilities.

Discussion: The Department of Indian Affairs and Northern Development is responsible for the prevention of pollution of Arctic waters from sources on land or on the sea-bed, for the regulation of activities likely to cause such pollution, and for the development of standards for buildings and installations to minimize the risks of pollution occurring. The Department foresees a need for aerial surveillance to detect pollution and the sources of pollution when it occurs, and believes that airborne sensors may be useful for this purpose.

Support Required from the Canadian Armed Forces: The Department of Indian Affairs and Northern Development is interested in the following support from the CAF:

(i) Aerial surveillance of northern waters, including the operation of airborne sensors, to detect pollution and the sources of pollution.

c. Interest Identified: Protection and Conservation of Migratory Birds and other species of Wildlife.
Governing Legislation: Migratory Birds Convention Act.
Responsible Minister and Department: Indian Affairs and Northern Development (Canadian Wildlife Service). The Canadian Wildlife Service is shortly to be transferred to the new Department of Environment.
Nature and Source of Challenge: not applicable.

Discussion: The Canadian Wildlife Service is responsible for the conservation of migratory birds in Canada and for the protection of their nesting areas. An extensive program of aerial surveillance in relation to migratory birds is carried out over Canada under cooperative arrangements with the US Department of the Interior and using aircraft made available by that Department. Additional aerial surveillance is required to report on ice movements and the disappearance of snow in the Arctic Islands, to carry out bird counts in nesting areas, and to observe movements and carry out counts of caribou, polar bears and other rare species.

Support Required from the Canadian Armed Forces: The Canadian Wildlife Service has expressed interest in the following support from the CAF:

(i) During the appropriate seasons, provision of observer spaces on aircraft engaged in northern surveillance operations to permit wildlife observations.

(ii) Occasional use of air transport for special wildlife investigations.

SURVEILLANCE AND CONTROL OF CANADIAN AIRSPACE

11. The volume and extent of Canada's airspace and the length of its perimeter are amongst the greatest of any nation in the world. Canadian airspace is, moreover, traversed by international air routes, some of which are already amongst the most important and heavily travelled and others of which are likely to become of increasing importance in the future. Canada's airspace is also of considerable strategic importance since the shortest military air routes between the USA, on the one hand, and the USSR and China on the other, pass through it. From most foreign countries, the air and air travel provide the major alternative means to the sea for gaining access to Canada and to Canada's resources.

a. Interest Identified: Safety of Flight and Control of Air Traffic in Canadian Airspace.
   Governing Legislation: Aeronautics Act.
   Responsible Minister and Department: Transport.
   Nature and Source of Challenge: A large volume of international air traffic uses the great circle routes from Europe to widely dispersed destinations in Canada and the US with the greatest volume of this traffic proceeding to the New York area. Other routes with increasing traffic densities are from various points of origin in the US to the Far East via Alaska as well as a significant volume of traffic from Europe to the Far East over the northern part of Canada. Trans-continental domestic traffic is over the southern and more heavily populated regions of Canada. Modern means of surveillance and of air traffic control are essential to permit safe flight and prevent collisions on these routes.

   Discussion: The Ministry of Transport is responsible for the regulation of civil air traffic entering or operating within Canadian airspace. The Ministry interprets its responsibility as being to ensure that a suitable system exists which will permit safe flight and

A Tracker aircraft on patrol over an icefield. (LAC)

prevent collisions or other air accidents and it operates on the basis of mandatory adherence to Canadian regulations while operating within Canadian airspace. In fulfillment of its responsibilities the Ministry licenses civilian pilots, certifies and licenses civil aircraft, operates airports, investigates accidents, and operates surveillance radars and other equipment required for air traffic control. The Ministry has a continuing requirement for surveillance information obtained from some of the military air defence radars operated by the Canadian Forces and has expressed some interest in the co-location of a new Air Traffic Control Centre, which it plans to establish for the Toronto area, with the military facilities at North Bay.

Support Required from the Canadian Armed Forces: The Ministry of Transport indicates interest in the following support from the CAF:

(i) Continued joint use of certain air defence radars.
(ii) Possible co-location of an Air Traffic Control Centre with the military facilities at North Bay.

b. Interest Identified: Customs control of Foreign Aircraft and Prevention of their Unlicensed Operation in Canada.

Governing Legislation: Aeronautics Act: Customs Act.

Responsible Minister and Department: National Revenue (Customs and Excise Division). The RCMP is the enforcement agency under the Customs Act.

Nature and Source of Challenge: Charter aircraft from the USA carry out some unlawful and unlicensed commercial operations in Canada in contravention of the sabotage regulations. The principal concerns are with small US aircraft transporting sportsmen and hunting parties between points in Southern Canada mainly in the Lakehead area, and with larger US aircraft from Alaska flying and transporting equipment between points in Northern Canada mainly in support of resource exploration and exploitation activities.

Discussion: The Customs Regulations require that aircraft entering Canada from abroad land and submit to customs check at recognized ports of entry. In Northern Canada, captains of such aircraft are required to report to the RCMP. Under the Aeronautics Act, aircraft are permitted to engage in commercial operations in Canada only under license from the Canadian Transport Commission. Violations of these regulations by US charter aircraft have been reported particularly in the Lakehead area and in the North. The Department of National Revenue would welcome support by the Canadian Armed Forces when they are stationed or operating at locations near the Alaskan border in providing surveillance of aircraft operations across the border in order to detect and report such violations and to identify the aircraft involved. The Department is concerned less with detection of aircraft in the air than with the observation of landing and departure on the ground and the identification of destination from one point in Canada to another.

Support Required from the Canadian Armed Forces: The Department of National Revenue (Customs and Excise Division) has expressed interest in the following support from the CAF:

(i) Limited surveillance of operations by US aircraft in the Canadian North near the Alaskan border.

III. OTHER AREAS OF SUPPORT

12. In the course of consultations with them, several departments have indicated interest in various kinds of support from the Canadian Armed Forces for activities not directly or clearly related to the maintenance of Canada's territorial integrity or national jurisdiction. Amongst the areas of interest, the following appear to be important:

a. Containment and Clean-up of Major Spills of Oil or Other Pollutants: The Departments of Indian Affairs and Northern Development and of Energy, Mines and Resources and the Ministry of Transport all attach major importance to the availability of the organizational and technical skills and of the communications and other equipment of the Canadian Forces to assist in the containment and clean-up of major pollution of waters from spills of oil or other pollutants.

b. Prevention and Fighting of Forest Fires: The Department of Indian Affairs and Northern Development has indicated considerable interest in support by the CAF in the summer season to carry out surveillance of forest areas in the Territories and in the national parks to detect forest fires and of support by the armed forces in the fighting of such fires when they occur.

c. Air Transport: The Departments of Indian Affairs and Northern Development and of Energy, Mines and Resources have displayed interest in the use of service aircraft and helicopters to transport technical inspectors to sites of oil and gas exploration in the North and offshore. The RCMP are interested in the use of service aircraft to transport personnel from one part of the country to another in an emergency and in helicopter support for police search operations. The Department of Indian Affairs and Northern Development has suggested possible heavy airlift by Hercules aircraft in case of disastrous occurrences such as blow-outs or fires where commercial facilities prove inadequate.

d. Search and Rescue: The Department of Energy, Mines and Resources suggested possible assistance in search and rescue operations related to offshore mineral resource operations.

4-3. Donald S. Macdonald, Minister of National Defence, to Hon. Mitchell Sharp, Secretary of State for External Affairs, 2 March 1971.[42]

In anticipation of the imminent proclamation of vital changes to the Canada Shipping Act, including extending the limits of Canadian territorial waters, it appears to me that we should consider now the operational measures which will be necessary to enforce this new legislation. Although, by statute, this will be the prime responsibility of other departments, the protection of Canadian sovereignty, should other departments require assistance, will fall on the Canadian forces.

The present situation in the Gulf of St. Lawrence indicates that there is a requirement for operational co-ordination of the measures needed to be taken by the Government and I believe it would be useful if this matter could, at least initially, now be looked at on an interdepartmental level. Perhaps an interdepartmental meeting could be held at which, hopefully, some agreed principles could be evolved which would further facilitate bilateral talks and the working out of standard operating procedures. This meeting should include representatives of the departments concerned, e.g., Fisheries and Forestry, MOT, [Energy, Mines and Resources], and Solicitor General.

It seems to me that having regard to your primary concern and responsibility for matters touching upon sovereignty and our relations with other states, someone in your department would probably be the most appropriate person to chair such a meeting as is referred to above.

I would appreciate receiving your comments. Should you concur with my proposal, please advise me who in your department will be the responsible official. I will arrange for representatives of my department to get in touch with him, so that study of this important and complex question can be commenced as soon as possible.

42 LAC, RG 25, vol. 10322, file 27-10-2-2 pt.2.

4-4. Interdepartmental Committee on the Law of the Sea, Report of the Meeting of the Working Group on the Enforcement of Fisheries, Anti-Pollution, and Territorial Seas Legislation, 6 April 1971.[43]

The meeting was chaired by Mr. E.G. Lee, Director, Legal Operations Division, Department of External Affairs. A list of the departmental representatives who attended the working group is attached.

Terms of Reference

The meeting took as its terms of reference a letter of March 2nd from the Minister of National Defence to the Secretary of State for External Affairs in which the Minister made the following comment:

"The present situation in the Gulf of St. Lawrence indicates that there is a requirement for operational co-operation of the measures needed to be taken by the Government and I believe it would be useful if this matter could, at least initially, now be looked at on an interdepartmental level. Perhaps an interdepartmental meeting could be held at which, hopefully, some agreed principles could be evolved which would facilitate further bilateral talks and the working out of standard operating procedures. This meeting should include representatives of the departments concerned, e.g. Fisheries and Forestry, MOT, EMR, and Solicitor General. It seems to me that having regard to your primary concern and responsibility for matters touching upon sovereignty and our relations with other states, someone in your department would probably be the most appropriate person to chair such a meeting as is referred to above."

The chairman drew the attention of the group to certain of the contents of the draft 1971 white paper on defence policy (pages 16-18 and pages 34-36- see attached) which was offered as further guidance for the working group in its examination of the enforcement of Canadian jurisdiction and sovereignty and the role of the Department of National Defence.

43 LAC, RG 25, vol. 10322, file 27-10-2-2 pt.2. Originally classified as "Confidential."

General Comments

As a basic working paper for the meeting, the chairman proposed a detailed examination of a paper prepared in the Department of National Defence based upon consultations with other government departments and agencies entitled "Role of Canadian Armed Forces in Relation to Sovereignty" (copy attached). It was pointed out that the draft white paper seemed to suggest that there were two distinct areas where DND might have surveillance and control function to perform. The first of these flowed from government legislation which defined the precise enforcement requirements and assigned them as appropriate to the civil ministry or agency, and a second which fell outside this area where regulatory needs had not been clearly defined. The working paper on the role of the Canadian Armed Forces was useful with respect to the first area but not the second. After some further discussion it was concluded that the working group should try to identify all of the specific surveillance and control activities DND might be required to perform, even those of an ad hoc nature, before attempting to speculate upon areas where there was no clearly defined requirement. It may be, upon further examination, that in carrying out normal military surveillance and surveillance activities in response to specific departmental or regulatory needs, DND could be regarded as discharging at the same time responsibility for overall surveillance, as described on page 17 of the draft white paper.

Fisheries Protection

The representative of the Department of Fisheries and Forestry approved the contents of the DND report.... He added that guidelines for the utilization of DND services for fishery protection purposes had been worked out at a meeting in Halifax on March 4 whereby it was suggested that Maritime Command should liaise closely with the Regional Director of Fisheries and would respond as required to requests for assistance. The question of regional co-ordination was discussed and it was observed that this was not always the most appropriate procedure since some of the activities involved might have broader domestic or foreign implications. With respect to fisheries protection it was necessary for DND to be fully informed about the areas where and period when surveillance was required and this should be approved at headquarters rather than at the regional level. It was further suggested that DND should simply report to headquarters of the appropriate department what they observed and should not be required to interpret these observations.

The following guidelines were agreed as the basis for the establishment of standard operating procedures:

(a) With respect to DND surveillance activities there should be regional co-ordination within agreed limitations.

(b) DND units should not interpret observations and the Department of Fisheries should decide the significance and status of a reported activity.

(c) With respect to control (i.e. enforcement and arrest) this should normally fall to Fisheries control vessels and the utilization of DND facilities for this purpose should be subject to approval of Department of Fisheries and Forestry headquarters in consultation with DND and External Affairs.

(d) Utilization of DND facilities for enforcement measures should only be requested as a last resort.

Ice Reconnaissance

...

The meeting was informed that there was no firm decision yet whether DND facilities would be required for this role or not. The matter was still under discussion between DND and MOT.

Pollution Control

...

(a) Southern Waters

The areas involved in this discussion was the territorial sea and fishing zones of Canada south of 60 [North] Latitude.

The MOT [Ministry of Transport] representative observed that DND was already performing a useful role in spotting and tracking discharges of oil and oily wastes within the prohibited zones as established under the terms of the 1954 (amended in 1962 and 1969 (the latter not yet in force)) International Convention for the Prevention of Pollution of the Sea by Oil. Consideration was being given to the extension of this kind of surveillance to the Great Lakes. On surveillance requirements there was already informal and continuing co-ordination between DND and MOT but it was possible a more formalized procedure might be adopted to develop broad guidelines on surveillance requirements with details being worked out at the regional level. On the east coast, for example, MOT facilities were better equipped to perform both the surveillance and control function while the same capability did not exist on the west coast.

With respect to enforcement under the provisions of the recent amendments to the Canada Shipping Act (not yet in force) the Minister will have the power to designate MOT and other government officials as pollution control officers. At present it is not envisaged that DND officers will be designated to this role, although this would be possible within terms of the legislation.

It was agreed that:

(a) The principal role of DND units with respect to anti-pollution measures would be the surveillance and detection of pollution by ships as part of their normal operational activities.
(b) The enforcement of anti-pollution regulations would rest primarily with the civil enforcement agencies.

Northern Waters

This part of the discussion related to the territorial sea and arctic pollution prevention zones north of the 60 N Latitude. Under the provisions of the Arctic Pollution Prevention Act it is provided that the arrest of vessels at sea might be required. This, therefore, would involve the possible utilization of DND facilities not only for surveillance but also for control purposes. Even though arrest is likely to be rare, legislation authority for permitting direct enforcement action of this kind by the Canadian armed forces should be determined in advance and should not await the occurrence of a particular incident.

It was agreed that:

(a) The employment of DND facilities for the purposes of enforcement particularly in contentious areas of the Canadian jurisdiction should be authorized and should be exercised within precise guidelines to be worked out by the departments concerned.

(b) In contentious areas the exercise of force not only by DND officers but also by other Canadian enforcement agencies should be exercised with care and restraint, and only after specific approval from relevant departmental headquarters after consultation with External Affairs.

Offshore Exploration and Exploitation Activities…

Subject to certain amendments to be conveyed to DND, EMR [the Department of Energy, Mines and Resources] agreed with the contents of the DND report on this subject and confirmed that the requirements in this case was surveillance in the normal course of operations and not control. It was noted that in this area the Fisheries and Forestry oceanographic fleet undertake seismic probing work as well as Fisheries Protection vessels which are active in observing seismic and other exploratory activities carried out in offshore areas. The oceanographic fleet would be available if required to undertake surveillance duties. It is understood that any reports DND might make to EMR of seismic activities which could cause damage to fish and conveyed by EMR to the Department of Fisheries and Forestry as a matter of routine procedure.

It was agreed that the DND role in this case was a useful one and the method of reporting and co-ordination was satisfactory.

Customs Control

Customs had not requested any DND assistance although it has indicated that some surveillance up to the limit of the 12-mile territorial sea might be helpful on occasion, in the course of performing other activities.

Summary of Agreed Basic Guidelines

(a) The requirement of departments for DND surveillance support should be coordinated to enable, where feasible, multi-purpose reconnaissance activities.
(b) DND should not be required to interpret its observations which should be the task of the responsible ministry.
(c) Enforcement of Canadian legislation should normally rest with the department primarily responsible under the application legislation.
(d) Any direct DND involvement in enforcement measures should be decided at headquarters level in consultation with the responsible department and External Affairs, and should be regarded as an exceptional measure.
(e) If direct DND enforcement support should be required, precise regulatory authority for such action should be established in advance.
(f) Enforcement by DND units in contentious areas should be conducted with care and restraint.
(g) In further bilateral discussions between DND and civil agencies an attempt should be made to relate needs for surveillance for civil operational and regulatory purposes to military capabilities and activities in a manner which would constitute a cost-effective use of overall government resources. (For this purpose a distinction should be made between support activities which would involve DND in the specific allocation of resources and those which could be carried out by DND units during the normal course of other activities.)

Future Role of the Working Group

It was concluded that DND should continue bilateral consultations with various departments on the basis of the discussions of the working group with a view to preparing standard operating procedures for the use of DND in the exercise of their enforcement support function. These would be reviewed by the interdepartmental working group to assess their broader domestic and international implications, if any.

4-5. House of Commons Debates, 21 May 1971

Mr. Judd Buchanan (Parliamentary Secretary to Minister of Indian Affairs and Northern Development): Mr. Speaker, the motion makes reference to the "role of our armed forces at home – with particular reference to our north." I would like to discuss some of the ways in which the Department of Indian Affairs and Northern Development and the Department of National Defence are working together in our north.

As hon. members know, the Department of National Defence has had a presence in the north for some time, and its experience has been put to use in a number of ways. The special problems of communications in the north are being researched at a $325,000 operations building located four miles north of Inuvik. I think some of us in the south are very prone to take for granted the communications systems which we have readily available to us, but one has only to spend a limited amount of time in some of the more remote settlements of the north to realize how fundamental and essential proper communications are to their existence.

Other more mundane but vital developments have taken place in clothing and equipment for the Arctic. The Department of Indian Affairs and Northern Development and the Department of National Defence are co-operating to build airstrips in the north. The aim is to promote communication to the various outposts for year-round administration and health services. To allow the landing of Hercules aircraft, four airstrips are being extended at Chesterfield Inlet, Pond Inlet, Whale Cove and Cape Dorset. Two others are being constructed at Igoolik and Pangnirtung. The construction of these airstrips over the next five years will utilize as much local civilian labour as possible.

This summer, work will begin on a 360-foot steel and concrete bridge across the Ogilvie river in the Yukon Territory. This bridge is being built for the Department of Indian Affairs and Northern Development by the Department of National Defence. In addition to hiring Natives on construction sites, the Department of National Defence has been actively recruiting northern people for the armed forces. CFB [Canadian Forces Base] Borden has offered an aerospace and engineering course. This training program is sponsored by the Department of Indian Affairs and

Inuit children from Rankin Inlet are given a tour of HMCS Protecteur, August 1970. (LAC)

Northern Development. It is designed to meet the demand for civilian pilots in Canada's north and to involve native peoples in the development of the north. The Department of National Defence has special programs for the native youth. Many young men have participated in many youth programs such as the Young Voyageurs, Sea Scouts and cadets. The feeling is that the broadening of their horizons through such activity will be a vital factor in helping the native youth to adapt to changes in their environment.

The Department of National Defence has a special role in Arctic search and rescue operations. As members are well aware, Canadian forces planes are often called upon to aid in rescue operations and to transport emergency hospital supplies. Plans are being laid for the Department of National Defence to provide emergency airlift operations for disasters in our north such as the one which occurred recently when their was a gas blow-out on King Christian Island.

Arctic research is a vital area for cooperation in the north. Consideration is being given to having the Department of National Defence help in the aerial surveillance of mineral surveys, seismic activity and on underwater equipment, particularly during installation. Transportation is often provided for departmental personnel by DND. The Department of National Defence is providing vocational training for the native peoples of the north is doing a great deal to involve them directly in its development.

I know that my colleague the hon. member for the Northwest Territories (Mr. [R.J.] Orange) has some observations to make in this area, and other hon. members opposite. I shall close now, having listed the areas where there is a substantial amount of cooperation between the Department of National Defence and the Department of Indian Affairs and Northern Development.

…

Mr. R.J. Orange (Northwest Territories): Mr. Speaker I will leave to the experts of the defence committee the question whether we should be moving our armed forces into or out of Europe. I intend to direct my remarks today to what I believe to be the role of the armed forces in the Canadian north.

Historically, the first appearance of the Canadian armed forces in the Canadian north was back in the Klondyke days, the days of the Yukon gold rush. In 1898, a regular force officer, Colonel Evans, led the Yukon field force into the Yukon to work with the Northwest Mounted Police to maintain order and discipline in that unruly era. The field force remained in the Yukon for many years before moving on.

During the course of the years the communications system in the Yukon and the Mackenzie was manned by the northwest signal corps. When it became apparent that the private sector was able to take over communications in the territories, the signal corps left. After the Second World War, the United States army moved out of the Yukon, the responsibility for maintaining the Alaska Highway, the northwest highway system, was left to the military.

With the growth of civilian services in the region in the area this arrangement, too passed from the scene and for a number of years the presence of the military in the Canadian north was limited to a number of installations, primarily communications stations at Frobisher Bay, Alert and Inuvik. Last year, however, on May 15, the then Minister of National Defence announced the establishment of a northern region command. When Mr. Cadieux made his announcement he indicated that one of the purposes of establishing a northern headquarters was to strengthen Canada's military presence north of the sixtieth parallel. A small aircraft-servicing detachment was established at Frobisher and increased air surveillance coverage was provided.

Together with some of my hon. friends in the House I had the opportunity of joining the committee on national defence and the minister last week in Yellowknife to celebrate Northern Command's first year and to dedicate Colonel Evans' headquarters' building in Yellowknife. In the past year we have seen the development of a reasonably effective plan for the presence of the armed forces north of the sixtieth parallel. Reasonably enough, the size of the permanent force at this stage is limited. They are responsible for logistic and technical support for all commands as they go north of the sixtieth parallel. These commands, whether their forces are seaborne or ground forces, have a responsibility to work with the northern region command so as to carry out an effective exercise in any part of the territories.

In the past year a considerable number of exercises have taken place in various parts of the north to determine the ability of our forces to move and survive in various parts of the Arctic in both summer and winter conditions, to develop new techniques of search and rescue and so on. So we have seen a start on the infrastructure. I think I can say that northern people welcome this initiative, not only in terms of the national scene but because they are delighted to have a military presence back again north of the sixtieth parallel.

Other hon. members, especially the Parliamentary Secretary to the Minister of Indian Affairs and Northern Development (Mr. Buchanan) have indicated there were many areas in which military presence could play an effective role in helping develop the Canadian north. My hon. friend made reference to a joint program of building airstrips in cooperation with the Department of Indian Affairs and Northern Development. A program for building these airstrips has been set out for seven or eight years based on the availability of funds to be provided by one department, the Department of Northern Affairs. However, because of the military involvement this program can now be completed much earlier and many northern communities will be served by adequate airstrips much sooner than would have been the case under the old arrangements.

The engineering corps has undertaken the responsibility of building a bridge across the Ogilvie River. This is a bridge which would have been completed eventually by the civil authority, but because the military were able to undertake this task, funds were released enabling the highway approaches to be completed, incidentally opening access to the Arctic Ocean from the Yukon territory. There are many other areas in which military forces could make a positive contribution.

The minister referred to his visit to Fort Smith last Sunday when the mayor of that community, Mr. Paul Kaeser, directed his attention to the proposal to use young people in the north who are undergoing vocational training, in cooperation with the technical abilities of the armed forces, to complete a stretch of road which is so low on the list of priorities for northern development that I doubt it will be completed in the seventies.

However, a program is now being worked out between the various government departments to use the skills of young northerners, under supervision of experts in the armed forces, to complete one other step in the process of northern development and thus fulfill the dream and the hope of many of the people in that area. When we had the opportunity of introducing the minister last Sunday, and following the mayor's eloquent plea for the building of this road, I could not help but think that if the Minister of National Defence (Mr. Macdonald) were able to pull it off, this highway should be named after him.

We must also look at the relationship between the military and the civilian community of the north. I have already indicated that this particular road is low in the order of priorities and probably would not be completed during this decade. However, I think that the military have the responsibility for ensuring that their activities, be they in the field of engineering, search and rescue or something else, do not conflict with the interests of civilian operators and people engaged in private enterprise. I believe the military are conscious of that and are making a serious attempt to ensure that there is no such conflict. However, we cannot repeat too often that we must keep close surveillance of and observation of the relationships between the military and the civilian community.

In the field of search and rescue, Northern Command will be setting up a small aircraft fleet in Yellowknife. From time to time there will be pressure to provide services that are normally provided by the civilian operators, and I believe we should insist there be no conflict here. There will be cases as happened last week, when a civilian operator is unable to provide the service. Since the military had available the equipment to meet a very serious situation facing one mining community, the mining community, the management, the military and civilian operators were able to work out a mutual agreement satisfactory to all and at the same time meet an emergency situation.

With regard to airstrips, by and large there are no communities in the north with civilian operators who can provide equipment to build airstrips. However, in one particular community, Igoolik, it is proposed to go ahead with the development of an airstrip. At the same time, there is an Eskimo community with the necessary equipment to build the airstrip and I think all concerned have agreed it would be better to move its project to another community rather than to conflict with the interests of the Eskimos at Igoolik.

There are still many areas in the north with which the Department of National Defence can concern itself. Last week, during his stop in Yellowknife, the Minister of National Defence announced an exciting new program of recruitment to interest young northerners in a career in the armed forces. The minister indicated that an attempt will be made to recruit 100 men and women for training in the administrative, transportation, supply, food services and communications fields. He went on to say that on completion of their training these young people from the north will be qualified to serve any armed services unit; however, particular emphasis will be placed on locating them in the north.

The minister indicated that opportunities were manifold for northerners, but possibly most important of all was that increased activity of armed forces personnel in the north and by arrangement with northern headquarters a requirement has been developed in the north for people with special knowledge of local working and living conditions and the terrain in the north, to kick off this program. Recruiting teams from various parts of southern Canada are planning to visit the major communities of Yellowknife, Inuvik, Whitehorse, Frobisher Bay, Fort Smith, Hay River and Churchill within the next month to meet and talk with young people coming out of the high schools.

Under this program, initially these young people will go off to Cornwallis in Nova Scotia to follow whatever trade they choose. They will be trained in groups and ultimately will move back to the north if they so wish. I believe this is an exciting program that will accomplish a lot of things and will provide an opportunity to develop expertise in the north within the armed forces. It also gives young people of the north a chance to have a career in the armed forces. Following their training and service, many of them leave the armed forces and use their skills I some other capacity in the north.

There are also other areas in which the armed forces can participate. For example, over the years the Ranger Corps has been a very successful operation. It was developed at the end of World War II and had been kept together primarily by a number of very dedicated officers of the armed forces. However, with Northern Command it seems to me the Ranger Corps should be expanded so as to use the talents and knowledge of northerners for surveillance purposes and to assist the military.

Another area that I hope the minister will take a look at is the use in years to come of young Canadians from the south as part of the armed forces team working during the summer months in the Canadian north carrying out a number of projects. For example, following the end of World War II the United States abandoned all of its equipment along the Canol Pipeline. This has been a disaster in terms of the amount of debris that is scattered along the line. I do not think that at this stage the civilian authority is in a position to divert funds to employ people to clean the area, but this might well provide an opportunity for a number of young Canadians to work on such a project over a period of time. It would enable them to see something of the north while providing a very useful service.

Development of canoe routes and preservation of historical sites are two more endeavours for our young people, under the direction and supervision of the military forces, which would enable them to perform a very useful and functional role in the north in years to come. I suggest that the talents of our young people could also be used in the building of emergency airstrips along, for example, the Mackenzie River Valley....

I have indicated that we welcome the armed forces presence in the north. In certain areas there can be conflict with civil services in terms of engineering projects or aircraft services in relation to search and rescue work. I believe the Canadian north will be a much richer place because of the presence of members of the Canadian forces and their families. I am personally happy to have had the opportunity of participating in this debate, and I wish the armed forces great success north of the sixtieth parallel.

5 The White Paper on Defence

5-1. DEXAF, Michael Shenstone, OMD (North American Defence & NATO Division) to FLE (Legal Division), 28 January 1971.[44]

Attached is a copy of a draft White Paper on Defence Policy which has just been made available to us by DND for comment on an unofficial and informal basis. The draft originated in the office of the Minister of National Defence, Mr. Donald Macdonald, and is now being studied in various branches of the defence staff. We have been asked to let DND have our preliminary departmental views on this draft by Friday, February 5. The Department will have further opportunities to comment on the White Paper at a later stage before publication but you will understand the importance of bringing our views to bear in a timely fashion at a stage when there may be a maximum flexibility in the drafting process. DND have particularly stressed the importance they attach to our comments on legal aspects, and we understand that the Under-Secretary has spoken to you in this regard.

2. As you will see there are a number of areas in the draft of direct interest to your Division. One of the major themes in the paper is a re-orientation of Canadian defence priorities towards a greater emphasis on the role of the forces in protection of sovereignty, as envisaged in the P.M.'s statement on defence policy of April 3, 1969.

3. Some of the questions raised by this paper in relation to Canadian sovereignty appear to be of a political rather than a legal nature. The paper acknowledges, for example, that the postulated objective of "an effective surveillance and intercept capability for all Canadian territory...

44 LAC, RG 25, vol. 10322, file 27-10-2-2 pt.2. Originally classified as "Confidential."

is as much or perhaps even more a political as a military imperative of our being a sovereign state".... Nevertheless, it is clear from the presentation that Canadian needs in terms of protecting our legal title to sovereign jurisdiction and in terms of protecting our legal title to sovereign jurisdiction and in relation to law enforcement are considered by the drafters as important ingredients in this "political imperative." In this light it would seem to us to call for careful consideration from a legal viewpoint.

4. There will be other issues or points of drafting on which you may wish to comment but we thought it would be useful in the first instance to set out below some of the questions which strike us as having important legal implication.

(1) Law Enforcement and Legal Validity of Jurisdictional Claims

It seems to us that at several points the draft paper tends to confuse the problem of law enforcement with the problem of strengthening the legal basis for jurisdictional claims. This was a problem which you noted earlier in relation to other DND papers examining the role of forces in relation to sovereignty (e.g. ... it is stated that "effective occupation and control clearly requires more comprehensive surveillance and identification.") Similarly ... there is a reference to "effective occupation" and the indirect implication that Canada does not exercise such "effective occupation" in the great expanses of the North outside "more settled areas." We would welcome your view as to whether, in an important state document of this kind, a clearer distinction should not be made between "effective occupation" (which, as we understand it, is no problem from a legal viewpoint, even in the North) and law enforcement or administrative needs (where there are clearly going to be increasing demands on overall government resources). An emphasis in this paper on "occupation" and on surveillance for the sake of surveillance, and for the sake of "demonstrating a presence" ... may give a misleading impression that is concerned to shore up a weak legal claim to sovereign jurisdiction in the North. As the P.M. has said on several occasions in the House, Canadian sovereign title to the northlands and the islands is unassailable and undisputed. Minor redrafting of the few passages involved may suffice to avoid any implication to the contrary.

(2) DND Responsibility for Law Enforcement

As it now stands, the paper seems to envisage assigning "concurrent authority and responsibility" to DND (together with civil agencies) for law enforcement in respect of Canada's 12-mile territorial limits, fishery zones and pollution control zones.... Canadian forces are also to be assigned law-enforcement responsibility in relation to exploitation of the seabed.... It is not spelled out in the paper whether this would involve amending present legislation. The relationship between the forces and the civil agencies primarily responsible for regulatory and law-enforcement duties in these areas is described at various places in the paper.... The role of the forces in this regard is however left somewhat vague, and we have in mind suggesting to DND that the paper might be strengthened by giving concrete examples of areas where there are or could be problems of surveillance and law enforcement beyond the capabilities of the responsible civil agencies. We would appreciate your views on what the implications might be in this regard in relation to the Territorial Sea and Fishery Zones Act and the Arctic Waters Pollution Prevention Act.... You may also wish to comment from the viewpoint of ongoing negotiations with the USA concerning a possible international convention on Arctic waters.

5. We are currently preparing comments on other aspects of the draft, from a foreign policy viewpoint, and hope to submit a collation of Departmental views to the [Under Secretary of State for External Affairs] on Wednesday, February 3. For this purpose could we have your comments by Tuesday, February 2.

5-2. DEXAF, L.H.J. Legault (FLO) to J.A. Beesley (FLP), re: Draft White Paper on Defence Policy – Sovereignty Aspects, 2 February 1971.[45]

The protection of Canadian sovereignty has been fixed as the priority objective of Canadian defence policy and is one of the major themes of the draft White Paper on Defence Policy. A proper understanding of the concept of sovereignty is thus essential to the examination of the issues raised in the White Paper.

2. While the White Paper nowhere attempts a definition of sovereignty, it appears to view the protection of sovereignty, if not the concept itself, in terms which are simultaneously restrictive and sweeping: restrictive in that the White Paper seems to suggest that the protection of sovereignty does not include defence against armed attack by foreign forces; sweeping, in that it also seems to suggest that sovereignty is challenged on every hand in other ways than armed attack, and that it is to these challenges that the protection of sovereignty must be directed. Thus, on the one hand, the White Paper does not categorize Canada's cooperative arrangements with the USA for the defence of North America as constituting protection of sovereignty; instead this cooperation is described as "an act of sovereignty" which does not "detract from sovereignty." Thus also, on the other hand, the White Paper posits a requirement for the provision of "security" in relation to undefined "political concerns;" it refers ambiguously to "effective control;" it suggests that something is lacking in Canada's "effective occupation" of its territory; and it prescribes "more comprehensive surveillance" as the universal panacea. All in all, the White Paper's discussion of the protection of sovereignty and the role of the armed forces therein is confused and deficient. The importance of having it clarified from the legal and other points of view cannot be too strongly emphasized.

Threats to Sovereignty

3. Perhaps the simplest method of achieving a proper understanding of sovereignty, and hence of the DND role in its protection, is to

45 LAC, RG 25, vol. 10322, file 27-10-2-2 pt.2. Originally classified as "Confidential."

examine the possible threats to which it may open. The first, most obvious and most dramatic of these is, of course, the direct military threat or threat of armed attack. Associated with that threat are such activities as intelligence gathering by military and para-military surface vessels, submarines or aircraft of a potential enemy, which may or may not involve an actual territorial violation by way of an intrusion into the internal waters, territorial sea or air space of Canada. (The likelihood of such intrusions into land territory in any operation short of full-scale armed attack has been discounted by the defence authorities.) The second area of concern is the non-military threat, which is not less clear although its effect may be less obvious for being less dramatic and immediate. That threat can assume a number of forms but consists essentially of infringements of certain Canadian legislation by foreign agencies or nationals in circumstances where such infringements involve a direct or indirect challenge to Canadian jurisdiction or sovereignty. It is difficult to conceive of infringements of legislation on land territory which might, in the normal course, involve such a challenge. For all practical purposes, it is infringements of Canadian legislation in maritime areas (and perhaps to a lesser extent in sovereign air space) which are relevant in the context of the White Paper. The maritime areas in question are Canada's internal waters and territorial sea (over which Canada exercises full sovereignty), Canada's fishing zones and pollution control zones (over which Canada exercises jurisdiction only, but without prejudice to possible claims to sovereignty), as well as Canada's continental shelf (over which Canada enjoys "sovereign rights" in respect of the exploration and exploitation of mineral resources and sedentary species of fish). The Canadian legislation applicable to these areas includes the Territorial Sea and Fishing Zones Act, the Coastal Fisheries Protection Act, the Arctic Waters Pollution Act, the anti-pollution provisions of the Canada Shipping Act, and a variety of laws regulating offshore mineral exploration and exploitation.

Implication of Direct Military Threat

4. With respect to the direct military threat or threat of armed attack, there would appear to be little need for discussion of what sovereignty means and how it can be affected if a threat of this kind were in fact to

be carried out. I would suggest, however, that it would be appropriate for DND to review the White Paper's treatment of defence against armed attack in the light of a less restrictive view of what constitutes the protection of sovereignty. In this connection, the White Paper rightly points out that Canada's collective security arrangements do not detract from Canadian sovereignty, but clearly the raison d'être of these arrangements must be something more than that – i.e., the protection of sovereignty. At the same time, of course, very difficult questions arise as to how far any country can go in relying on alliances for its defence. At what point, if any, does the protection of sovereignty in this way become transformed into the surrender of sovereignty? Or, in more extreme terms, if your friend is your sole defence, then who defends you from your friend? I do not suggest that the White Paper should explore these essentially hypothetical questions but I do consider that they are of some indirect political relevance in the discussion of "effective occupation" in the Arctic (which I examine later in this memorandum).

Implication of Non-Military Threat

5. With respect to the enforcement of Canadian legislation in the areas and circumstances described in paragraph 3 above, the importance of this factor in the maintenance of Canadian jurisdiction and sovereignty is not self-evident as in the case of defence against armed attack. Law enforcement is, of course, an objective in its own right, but the implications of enforcing legislation go beyond that. Even where there is no doubt or dispute, in terms of international law, as to the validity of a claim to maritime jurisdiction or sovereignty, a demonstrated and persistent incapacity to enforce legislation represents a serious diminution of the exercise of jurisdiction or sovereignty, even if it does not destroy the legal validity of the claim. In cases where a claim to maritime jurisdiction or sovereignty is in fact disputed or in doubt in terms of international law, the effect of enforcement or non-enforcement of legislation is much wider ranging. It is true, of course, that there is a distinction between law enforcement and a claim to jurisdiction or sovereignty. The legal validity of a claim is not necessarily destroyed if it is not necessarily established because it is effectively enforced. Nevertheless, effective enforcement is a very important factor in the weakening or destruction of such claims.

Inuit from Pond Inlet line up for a picture in front of a Hercules resupplying the town, April 1974. (LAC)

6. On the basis of the considerations outlined above, I would agree with DND's general assessment that there is an important requirement for the protection of sovereignty and jurisdiction against non-military threats, and that the Canadian armed forces could have an important role to play in assisting civil agencies in this respect. The White Paper is, however, seriously deficient in its treatment of this subject. It does not clearly define the nature of the threat, the specific forms its can take, the areas involved, and the role to be played by the armed forces. Instead it indulges in vague generalities and catch-words where it should be precise and concrete, and it sometimes seems to view "surveillance" as a sort of mystic rite rather than a functional requirement to meet well defined needs. I consider that the White Paper could be very substantially improved if it were to take into account, and to be revised in the light of, the recent DND report on consultations with other Government departments and agencies "charged with statutory responsibilities for surveillance and control of Canadian territory and the exercise of

Canadian jurisdiction in relation to the activity of foreigners and foreign interests." That report defined much more precisely and realistically the role which the Canadian armed forces can play in assisting civil agencies in the enforcement of Canadian legislation, particularly with respect to surveillance activities.

Effective Occupation in the Arctic

7. Another major source of difficulty and confusion in the White Paper is the question of effective occupation of Canada's Arctic mainland and islands. The essential consideration to be borne in mind here – and which is not brought out in the White Paper – is that Canada has complete and unchallenged sovereignty over its Arctic lands. The legal basis for that sovereignty is effective occupation, and there can be no reasonable doubt that Canada's occupation of this region is indeed fully effective. (One leading international authority, Gustav Smedal, cites Canada's handling of its Arctic land territories as a good precedent of how to take effective possession of polar regions.) Accordingly, I cannot agree with the White Paper's suggestion that Canada's occupation of the Arctic may not be sufficiently effective and that something more is needed to perfect Canada's title, such as "more comprehensive surveillance." Indeed that suggestion is prejudicial to the very objective of protecting sovereignty, for if Canada persistently calls into doubt its sovereignty in the Arctic then others too may begin to entertain such doubts.

8. All of this is not to say that there is not a requirement for greater administrative machinery in Canada's Arctic lands, or that there is not a requirement for more comprehensive surveillance, or that DND has not greater role to play in these matters than that which it fills at present. These possible requirements and this possible role, however, should not be assessed on the basis of some imagined need to satisfy legal formalities. Functional needs should be the touchstone, while bearing in mind the political sensitivity of the very phrase "Arctic sovereignty."

9. An issue of special political sensitivity with respect to the Arctic is the joint Canada-USA military effort in this area in the context of North American defence arrangements, particularly where the USA has

assumed the major financial burden and responsibility. Questions have been raised from time to time as to whether such arrangements, even with all possible safeguards and the best of intentions on both sides, could ultimately lead to a situation in which effective authority in the Canadian Arctic, in fact if not in law, would be in the hands of the United States. Concern about this aspect of joint defence arrangements does not, however, detract from the fact that Canada's title to its Arctic lands is unassailable in law and not affected in any legal sense by the joint arrangements with the USA.

10. The attitude of the USA in questions relating to the Canadian Arctic is, of course, of major importance with respect to the political sensitivity of Arctic sovereignty and joint defence arrangements. The well-publicized opposition of the USA to Canada's claims to sovereignty or jurisdiction in Arctic waters beyond the once traditional three-mile limit have, unfortunately, complicated matters by giving rise to a certain popular impression that the USA was challenging Canada's sovereignty over its Arctic lands as well. More disturbing, perhaps, is the choice of language in an Aide-Memoire presented to the Department of External Affairs by the US Embassy on April 5, 1969 (which was not made public). In that document the Embassy stated, with reference to "recent public discussions regarding the islands of the archipelago north of the Canadian mainland" that the US Government "asserts no claim of sovereignty to these islands." The Aide-Memoire did not suggest, even indirectly, that the USA <u>recognizes</u> Canada's sovereignty over the Arctic islands. In replying to that Aide-Memoire, the Canadian Government stated that although it was "grateful for confirmation of the position of the US Government on this matter, Canada's sovereignty over its Arctic regions, including the islands of the Arctic archipelago, is long since well established and beyond dispute in fact and law."

11. [Still classified.]

12. In light of the foregoing considerations it would seem appropriate to conclude that while Canada's legal title to its Arctic lands does not require buttressing, it would nevertheless be desirable to ensure that

whatever "presence" is required in the Arctic for practical, functional, purposes should, to the greatest possible extent, be a Canadian presence.

General Conclusions

13. The White Paper, in my view, needs radical revision. It should above all avoid giving the impression that Canada's sovereignty is legally insecure. I have attached a supplementary memo commenting on specific sections of the White Paper and making suggestions as to how they may be revised. Those suggestions, however, should only be considered as guidelines since the White Paper requires a more fundamental revision than simple "patching up" here and there it is to be given the desired precision and clarity.

5-3. DEXAF, J.A. Beesley, Director General, Legal and Consular Affairs, to Director General, Office of Politico-Military Affairs, 5 February 1971.[46]

Attached is the commentary on the draft White Paper on Defence Policy incorporating the comments and the drafting changes which Mr. Legault and I suggested during our meeting in your office on February 3 with you and Messrs. Shenstone, Walker, Wang and Gordon Smith. This paper had been prepared with a view of turning it over directly to Gordon Smith if you approve of the drafting changes suggested.

2. I am also attaching an analysis prepared by Mr. Legault of the legal aspects of the concept of sovereignty insofar as it relates to the issues raised by the paper. This second paper should not, of course, be passed to DND.

3. I should like to confirm our understanding that it was agreed during the discussion in your office that a basic conceptual change should be

Legal advisor Alan Beesley of the Department of External Affairs later played a key role in the complex negotiations that led to the United Nations Convention on the Law of the Sea in 1982. (UN Photo/Yutaka Nagata)

46 LAC, RG 25, vol. 10322, file 27-10-2-2 pt.2. Originally classified as "Confidential."

made in the treatment of the sovereignty question in the White Paper. In brief the paper seems to treat protection of Canadian sovereignty and national defence as two mutually exclusive concepts and implies that the first of these objectives can be achieved by means of surveillance as an end in itself. It is our view that the priority objective of national defence comprises the essence of the protection of sovereignty and that while certain activities would be directed towards the one objective rather than towards the other, many activities could and should be directed towards the attainment of both objectives, which overlap to a considerable extent. The specific drafting changes contained in the attached paper are intended to reflect an essentially functional approach to the problem specifying which activities should serve which ends.

4. I consider that I should also record my view, which is shared by Mr. Legault, that even with the inclusion of the drafting changes suggested, the White Paper will still need some considerable reworking in order to adequately reflect the conceptual approach suggested above. We understand that we will be given an opportunity to see a further redraft of the paper.

5-4. DEXAF, Draft Paper on Defence Policy: Comments on draft dated January 18, 1971, 11 February 1971.[47]

General

In general, we consider that the draft provides a statement of defence policy which accords well with the broad lines of Canadian national aims and interests as indicated in Foreign Policy for Canadians. It develops the themes of the Prime Minister's statement of April 3, 1969, placing them in their broad foreign policy context. It reaffirms continued Canadian cooperation with our allies in North American defence and NATO in ways consonant with Canada's views on the changing world strategic situation. And as a contribution to Canada's bilateral relations with the USA, it incorporates decisions to approve several long-standing U.S. proposals which have been held in advance pending the defence review, namely U.S. interceptor dispersal (in time of crisis only) … and SAC refueling and emergency overflight privileges.

2. Its principle shortcoming is that, although the protection of Canadian sovereignty has been established as the priority objective of defence policy, the paper does not explain clearly what is meant by this term. It appears to treat the protection of Canadian sovereignty and national defence as two mutually exclusive concepts; this in turn leads to conceptual difficulties in the discussion of the role of surveillance in protecting Canadian sovereignty. A critique of this aspect of the paper is set out below (paras. 7-12) along with specific drafting suggestions at Annex A.…

Sovereignty

7. While the White Paper nowhere attempts a definition of sovereignty, it appears to view the protection of sovereignty, if not the concept itself, in terms which are simultaneously restrictive and sweeping: restrictive, in that the White Paper seems to suggest that the protection of sovereignty does not include defence against armed attack by foreign forces; sweeping, in that it also seems to suggest that

47 LAC, RG 25, vol. 10322, file 27-10-2-2 pt.2. Originally classified as "Confidential." Sovereignty excerpts only.

sovereignty is challenged on every hand in other ways than armed attack, and that it is to these challenges that the protection of sovereignty must be directed.

8. Perhaps the simplest method of achieving a proper understanding of sovereignty, and hence of the DND role in its protection, is to examine the possible threats to which it may be open. The first, most obvious and most dramatic of these is, of course, the direct military threat or threat of armed attack. Associated with that threat are such activities as intelligence gathering by military or para-military surface vessels, submarines or aircraft of a potential enemy, which may or may not involve an actual territorial violation by way of an intrusion into the internal waters, territorial sea or air space of Canada.

9. The second area of concern is the non-military threat, which is no less clear although its effects may be less obvious for being less dramatic and immediate. That threat can assume a number of forms but consists essentially of infringements involving a direct or indirect challenge to Canadian jurisdiction or sovereignty. It is difficult to conceive of infringements of legislation on land territory which might, in the normal course, involve such a challenge. For all practical purposes, it is infringements of Canadian legislation in maritime areas (and perhaps on a lesser extent in sovereign air space) which are relevant in the context of the White Paper. The maritime areas in question are Canada's internal waters and territorial sea (over which Canada exercises full sovereignty), Canada's fishing zones and pollution control zones (over which Canada exercises jurisdiction only, but without prejudice to possible claims to sovereignty) as well as Canada's continental shelf (over which Canada enjoys "sovereign rights" in respect of the exploration and exploitation of mineral resources and sedentary species of fish).

10. With respect to the direct military threat or threat of armed attack, there would appear to be little need for discussion of what sovereignty means and how it would be affected if a threat of this kind were in fact to be carried out. We would suggest, however, that it would be appropriate to review the White Paper's treatment of defence against

armed attack in the light of a less restrictive view of what constitutes the protection of sovereignty. In this connection, the White Paper rightly points out that Canada's collective security arrangements do not detract from Canadian sovereignty, but clearly the raison d'être of these arrangements must be something more than that, i.e., the protection of sovereignty.

11. In cases where the threat is non-military…, and even where there is no doubt or dispute as to the validity of a claim to maritime jurisdiction or sovereignty, a demonstrated and persistent incapacity to enforce legislation represents a serious diminution of the exercise of jurisdiction or sovereignty. Where a claim to maritime jurisdiction or sovereignty is disputed, the effect of enforcement or non-enforcement of legislation is much wider ranging. In essence we would support the proposition in the paper that there is an important requirement for the protection of sovereignty and jurisdiction against non-military threats and that the Canadian armed forces could have an important role to play in assisting civil agencies in this regard. In clarifying Canadian concerns in this area the emphasis should be on functional requirements in the protection of defined Canadian interests rather than quasi-symbolic activities such as "presence" or "surveillance" for their own sake. The approach adopted in the DND report on interdepartmental consultations should be the basis for a further definition and examination of the role of the forces in these areas relevant to the protection of Canadian sovereignty in cases of non-military threats.

12. References in the paper to the question of "effective occupation" of Canada's Arctic mainland and islands could be a source of misunderstanding and doubt inasmuch as Canada already has complete and unchallenged sovereignty over its Arctic lands and the legal basis for that sovereignty is effective occupation. (One leading international authority cites Canada's handling of its Arctic land territories as a good precedent for how to take effective possession of polar regions.) This does not rule out the possible need for greater administrative machinery in Canada's Arctic lands, a possible need for more comprehensive surveillance, or a greater role for the DND in these respects. However,

these requirements should not be assessed on the basis of some imagined need to satisfy legal formalities. Functional needs should be the touchstone. It is most important to avoid in this policy paper the impression that Canada's sovereignty is insecure.

Annex A
Commentary on Draft White Paper on Defence Policy Sovereignty Aspects

...

The section entitled "National Concerns" ... could explain more clearly how and why certain developments which have taken place in Canada are "of particular importance to defence policy." The reference to "effective occupation and control is difficult to relate to the proceeding discussion, especially since the concept of "effective occupation" can not apply to the sea or sea bed. The reference to that concept could, moreover, suggest that there is some doubt as to the validity of Canada's legal "title" to some part of its land territory which, of course, is not the case, in the Arctic as elsewhere. Similarly, the functional requirement for "more comprehensive surveillance and identification" is not made clear. Greater clarity would be achieved if this section could be revised ... as follows:

> "...The Government has moved to channel development in this area and to ensure that it is compatible with environmental preservation, for instance by adopting legislation to prevent pollution in the Arctic and Northern inland waters. Canada's coastal interests as a whole, in southern as well as Arctic regions, have assumed increasing importance, as reflected in the heightened pace of exploration for offshore mineral resources, the extension of Canada's territorial sea, and the establishment of fisheries protection and pollution control zones on the Atlantic and Pacific coasts.
>
> While the defence forces do not have exclusive responsibility in any of these fields, their role in support of the civil agencies needed to be examined. With respect

> to coastal interests in particular, more comprehensive surveillance is clearly required for the enforcement of legislation in the maintenance of Canadian sovereignty and jurisdiction."

…

The first sentence of the section entitled "Scope for Canadian Military Activity" appears to have become garbled and should presumably refer not to the "maintenance of Canada's political identity" but rather to the "maintenance of Canada's security as an independent political entity" (consistent with the first of the national aims …). …The entire section might be revised along the following lines:

> "The primary purpose of the Canadian armed forces, one which they share with other agencies of the government, is the maintenance of Canada's security as an independent political entity. In Canada's case this involves a definition of security more fundamental than one which would involve only the threat of direct military attack. The security which the armed forces provide must relate not just to military threats but also to infringements of Canadian sovereignty and jurisdiction which do not constitute a military threat as such. In other words, the armed forces have tasks, such as assisting in the enforcement of certain Canadian legislation, which go beyond those which would flow from a strict definition of what is required for the defence of Canada against overt military attack but are nevertheless related to the same basic objective of maintaining sovereignty and jurisdiction."

…

The section entitled "Territorial Integrity" should make clear that surveillance is a functional activity directed variously to the detection of military threats (e.g. submarine operations and intelligence activities by potentially hostile ships and aircraft), territorial violations not strictly military in nature (e.g. unauthorized over flights), and infringements of Canadian jurisdiction or legislation (e.g. unauthorized foreign fishing in Canada's fishing zone). Any suggestion that surveillance might be a quasi-symbolic activity required to meet certain legal formalities of sovereignty would be inaccurate and should be avoided. This section accordingly might be revised as follows:

> "By being able to maintain surveillance over Canadian territory, whether land, sea or air, the armed forces help safeguard sovereignty and independence against overt military threats as well as non military forms of territorial violations of infringements of Canadian jurisdiction or legislation. The requirement for surveillance will, of course, vary with the kind of threat, violation or infringement which it is anticipated may be detected or must be deterred. Should Canadian territory be violated, or should Canadian jurisdiction be challenged or Canadian legislation be infringed by other countries or their nationals, the armed forces are ready to respond with the appropriate means at the direction of the government. Thus the armed forces in conjunction with civil agencies provide the capability for exercising effective control over national territory and for the full exercise of Canadian jurisdiction. This includes but is not necessarily restricted to providing a direct defence against armed attack. For the purpose of deterring territorial violations or infringements of jurisdiction or legislation, it may be sufficient to ensure, first, that they will be detected and, secondly, that some measure of force short of warlike force can be brought to bear if they are continued.
>
> Canada's geographical position on the top half of the North American continent between the two superpowers results in certain imperatives for the Canadian armed forces which cannot be ignored. Safeguarding sovereignty and independence involves the maintenance of territorial integrity, the exercise of effective control over that territory, and the enforcement of jurisdiction

> and legislation; and the role of the armed forces in these tasks is in some respects complementary to that of the civil authorities. The proportionate requirement for the military, however, is higher in the remote regions until a more advanced stage of development is reached and the associated expansion of civil agencies and resources occurs. Similarly, a shortage of civil resources for the policing of coastal waters may require an expanded role for the armed forces in this respect."

...

The section entitled "The North" appears to use the terms "security control," "effective control" and "effective occupation" interchangeably. The latter term embodies a legal concept with respect to the acquisition and consolidation of "title" to territory. The manner in which it is used in this section tends to suggest that there is some doubt or something more to be done as regards Canada's sovereignty over its Arctic lands. Revision of this section along the following lines would be appropriate:

> "...In more settled areas effective control is largely ensured by various levels of civil administration – federal, provincial and municipal. In the great expanses of the North, which is in a sense the last frontier of Canada, the same control is maintained by special kinds of administration, including the activities of the Northern Administration, the Ministry of Transport, the Department of Indian Affairs and Northern Development, the Royal Canadian Mounted Police, and also, very importantly, the Department of National Defence...etc."

...

The second paragraph of the section entitled "Pollution Control" would be improved by being redrafted as follows:

> "Legislation provides for the exercise of pollution-control jurisdiction in an area extending generally 100 miles from the mainland and islands of the Canadian Arctic. The Government is required to take special stops to

> ensure that the legislation and that jurisdiction are fully respected."

...

The section entitled "Territorial Sea, Fishing Zones and the Seabed" would be improved by being amended as follows:

> "This Government has also taken decisions with respect to the limits of Canada's territorial sea and fishing zones. Legislation has extended Canada's territorial sea from three to twelve miles and, having incorporated the former nine-mile contiguous fishing zone within the extended territorial sea, has provided for the creation of new Canadian fishing zones in areas of the sea adjacent to the coast. An Order in Council has been promulgated establishing such fishing zones in Queen Charlotte Sound, Dixon Entrance and Hecate Strait in the west coast, and in the Gulf of St. Lawrence and the Bay of Fundy on the east coast – a total of 80,000 square miles. Pollution control jurisdiction is also to be exercised in these areas.
>
> Canada also has the exclusive sovereign right to explore and exploit the resources of the continental shelf adjacent to its coasts. This area extends to the "limits of exploitability," which Canada interprets as comprising the submerged continental margin extending as far as 350 miles off Newfoundland and 130 miles off Nova Scotia. The Canadian forces do not have sole responsibility for ensuring respect for Canadian jurisdiction and legislation in the territorial sea and fishing zones and on the continental shelf, but their contribution in the way of ensuring effective control can be an important one.
>
> ...The role of the armed forces in enforcing pollution control legislation in the North and in the Canadian fishing zones will be their major contribution to the preservation of an unspoiled environment."

...

The section entitled "Surveillance of Canadian Territory and Coastlines" (like the section entitled "Territorial Integrity" …) could give a clearer treatment of the role of surveillance in the protection of Canada and Canadian interests. The kinds of "challenges" which might arise are not defined (perhaps deliberately); nor is it brought out here that surveillance is a civil as well as military function. The distinction between surveillance and "monitoring" (if any) is not established; the reference to the resources of the sea and seabed is not clearly related to surveillance activities; the use of the term "foreshore" (that part of the shore between the level of high tide and low tide) is puzzling and seemingly irrelevant; and the reference to violations of "Canadian waters" not strictly accurate. This section could be improved by amending the relevant portions as follows:

> "…In addition, if Canadian jurisdiction over the Arctic waters as established by Parliament for purposes of pollution control is to be observed, there must be a capability for conducting surveillance of these waters and detecting infringements of the relevant legislation. The same considerations apply to Canadian jurisdiction in the fishing zones which have been established on the east and west coasts and in which it is also proposes to exercise Canadian pollution-control jurisdiction. Unless it is known that Canada has such a surveillance capability, it could be difficult to ensure respect for Canadian jurisdiction and Canadian legislation in these areas. Violations of Canada's former contiguous fishing zones have occurred in the past and offenders have been prosecuted but the area involved is now much larger and the problem of surveillance correspondingly greater with the establishment of the new fishing zones."
>
> Exploitation of the resources of the continental shelf will become increasingly important in the years to come. Surveillance will also be required in this area to ensure the detection and deterrence of unauthorized exploration and other activities which might be incompatible with

Canada's exclusive sovereign rights over offshore mineral resources."

...

The section entitled "Relationship to Civil Authorities" could give more detail and precision to the respective roles of the armed forces and the civil agencies with respect to surveillance and enforcement of jurisdiction and legislation. (The DND "Report on Consultation with other Government Departments and Agencies" [*doc. 4-2*] provides useful background information for this purpose.) Apart from this consideration, the section would be improved if amended as follows:

> "The Canadian forces will support the civilian departments and agencies of Government in their discharge of responsibilities for carrying out surveillance and for exercising effective control over Canadian land territory and Canada's internal waters and territorial sea and air space, as well as those marine areas in which Canada asserts jurisdiction for purposes of fisheries protection, pollution control, and exploration and exploitation of the resources of the continental shelf, within the limits established by Canadian legislation. The forces will carry out surveillance and provide means to exercise effective control in those areas in which the capabilities provided by the civil departments and agencies of government in the discharge of their normal responsibilities are inadequate to provide full protection of Canadian interests.
>
> Beyond surveillance and the detection of territorial violations or infringements of jurisdiction or legislation, a capability for enforcement is required. While other Government departments share in the responsibility for these tasks, and in some cases have primary responsibility, a major role belongs to the Canadian forces."

...

This section entitled "The Nature of the Problem" seems to be restricted to maritime areas, and we wonder if this was intentional. We wonder too whether the nature of the problem is really "unclear" and whether any such lack of clarity may not arise from some uncertainty as to the functional objectives of surveillance. This section would be improved by being amended as follows:

> "This is a complicated problem. The area to be covered is vast, and in certain maritime and other areas of particular interest adequate facilities are lacking and weather conditions are generally adverse. Indeed Canada has the longest coastline of any country in the world. The problem would in a sense be simpler if it were restricted to clear threat of attack from a known enemy, the more traditional military problem. Instead the problem is a wider one and involves less direct challenges or pressures. Potential intruders or offenders might be civil as well as military, or private entities as well as foreign government agencies, such as, for instance, a fishing vessel, an oil tanker or a private aircraft instead of a bomber or a submarine. But the principle involved – discussion – is a well-known one. By establishing the known capability to conduct surveillance and thereby detect infringements of jurisdiction or legislation, or violations of territory, it is possible to discourage such actions."

...

The section entitled "The Government's Objective" does not clearly distinguish between the need for surveillance and "intercept" capability as against a direct military threat and against a less direct challenge to sovereignty or jurisdiction, or against infringements of legislation. The statement that the Government's objective is "as much or perhaps even more a political as a military imperative of our being a sovereign state" is ambiguous and tends to suggest that surveillance is required for its own sake rather than for functional purposes (which, in legal terms at least, is not the case). The section should be revised along the following lines:

> "The objective of the Government is to have an effective surveillance and enforcement capability for all Canadian territory as well as certain maritime areas where Canada exercises jurisdiction rather than full sovereignty. This is

> not a purely military imperative but is directed as well at the protection of the broadest range of Canadian interests which might be prejudiced in non-military ways. Such a surveillance and enforcement capability would permit the full exercise of sovereignty and jurisdiction through the enforcement of legislation, while at the same time protecting sovereignty against armed attack by contributing to North American defence in providing early warning and enhancing the possibility for a forward defence. Naturally it will have to defend etc...."

...

It is not clear whether the last sentence of the section entitled "Maritime Forces" refers only to northern waters and, if so, why? The sentence might simply be deleted.

...

The section entitled "rationalizing Canada's maritime fleets" contains some detailed information which might be useful in giving clarity to the earlier section entitled "Relationship to Civil Authorities".... [T]his section would be improved if it were amended as follows:

> "...The Government is prepared now to assign complimentary authority and responsibility to DND and the Coast Guard for the enforcement of Canadian legislation in the maintenance of Canadian sovereignty and jurisdiction, particularly with respect to violations of the 12-mile territorial sea and the fishing and pollution control zones."

...

The section entitled "Sub-surface Detection in the Arctic" raises difficult questions in the statement that there is already evidence that foreign submarines have been operating in the Arctic and that activity will almost certainly increase in the years to come. Our understanding is that the only submarines which have been detected in this area have been US submarines. We wonder whether it would be appropriate in a public document to draw attention to such operations by US submarines and to provoke questions as to whether or not they are being conducted with the prior knowledge and consent of the Canadian Government. So far as Canada's claim to sovereignty over the waters of the Arctic archipelago is concerned, the question does arise, of course, whether the unauthorized transits by US submarines might seriously prejudice the claim in question. This is not, however, a question which would appear appropriate for discussion in a public document.

...

The phrase "surveillance and enforcement of territorial integrity" ... is obscure and should be replaced by the phrase "surveillance of Canada's coastal waters and the enforcement of Canadian legislation in the maintenance of Canadian sovereignty and jurisdiction."

...

The section entitled "The Deterrent System" posits that only direct threat to Canada's national security is that of a large scale nuclear attack on North America. It does not make clear that such a threat is, of course, a threat to Canada's sovereignty in the sense of both territorial integrity and independence, but rather stresses that cooperation with the USA in the defence against this threat does not "detract from sovereignty" and is indeed "an act of sovereignty." This rather negative approach seems to reflect the view (which is also manifested in other ways through the White Paper) that the protection of "sovereignty," "territorial integrity" and "independence" is a "political concern" not directly connected to the threat of armed attack. There are no grounds in international law for such a restrictive view of sovereignty.

...

The section entitled "Surface Vessels" makes the point that the maintenance of Canadian pollution control jurisdiction in the Arctic waters will require the capability to enforce the relevant legislation. This is, of course, quite accurate but we wonder if sufficient thought has been given to the fact that perhaps the strongest opposition to the exercise of Canadian jurisdiction in the Arctic waters comes from the USA. While Canada and the USA are holding discussions on the possibility of elaborating a multilateral treaty regime on safety of navigation and pollution control in Arctic waters, and while there are grounds for optimism that such a regime may in fact be established, the need for national enforcement of anti-pollution regulations – whether internationally agreed or otherwise – will remain. The potential difficulties involved in having Canadian naval vessels enforce such regulations against US naval vessels is sufficiently obvious not to require elaboration. In this respect at least, without minimizing the role which could be played by DND in assisting civil agencies to enforce anti-pollution regulations, there would appear to be certain advantages to assigning primary responsibility for such enforcement to civil agencies. With respect to more purely legal concerns, the third sentence of the first paragraph of this section would be improved by amendment as follows:

> "If Canadian pollution control jurisdiction is to be maintained in these waters, it is important that the Government have the capacity to enforce the relevant legislation."

5-5. DEXAF, J.A Beesley, Director General, Bureau of Legal and Consular Affairs (FLP), to Defence Foreign Relations [DFP], re: White Paper on Defence Policy, 8 April 1971.[48]

We understand that the March 16 version of the draft 1971 White Paper on Defence Policy will be discussed in Cabinet Committee in the first week of May at the earliest. While we consider that this revised version generally reflects the comments made by us with respect to earlier drafts, there remain a number of less important points on which we would wish to suggest further drafting changes as outlined below before the paper is taken up in Cabinet Committee.

2. Page 13 – We have reservations concerning the use of the word "challenges" in the first sentence of the second paragraph of the section entitled "External Challenges." Despite the section heading, we assume that the word "challenges" in this sentence is not used in the sense of "external challenges" (i.e. challenges by foreign agencies) but rather in the sense of climatic and geographic difficulties for effective administration and control. This, however, is not clear from the present wording which could suggest that other states are questioning Canada's sovereignty over its Arctic lands. Accordingly, we would recommend that the sentence be revised as follows: "The Canadian North, in a sense the last frontier of Canada, is a unique physical environment presenting special problems of administration and control."

3. Page 16 – The second paragraph on this page suggests that it is possible to "occupy effectively" Canadian airspace and waters, whereas in fact the concept of effective occupation cannot, in our view, apply to such areas in either physical or legal terms. Moreover, the phrase "waters off the coasts over which Canada exercises sovereignty or jurisdiction" is ambiguous and does not make clear that it is the coastal waters and not the coasts themselves to which reference is being made. Accordingly, we would recommend that the first sentence of this paragraph be amended as follows: "The Government's objective is to continue to occupy effectively all Canadian territory and to have surveillance and

48 LAC, RG 25, vol. 10322, file 27-10-2-2 pt.2. Originally classified as "Confidential."

control capability to the extent necessary to maintain authority over that territory and over the airspace and coastal waters over which Canada exercises sovereignty or jurisdiction."

4. Page 33 – The first sentence of the first paragraph on this page does not clearly distinguish between the two kinds of surveillance to which we presume reference is made, i.e. (a) surveillance for the enforcement of jurisdiction and legislation, and (b) surveillance for more strictly military purposes. The distinction would be more clearly brought out if this sentence were amended as follows: "The Government believes that the next generation of aircraft should meet the full variety of surveillance tasks required under the defence priorities, for example, surveillance of the sea for hostile submarines and surveillance for other purposes in the North and on the east and west coasts of Canada."

5. Page 38 – The last sentence on this page appears to contradict itself since it states, on the one hand, that present naval ships do not have the capability of operating safely in ice covered waters or above 65 degrees North latitude at <u>any</u> time of the year but, on the other hand, these ships are nonetheless being employed to a greater extent during the summer months. This difficulty could be met by substituting the words "all times of the year" for the present wording "any time of the year."

6. Page 40 – Sub-paragraph (b) on this page appears to limit DND's enforcement in respect of pollution cases involving the actual discharge of pollutants. The provisions of both the Arctic Waters Pollution Prevention Act and the recent amendments to the Canada Shipping Act, of course, go far beyond the simple prohibition of the discharge of pollutants and indeed make it an offence for vessels even to enter certain areas unless they meet Canadian safety standards. This sub-paragraph, accordingly, should be amended as follows: "occasional arrest within territorial waters and pollution control zones of foreign ships in breach of Canadian anti-pollution regulation.

7. While we appreciate that it is not within our terms of reference to comment on the non-legal aspects of the White Paper, we wonder

whether the references to the military threat posed by the USSR … might not be toned down and made in a rather more oblique fashion, taking into account the fact that the release of the White Paper will follow hard on the heels of the Prime Minister's visit to the USSR. Finally, if we may be permitted to stray yet further from our bailiwick, we wonder too why the White Paper does not explore the implication which might ultimately arise for Canada as a result of the triangular relationship between the USA, USSR and the People's Republic of China. (A Stanley Kubrick might well envisage a scenario in which the Chinese would make a quick dash into the Arctic archipelago to fire one missile in the direction of the USA and one in the direction of the USSR, and then sit back and watch the results.)

5-6. Privy Council Office, Record of Cabinet Decision, meetings of 8, 15, 22 July 1971.[49]

Record of Cabinet Decisions
Meetings of July 8, July 15, and July 22, 1971

The White Paper on Defence

The following decision of Cabinet draws together the decisions of substance on Defence policy taken during three Cabinet meetings devoted to consideration of this subject on July 8, July 15 and July 22.

The Cabinet agreed that:

a) the 1971 White Paper on Defence should be published, suitably amended to take into account the decisions reached during Cabinet discussion of that paper and its policy recommendations;

Protection of Canada

b) the Canadian Forces should expand maritime operations in the Arctic and should study the need for a greater submarine detection capability in the Arctic;
c) if the results of the systems analysis concerning overhaul of the Argus aircraft indicated that it would not be cost-effective to carry out such an overhaul, the Minister of National Defence would return to Cabinet with his recommendation for long range patrol aircraft requirements generally and Argus replacement specifically;
d) CF-5 aircraft will be employed to provide a quick response photographic reconnaissance capability in Canada and over offshore waters in peacetime; CF-104 aircraft from the Operational Training Squadron at Cold Lake, Alberta, will be used to provide Canada with its own identification and interception capability in the Prairie area; and CF-101 VOODOO aircraft operating from eastern Canada bases will carry out identification and interception tasks on the eastern approaches to Canada;
e) the Department of National Defence should be prepared, when required, to render increased assistance to other departments in fields relating to national development, this without any

49 LAC, RG 25, vol. 10322, file 27-10-2-2 pt.2. Originally classified as "Confidential."

degradation to their ability to respond to their basic defence roles; joint operations centers would be established on the east and west coasts to facilitate better co-ordination between DND and other departments and agencies; and that a study should be initiated to enquire into and make recommendations to Cabinet with a view to effecting greater centralized co-ordination and control over the operation of all government vessels and aircraft belonging to those departments and agencies having coastal functions and responsibilities;

f) increased emphasis will be placed on Land Force presence and operations in the North; ….

5-7. Donald S. Macdonald, Minister of National Defence, *Defence in the 70s*. White Paper on Defence, August 1971. Excerpts.

National Concerns

There have been developments within Canada of particular importance to the employment of our defence forces. Defence responsibilities required re-examination as a result of Government decisions to regulate the development of the North in a manner compatible with environmental preservation, and with legislation enacted to prevent pollution in the Arctic and the Northern inland waters. Other relevant developments included the extension of Canada's territorial sea, the establishment of fisheries protection and pollution control zones on the Atlantic and Pacific coasts, and the heightened pace of exploration for offshore mineral resources. Finally, the threat to society posed by violent revolutionaries and the implications of the recent crisis – although the latter occurred well after the defence review began – merited close consideration in projecting Canadian defence activities in the 1970s.

...

The Basis for Defence Policy in the 1970s

DEFENCE AS PART OF NATIONAL POLICY

Defence policy cannot be developed in isolation. It must reflect and serve national interests, and must be closely related to foreign policy, which the Government reviewed concurrently with defence. In the course of these reviews the principle that defence policy must be in phase with the broader external projection of national interests was underlined. In addition, internal aspects of national defence were also considered; these included aid of the civil power and assistance to the civil authorities in the furtherance of national aims.

National Aims

In the foreign policy review general national aims were defined as follows:

- that Canada will continue secure as an independent political entity;

- that Canada and all Canadians will enjoy enlarging prosperity in the widest possible sense; and
- that all Canadians will see in the life they have and the contribution they make to humanity something worthwhile preserving in identity and purpose.

Policy Themes

To achieve these aims, the themes of Canada's national policy were more specifically defined as seeking to:

- foster economic growth
- safeguard sovereignty and independence,
- work for peace and security,
- promote social justice,
- enhance the quality of life, and
- ensure a harmonious natural environment.

...

SOVEREIGNTY AND INDEPENDENCE

Canada's sovereignty and independence depend ultimately on security from armed attack. In this sense, the contribution of the Canadian Forces to the prevention of war is a vital and direct contribution to safeguarding or sovereignty and independence. Defence policy must, however, also take into account the possibility that other challenges to Canada's sovereignty and independence, mainly non-military in character, may be more likely to arise during the 1970s. They could come both from outside and from within the country, and to deal with them may in some ways be more difficult. While deterring war is not an objective Canada alone can achieve, and is therefore one which must be pursued through collective security arrangements, the other challenges to sovereignty and independence must be met exclusively by Canada. The provision of adequate defence resources for this purpose must therefore be a matter of first priority.

External Challenges

By assuming the general responsibility for surveillance and control over Canadian territory, waters and airspace, in conjunction with civil agencies, the Canadian Forces help safeguard sovereignty and independence. Challenges could occur through actions by foreign agencies or their nationals involving territorial violations or infringements of Canadian laws governing access to and activity within these areas. This is not a new role for the Canadian Forces, but its dimensions are changing.

The North, in a sense the last frontier of Canada, has a unique physical environment presenting special problems of administration and control. Modern industrial technology has in recent years stimulated a growth of commercial interest in the resources potential of the area, and contributed to a major increase in oil and gas exploration in the Territories, especially on the Arctic Islands. These activities, in which foreign as well as Canadian companies are involved, have brought with them a need to ensure that exploitation of the resources is carried out in accordance with Canada's long-term national interests. There is a danger that this increased activity with its inherent danger of oil or other pollution might disturb the finely balanced ecology of the region. The Government therefore decided to take special measures to ensure the environmental preservation of this uniquely vulnerable area, and to ensure that these measures are fully respected. Strict regulations governing land use and mineral exploration and exploitation are being brought into effect. Legislation provides for the exercise of pollution control jurisdiction in an area extending generally 100 miles from the mainland and islands of the Canadian Arctic.

Canada is a three-ocean maritime nation with one of the longest coastlines in the world, and a large portion of the trade vital to our economic strength goes by sea. The Government is concerned that Canada's many and varied interests in the waters close to our shores, on the seabed extending from our coasts, and on the high seas beyond, be protected.

...

Exploration and exploitation of the resources of the continental shelf are regulated under the Oil and Gas Production and Conservation Act. This area extends to the limits of exploitability, which Canada interprets as comprising the submerged continental margin. Although less extensive off the West Coast, it extends hundreds of miles off the East Coast, and encompasses large areas off the Arctic mainland and islands.

In recent years there has been a tremendous increase in technological capability for exploitation of this resource potential.

Departmental Responsibilities and Relationships

The Government's objective is to continue effective occupation of Canadian territory, and to have a surveillance and control capability to the extent necessary to safeguard national interests in all Canadian territory, and all airspace and waters over which Canada exercises sovereignty or jurisdiction. This involves a complex judgment on the challenges which could occur and on the surveillance and control capability required in the circumstances.

The Canadian Forces do not have sole responsibility for ensuring respect for relevant Canadian legislation but they do have a general responsibility for surveillance and control over land, sea and airspace under Canadian jurisdiction. In peacetime this role of the Forces is in many respects complementary to that of the civil authorities. The requirements for military assistance is generally greater, however, in more sparsely settled regions until a stage of economic and social development has been reached, justifying an expansion of civil agencies and resources. Similarly, where the Canadian Forces have the capability to meet a shortage in civil resources for the policing of waters off the coasts, their role can be expanded.

The area to be covered is vast. In certain regions facilities are limited and weather conditions are often adverse. The problem would perhaps be simpler if it were restricted to the more traditional security threat of direct military attack from a predictable enemy. Instead, challenges could arise in more ambiguous circumstances from private entities as well as foreign government agencies. Incidents may involve, for instance, a fishing vessel, an oil tanker or a private aircraft. But the principle involved is well established. By creating a capability for surveillance and control which is effective and visible, the intention is to discourage such challenges.

Other departments of government already have specific responsibilities in many instances for regulating activity in Canadian territory, and these lead to requirements for carrying out surveillance and exercising control. National Defence has, however, ultimate responsibility to ensure that overall an adequate Canadian surveillance and control capability exists for the protection of Canadian sovereignty and security.... Close consultation between National Defence and the civil departments concerned will be maintained on a continuing basis to ensure that surveillance and control is being exercised when, where, and to the extent necessary to satisfy the Government's requirements in the most economical way.

...

NATIONAL DEVELOPMENT

Although maintained primarily for purposes of sovereignty and security, the Department of National Defence provides an important reservoir of skills and capabilities which in the past has been drawn upon, and which in the future can be increasingly drawn upon, to contribute to the social and economic development of Canada. By their service and devotion to duty the members of the Armed Forces, and the civilians who support them, have made a significant contribution to preserving a democratic society in Canada against the threat of external challenges.

...

The Canadian Forces have made major contributions to the development of the North. The Northwest Territories and Yukon Radio System, established in 1923, pioneered development of communications in the North. Both before the Second World War and in the post-war years, the Forces carried out extensive aerial photographic and survey activities which played a key part in mapping the Arctic and in opening it up for air transportation.

The construction of defence installations in the North developed new techniques for dealing with permafrost and other Arctic conditions which have been invaluable to subsequent northern development. Much has been done to understand and deal with the special problems of communications and navigation in the Arctic. An icebreaker operated by the Forces was the first large ship to navigate the Northwest Passage. The Forces, with the help of the Defence Research Board (DRB), have been in the forefront of the opening of the North and have pioneered in finding solutions to the problems of its development. This role will be enhanced in the future, particularly where National Defence engineering and construction resources can be utilized.

The Forces will make a major contribution to the preservation of an unspoiled environment and an improved quality of life by supporting the civil agencies in exercising pollution control on the North and off Canada's coasts. The Forces and the Canadian Emergency Measures Organization will continue to play an important part in providing relief and assistance in the event of natural disasters or other civil emergencies, including those resulting from oil spills or other forms of pollution.

...

PRIORITIES FOR CANADIAN DEFENCE POLICY

The policy announced by the Prime Minister on April 3, 1969, initiated the process of adjusting the balance between Canadian defence activities to ensure that priorities for defence were responsive to national interests and international developments. Four major areas of activity for the Canadian Forces were identified in summary form as follows:

(a) the surveillance of our own territory and coast-lines, i.e. the protection of our sovereignty;
(b) the defence of North America in co-operation with U.S. forces;
(c) the fulfillment of such NATO commitments as may be agreed upon; and
(d) the performance of such international peacekeeping roles as we may from time to time assume.

This paper will next examine these four areas of defence policy in detail. Activity in each must be assessed in terms of the priorities which have been established, and of the cost-effectiveness and marginal return of various options. With the limited resources available for Canadian defence needs, it is desirable to have versatile forces and multi-purpose equipment rather than a high degree of specialization. Multiple tasking is also necessary in order to make the most efficient use of available resources.

Protection of Canada

Apart from the aid of the civil power, which will be considered separately, the two principal aspects of this role of the Forces are surveillance and control. Surveillance requires detection and identification to obtain information on what is happening on Canada's land mass, in her airspace and on and under her coastal waters; control implies appropriate enforcement action to ensure that laws and regulations are respected.

SURVEILLANCE

Military surveillance is required for the protection of Canada and Canadian interests, but it is also an essential contribution to North American defence and, in the broader context, to the security of the North Atlantic region. In our collective security arrangements, surveillance is conducted to provide warning of potentially unfriendly acts by foreign military forces. But Canada also has a national requirement for certain surveillance activities to provide information on events of importance occurring on land, at sea and in Canadian airspace.

Air

Almost all identification of aircraft in the Canadian airspace which is under air traffic control is performed by comparing radar tracks with filed flight plans, or by ground-to-air communication through the active co-operation of the aircraft concerned. The communications network required to make flight plans available in time is of considerable complexity. Since the function of civilian air traffic control requires much of the same data as the function of identification for air defence, full civil-military co-operation is the most effective approach. There is already a considerable degree of integration and more will be possible in the future, with benefits in both areas.

Extensive surveillance systems are now operated as part of the North American Air Defence Command (NORAD) but they also serve national purposes in covering a portion of Canadian airspace. A number of radar installations, many of which were operated by the U.S., have been closed in recent years to effect economies as the bomber threat declined. The U.S. earlier this year gave Canada notice of intention to close two radar stations it operated in Canada: Melville, near Goose Bay, Labrador, and Stephenville, Newfoundland. In order to continue the radar coverage in the Labrador area which is required for adequate surveillance as well as control on the East coast, the Government decided to operate Melville as a Canadian radar site.

Maritime and Land

A substantial capability for surveillance over Canada's waters in the temperate zone is currently available. Surveillance over Arctic land and waters can be carried out by long-range patrol aircraft but at present is limited by light and weather conditions. Surveillance by ships is restricted to ice free periods of the year. Because of the areas involved, general ground surveillance by land forces is not practicable. The Department of National Defence is assessing the challenges that might be expected in the Canadian North and, if warranted, will increase surveillance.

Surveillance over maritime and land areas is currently available from the Argus long-range patrol aircraft which was designed and bought specifically to detect and track submarines. The Tracker aircraft has similar capabilities, although its range is much shorter. Both the Argus and Tracker could be operated at least to the end of the decade, and therefore the question of a new generation of this type of aircraft need not necessarily arise for several years. The Argus would, however, have to be overhauled to ensure continued air worthiness. A comprehensive systems analysis of the alternatives is being undertaken.

...

Although Canada has a good capability to detect submarines in its waters in the temperate zone, it has only very limited capabilities to detect submarine activity in the Arctic. It might be desirable in the future to raise the level of capability so as to have subsurface perimeter surveillance particularly to cover the channels connecting the Arctic Ocean to Baffin Bay and Baffin Bay to the Atlantic. The Government is therefore undertaking research to determine the costs and feasibility of a limited subsurface system to give warning of any unusual maritime activity. The Defence Research Board is playing an important role in these studies. If found to be desirable, the system could be operated as part of the overall surveillance of North America against unknown submarines.

...

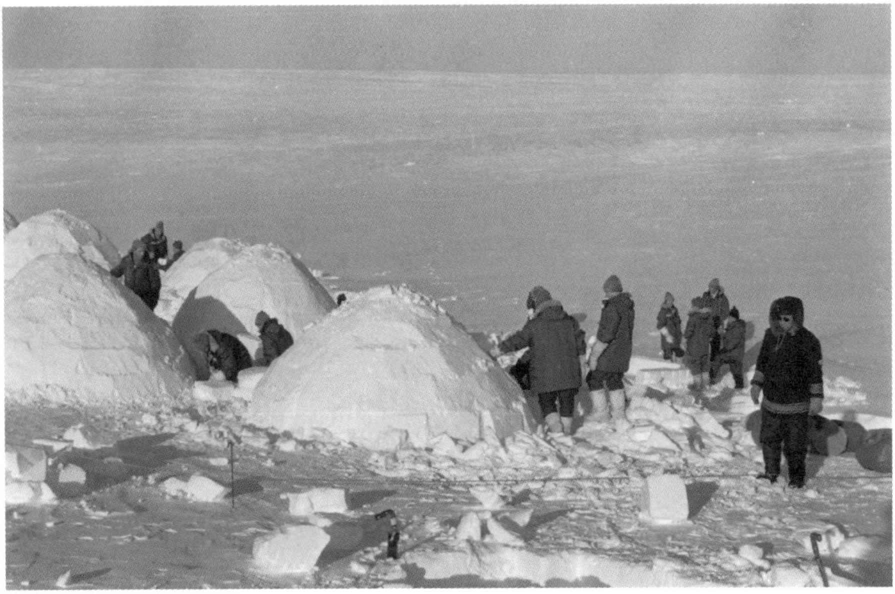

Two Ranger instructors demonstrate building an igloo on the first day of a training course at Resolute Bay. March 1971. (LAC)

Assistance to the Civil Authorities

The general surveillance of Canadian airspace and waters required for national security will permit greater support to other departments. Initial consultation with the civil departments responsible by legislation for the protection of various specific interests have already indicated several areas where a greater contribution by the Armed Forces will be necessary. They will be kept under review to ensure that the total national effort is both effective and efficient in the use of available resources to meet the Government's requirements.

Some of the activities identified are:

(a) general area surveillance of foreign fishing fleets off the coasts;
(b) specific reconnaissance missions on a quick response, short-term basis to locate those fishing fleets when they move and fail to appear when expected;
(c) area surveillance of offshore waters to detect and report suspected illegal seismic and other exploratory activities;
(d) assistance in ice reconnaissance operations;

(e) surveillance when needed of Canadian waters off the East and West Coasts and in the North to detect pollution at sea;
(f) surveillance of Canadian territorial waters to detect and report foreign vessels illegally present therein;
(g) surveillance of sites of mineral exploration and exploitation projects in the North when verification of their locations and status is required; and
(h) during the appropriate seasons, provision of observer space on aircraft engaged in northern surveillance operations to permit wildlife observations.

CONTROL

In addition to the requirements for surveillance a military capability for control is required as an adjunct to the other measures necessary for the protection of Canada and Canadian interests. This should include an ability to enforce these measures should laws not be respected. Such efforts to protect national interests are fully consistent with Canadian involvement in collective security against foreign military attack.

…

Maritime

Canada's sea and air maritime forces possess a considerable capability for exercising control in the territorial seas, in the fishing and pollution control zones, and in the waters above the continental shelf. It is through continuous operations and co-ordinated team efforts, often in co-operation with units of other government departments, that the necessary degree of control can be achieved. Although the present naval ships cannot operate safely in ice-covered waters, or above 65 ° N latitude at any time of the year, they are being employed in northern waters to a greater extent during the summer months.

…

The possibility of the Department of National Defence providing increased support to other departments in control activities has been studied and the results indicate a need for … occasional arrest within territorial waters and pollution control zones of foreign ships in breach of Canadian anti-pollution regulations.

The Forces will be prepared to respond when called upon by the appropriate authorities in such situations.

Land

The current capabilities of the Canadian Forces are generally adequate for surveillance and control. The three combat groups within Canada are air transportable and the Canadian Airborne Regiment provides a parachute drop capability well suited for operation in the North. In the event of a requirement to defend the land mass of North America, a mutual support arrangement exists with the United States.

More emphasis is being placed on training the Armed Forces to live and operate in the Arctic. A Northern Region Headquarters has been established at Yellowknife, and there is a military liaison staff at Whitehorse. Consideration will be given to establishing other small bases in the North, particularly in the Arctic Islands, and to the desirability of reconstituting the Canadian Rangers. National Defence is also examining the desirability of establishing a special training school for all personnel assigned to the North. The adequacy of existing equipment is also being studied with particular emphasis on over-snow vehicles.

6 Deploying the Forces

6-1. BGen R.M. Withers, "Northern Region Concept for Force Development," to All Officers NRHQ, 15 June 1971.[50]

NORTHERN REGION CONCEPT FOR FORCE DEVELOPMENT

References: A. FDO C1/71 CF Activities in the North 71-83
B. FDO A6/71 Search and Rescue 71/83

Brigadier General R.M. Withers. (LAC)

BACKGROUND

1. References A and B have now been received and I am in the process of preparing comments on them for CFHQ. Although we made our input to the initial development of both these FDOs [Force Development Objectives], we have learned a great deal over the last year and must now make available our revised philosophy on these matters. The purpose of this memorandum is to put our philosophy in writing as a guide to all members of the staff in considering Force Development within and for Northern Regions.

50 Northern Region file 3185-1 (COMD). Originally Confidential (Canadian Eyes Only), copy provided by CFNA (now JTFN).

2. We must all appreciate that the concepts we are developing in Northern Region are quite different from those which have guided Canadian Force structures of the past many years. Furthermore, we must remember that the shift of emphasis involved is of such a degree that it is difficult for some in the Canadian Forces to comprehend rapidly. After all, we have been involved in the alliance-type of operation for some three generations; to switch to a situation which all activities are to be Canadian requires some pretty big adjustments. And finally, we must remember that all of us have had the benefit of recent exposure to the North, its activities and its people; this is an advantage others in the CF have not had.

3. As an example of the difficulty faced by planners in the South when considering northern operations, we have noticed the continuation of thinking about enemy lodgments. This philosophy originated over 20 years ago when it was considered that an enemy would attempt medium-scale incursions into the North for various purposes an example of which is capturing an airfield for bomber deployment. We still find some thinking of deployments of combat-group size in the North under these circumstances. It has also been difficult for some to grasp the importance of threats and incursions which are not overt military actions.

AIM

4. The aim of this memorandum is to outline the Northern Region concept for Force Development.

THE SITUATION

5. For the past 50 years, Canada, in reality, has never faced an exclusive military threat. Because of Empire and Commonwealth ties and the alliance commitments in Hot and Cold war a rather narrow spectrum of options was imposed. Canada was committed to an "expeditionary" role and a deterrence support role which, in turn, dictated our Force Development. The shift of emphasis occurred in the April 1969 statement of the Government which saw a partial disengagement from the alliance and expeditionary Force concept. Thus a much wider spectrum of

options is now available and is being considered. Internal security and sovereignty have emerged as the primary and solid commitment.

6. Previous concepts for northern operations were based on deterrence and were directed against functional support lodgments as opposed to aggressive penetrations. Because of changes in technology, the lodgment possibility now has become remote and this threat along with other hostile land penetrations are assigned a low probability. Similarly, technology makes the threat of the Arctic launch of the submarine ballistic missile unlikely sometime after 1975.

7. On the other hand there are both definable and indefinable threats of a non-military nature to Canadian interests in the North. In the maintenance of sovereignty, Canada must demonstrate to the world that she is capable of knowing what goes on in the sparsely-populated regions of the Nation and that she is capable of taking effective action to enforce compliance with Canadian legislation and regulations. These requirements have been recognized and stated in our national objectives for the North, which have been approved by the Government and which should be promulgated shortly along with an indication of priorities.

8. The DND analysis of the new Defence policy and national objectives resulted in the establishment of Four Defence Objectives for the North as follows:

a. Contributing to the maintenance of Canadian Sovereignty by establishment of a military presence and by surveillance and reconnaissance of Canadian territory, territorial waters, air space and the approaches to them.
b. The maintenance of operational ready sea, land and air forces capable of defeating illegal and forcible entry into Canadian territory.
c. Provision of an effective search and rescue organization in the North.
d. Contributing to projects which further the economic development of the North.

9. It has also been stated that all departments involved in the North are to so arrange their activities that they contribute not only to the achievement of that department's primary objective, but also contribute to the extent possible to the attainment of all other national objectives for the North. It is my conclusion that DND has not yet grasped the importance of this last fact, that our activities be so designed as to make the optimum contribution to the attainment of other national objectives in the North. I admit that much has been done, especially over the last year, but there is still room for more. Coming back to my earlier point concerning the shift from an alliance philosophy to one giving priority to the nation itself, I consider that our planners are still giving emphasis to activities which have a dual application within the nation and to expeditionary or alliance activities rather than furthering activities which have a dual application within the nation and, therefore, activities which achieve their dual benefit by interaction with the programs of other government departments, particularly in the North.

10. I think that we have been able to see these points as we have become better educated during our first year of operation and, particularly, because of living and operating in the North over these last several months. We now must embark on the process of making our case for the allocation of resources; in other words, we must now influence the Force Development process in accordance with our convictions.

11. To summarize, the situation today is much different from that of even a few years ago. Gone are the scenarios of an enemy parachuting or air landing to seize some objective in Canada. While we must still possess the capability to deal with situations of this nature in the North, this type of activity is very low on the scale of priorities. We must now recognize the need to design activities and Force structures to achieve Four Defence Objectives for the North described above. It will be seen that these are in accordance with Canadian Defence priorities and include the requirement to design activities which will contribute to national development. We must promote Force Development activities which are as effective and as economical as possible over the spectrum of these Northern Defence Objectives and which take into account

the special considerations and conditions which apply in our region. In so doing, we must also employ resources which are easily identified as Canadian and, of even greater value, are proven performers in the North. Let us examine the activities which must be performed to determine a reasonable philosophy.

SURVEILLANCE AND RECONNAISSANCE

12. The surveillance and reconnaissance which is involved in our region is of a very different nature than that which the Canadian Forces have been carrying out in other roles such as contributions to an alliance. It is important that these differences are recognized and understood to enable us to state our concepts properly and to ensure that our Force Structure and equipment policies are the most appropriate.

13. To do this, let us examine some of the characteristics of northern surveillance and reconnaissance which differ from those we have been used to in Europe and on the Atlantic:

a. Target Density. The target density (possible targets per sq. mile) will be very low. Considering that we are involved with a region of some 1.5 million sq. miles with a rate of occurrence of no more than say two targets at any one time, target density is much lower than that normally encountered in the traditional military situation.
b. Sensor Space Ratio. The sensor space ratio, that is the probable available number of sensors usable at any one time related to the area to be covered, will always be low and probably below the ideal ratio unless inexpensive systems can be developed.
c. Targets. Differences between the traditional target and the northern target are outlined below:

Traditional Target	New Northern Target
1. Evasive	1. Not evasive & often cooperating
2. High ability to conceal & deceive	2. Overt & possibly cooperating
3. Hostile & responsive	3. Not hostile & probably not dangerous

4. Mobile	4. No or low mobility
5. Limited in variability	5. Complex & variable
6. Easily recognized & identified	6. Difficult to recognize often requiring sampling & data analysis
7. Countered mainly by fire power	7. Rarely if ever countered by fire power or force

14. In summary, surveillance and reconnaissance targets in the North in the current threat situation tend to be different and demand different systems in response. They are not hostile, probably do not deny or prevent investigation and can be approached, eliminating the old need for remote sensing. Since targets are less evasive, speed of pursuit is no longer of major importance. These targets may not try to conceal themselves but they may be more complex, difficult to identify, describe and establish accurately. Seldom, if ever, will they be countered by force, fire power or hostile acts. In the main, they will be investigated and countered more by documentation, accurate description, diplomatic response, interrogation, friendly presence and actual physical conversation. Target sensor ratios and the surveillance area size all point towards the need for inexpensive systems available in larger numbers.

15. All this suggests that on-the-ground investigation will be required a great deal of the time if not all the time. On-the-ground surveillance may become important because of target complexity and reconnaissance will involve more and more elements of ground investigation. The conclusions are:

a. Platforms for surveillance and reconnaissance should have a simultaneous air-ground capability.
b. The extent of employment of ground surveillance and reconnaissance systems is an essential requirement.
c. The human becomes an attractive part of the system concept because of the new conditions of operation, the need for special identification and his ability to be programmed to react to a wide variety of situations. This same human sensor can move to the

target area by air, ground (on ice) or on the surface of water. The platforms for him are all well within the state of the art and are now in use in the North and are proven items. As a result, there would be no development costs.

d. Finally, it will be seen that this same human with his platforms constitutes a system which can perform effectively in activities designed to attain the other Defence objectives.

16. In conclusion, these operations suggest a flexible, relatively unsophisticated, inexpensive surveillance and reconnaissance system consisting of the human sensor with the right kind of platform, principally the aircraft. Such a system would be capable of breaking off surveillance and starting ground reconnaissance on the spot. Deployment of such a system throughout the North would be co-ordinated with other activities to achieve effectiveness, efficiency and economy in the attainment of the full spectrum of Defence Objectives. Such a system would also allow exploitation of the resources which live in the North plus those which have been developed for northern activities. This in turn would allow a contribution to be made to the attainment of other national objectives.

OPERATIONAL READY FORCES

17. While the combat arms must be capable of operations anywhere in the nation and, therefore, must be trained and equipped to deal with a warlike situation in the North, the probability of occurrence of such a situation is extremely low. On the other hand, there is a high probability for troops to deal with emergency situations, particularly in assistance to civil authorities. As a generalization, such emergency situations fall into two categories:

a. the low level emergency, in which the timely intervention of a few men can achieve the required results; and,
b. the big affair, such as the fire in Wood Buffalo National Park, in which a large labor force is required for a relatively long time.

18. We must also remember that the internal security requirements of the South are such as to demand all available land force units now in the order of battle. Even then, we really do not have enough.

19. Considering these factors plus those of time and space involved in deployment of southern units to the North, it can be seen that timely intervention could be very difficult to achieve. The deduction is that it will be a great advantage to have troops available in the North, particularly to deal with the low level situation. Indeed if such resources are not available right within the region, timely intervention in the low level situation virtually would be impossible.

20. Therefore, it follows that small detachments located throughout the North and provided with the right kind of transportation would be effective in a number of emergency scenarios. If these detachments could be the same people as the human sensors of the surveillance and reconnaissance system and if their modes of transportation could be the same, two Defence Objectives could be achieved with the one resource. Equally, such detachments could be of considerable value in the large-scale scenario through their actions as on-site advance parties for larger temporary deployments.

21. As commercial and development activities increase in the North, so also increases the volume of civil aviation and, in turn, the search and rescue threat. This is borne out by the fact that the annual number of search and rescue incidents increased from 6 in 1966 to 32 in 1970. This trend is recognized in the [Search and Rescue Force Development Objective]. However, that same FDO states that 24 hours is an acceptable reaction time to a northern incident; US Alaskan Air Command considers 4 hours to be the maximum for a northern search inception. Clearly, the Alaskan standard is the correct one, for it appreciates the survival time involved under northern weather conditions. In Northern Region the only way in which the sensible reaction time can be attained is through the deployment of SAR resources throughout the region.

A Canadian Army unit establishes a campsite during a training course near the Bay of Woe, Ellesmere Island. 29 August 1974. (LAC)

22. While these resources are primarily aircraft, they also include ground search resources and, at times, surface-craft. It would be quite easy and thoroughly sensible to make these resources the same ones which deal with surveillance, reconnaissance and emergency situations.

NATIONAL DEVELOPMENT IN THE NORTH

23. One tends to think of national development projects in the North in terms of construction engineering because of the projects currently underway. It must not be forgotten that equal if not greater value can result from providing job opportunities and from engaging in a co-operative way with the development of commercial and government facilities in the region. Thus, if we were to raise a force from the manpower of the North and to support it by transportation and communication facilities living in the region, the following additional benefits would result:

a. job opportunities for northerners would be provided;
b. the purchase of local services such as fuel, food and lodging to name three would be a direct input to the northern economy;

c. the provision of communications for the purposes of command and control would enhance the underdeveloped communications network, particularly North of 70;
d. military training would provide skills to northerners; and,
e. the fact that essential Defence tasks were being performed by northerners would instill pride of accomplishment and dignity in an area where these qualities have perhaps suffered from the invasion of the southern way of life.

The Optimum Course Open

24. First of all, the principal deductions are as follows:
a. Canadian Defence policy having changed to give considerations of sovereignty and internal security first place, fresh options for the execution of our military activities are appropriate;
b. the four Defence Objectives for the North recognize the changed threat situation and, therefore, demand a new appreciation of our activities;
c. the desire for national identification and clear demonstration of Canadian control indicate that our northern activities should be performed with all Canadian, and preferably, northern resources;
d. activities and resources must not only achieve the Defence Objectives, but also should attempt to make maximum contribution to other national objectives for the North;
e. a surveillance system consisting of human sensors with suitable air, ground and sea platforms is quite suitable for the northern requirement;
f. in addition to operationally ready units which can be deployed into the North for emergencies, there is a need for local forces to handle small-scale emergencies in a timely manner;
g. to achieve the required reaction time, SAR resources have to be deployed throughout Northern Region;
h. a combination of northern manpower with suitable transportation and communications can carry out a very large part of the total spectrum of activities needed to satisfy all Defence Objectives in the North; and,

i. the creation of such a northern element in the Canadian Forces would have beneficial sociological affects.

25. I consider that the optimum course open is to form a battalion of the Canadian Rangers for service in Northern Region. This battalion would be supported by a STOL [short take-off and landing] squadron, probably equipped with the CC 138 Twin Otter which is already a proven northern performer and is of Canadian manufacture. Suitable communications, before the availability of a communications satellite, would require a network of HF SSB [high frequency single side band] radios to supplement the rather sparse existing communications system.

26. The battalion would offer full-time employment to northerners at selected settlements. Men would be enrolled in the Reserve and employed on continuous duty. This would allow them to change to other employment without complications and, at the same time, would allow the battalion commander to discharge an unsatisfactory member with minimum problem. Enrolment standards would be decided within the battalion, appropriate officers having wide scope and flexibility. In the beginning, the regular component of the battalion would have to provide not only leadership but also the necessary training and administrative skills. As the unit developed, leaders would be selected and appointed from within thus eliminating certain of the regular component positions. Many aspects of organization and administration remain to be worked out, however two are worthy of note at this time:

a. All existing services provided to northerners in the fields of health, housing and administration would continue to be performed by the Territorial Government or the Federal department concerned. These would not be a charge against DND. Hence the main cost to DND would be salary, making this a much cheaper option than employment of regulars in the South.
b. All members would wear the uniform of the Canadian Forces and, in addition, would be provided with a top quality parka which would both meet the needs of the environment and be attractive and distinctive.

27. The STOL squadron needed to support this battalion could easily meet the needs of SAR North of 60. In the course of time, it would be hoped that northerners who joined the Regular Force would qualify for positions on this squadron.

28. This option does not foresee the need for any large Canadian base in the North. To the contrary, it calls for making maximum use of facilities now available and those being developed in the North. In this way it will not only be a minimum capital outlay to DND, but also will contribute to the economic development of the North. I have discussed this concept with a great many people of experience in the North. These include the Commissioner of the Northwest Territories, Mr. Richard Hill the Mayor of Inuvik, officials of DIAND [the Department of Indian Affairs and Northern Development], educators and those engaged in industrial and social development. All have considered it to be an excellent concept which they hope will be implemented. In informal discussions with [the Minister of National Defence], the Deputy Minister and CDS there was great interest.

CONCLUSION

29. While this memorandum obviously has not covered the subject fully, it is a start point for a new approach to Force Development in the North. I ask all of you to consider it carefully and to offer suggestions for improvement and expansion.

6-2. Department of National Defence, Submission For Inclusion in the Advisory Committee on Northern Development Annual Report, "Government Activities In The North - FY 1971/72." Excerpts.

CANADIAN ARMED FORCES

Responsibilities

The Canadian Armed Forces are responsible for:

- the support of Canada's national policies by contributing to the maintenance of Canada's sovereignty;
- all aspects of maritime, land and air defence (in some areas these tasks are carried out in co-operation with our allies under international agreements);
- operation of rescue co-ordination centres, and the provision of aircraft search and rescue services;
- assisting other government departments and civilian agencies in national development projects, and in time of civil emergencies.

Long-term Plans

Within the context of these responsibilities the Department of National Defence will increase the scale of its activities in the Canadian Arctic. It has already embarked on a continuing surveillance of Arctic lands and waters, and is training troops to live, work and fight in both summer and winter Arctic conditions. In support of these operations, it has tested its ability to deliver airborne troops to isolated parts of the Arctic and to operate fighter aircraft in the north. Its transport operations are increasing, and it is co-operating with other government departments to improve the number and size of operational airstrips in the Arctic. During the past two years its naval forces have again started penetrating the Arctic seas with large ships. Recruiting of northerners for the Canadian Forces has started on an organized basis, and a meaningful role for the Canadian Rangers is being worked out. Coordinating all these activities is the new Northern Region Headquarters at Yellowknife.

Cutting snow blocks on an Arctic survival course. March 1971. (LAC)

Review of 1971 Operations

Maritime Forces

There was considerable naval activity in Canada's northern waters and airspace, largely in the surveillance role.

During the 12-month period Argus aircraft flew 43 missions into the Arctic for a total of 2,029 flying hours, and Tracker aircraft flew 290 hours on northern coastal patrols. The Argus aircraft flew from northern bases at Frobisher, Yellowknife, and Whitehorse, while the Tracker operated from Goose Bay and Frobisher Bay for surveillance of the coastal regions. A Maritime Command detachment was established at Frobisher Bay. Scientists and observers from other government departments were frequently on board these aircraft for special projects.

In August, a naval task force, composed of HMC Ships *Preserver*, *Assiniboine*, and *Margaree*, with a helicopter detachment on board, deployed for three weeks into Arctic waters. They visited Povungnituk, Ivujiuk, Sugluk, Wakeham Bay, Rigolet and Nain. During the voyage they were in contact with the Canadian Rangers in Labrador and northern Quebec, and carried out surveillance of foreign fishing trawlers in the Davis Strait. The medical officer from *Preserver* examined more than 160 patients and the dental officer attended a further 73 northern residents.

The ships also visited Frobisher Bay, Godthaab and Sondrestrom in connection with the visit of the Minister of National Defence to Greenland. During this phase of the voyage the ships conducted exercises north of the Arctic Circle, the first in our maritime history.

Shortly after, on the western side of the Arctic, HMCS *Provider*, HMCS *Qu'Appelle* and the submarine *Rainbow* were on an exercise off Alaska when a Soviet cruiser, two destroyers, three submarines, a submarine tender and a tanker were encountered. The Canadian ships were joined by an American group and the exercise became a surveillance operation. The Canadian and American ships and aircraft kept a watch on the Soviet units through the Aleutian chain, the Gulf of Alaska and south toward Hawaii.

At National Defence Headquarters in Ottawa a study was made of the long-term needs for Arctic and coastal surveillance. Also considered was the need for long-range maritime patrol against surface and subsurface vessels.

Land Forces

The scope of land force operations, training and manoeuvres expanded considerably during 1971.

Probably the biggest single advance was the establishment of Northern Region Headquarters at Yellowknife in the Northwest Territories, with a detachment at Whitehorse. It is important because it provides a permanent military co-ordinating authority in the north, close and continuing liaison with the Territorial governments, and a central data unit for military and civilian agencies who need information to operate in the north.

Northern Region is one of the six designated military regions of Canada and is geographically the largest. It comprises the Yukon Territory and the Northwest Territories, including the islands in Hudson Bay and James Bay, the islands of the Arctic archipelago, and extends to the geographic North Pole. The area is more than 1,500,000 square miles, representing 40 per cent of Canada.

The commander of the Northern Region co-ordinates the activities of the forces of other commands when they are deployed in the north. Only the units, personnel and material of the forces assigned solely to northern activities are based permanently in the north.

One continuing series of sub-unit exercises, which has been going on for the past three years, is called New Viking. These exercises are designed to prepare ground forces for surviving, working and fighting in summer and winter Arctic conditions. Apart from providing an almost continuous military presence in the north, they had by the end of December familiarized some 2,200 officers and men with the geography, terrain, climate, and operating difficulties from Churchill to the most northerly islands of the Arctic archipelago.

Headquarters and main support base for Exercise New Viking are at Churchill. Advanced bases during the winter are established at such points as Baker Lake, Coral Harbour, Rankin Inlet, Frobisher Bay and Yellowknife. In the summer, they are transferred to Sachs Harbour, Mould Bay, Isachsen, Ray Point and Eureka.

During the same period, a field survey was completed by 71 specialists from the Directorate of Mapping and Charting. The survey, codenamed *Arctic 71*, will eventually lead to the production of 347 tactical maps to a scale of 1/50,000 covering an area of 75,000 square miles from Coppermine to Melville Peninsula. The operation was supported by three military CH-113A Voyageur helicopters which logged 5,000 miles and positioned 500 drums of fuel for the civilian helicopters carrying survey parties.

Further north, members of the Canadian Forces manned the satellite triangulation stations at Cambridge Bay and Frobisher in co-operation with the Satellite Triangulation - North American Development Program.

In the Yukon, members of 3 Field Squadron, Royal Canadian Engineers constructed a steel and concrete bridge across the Olgilvie River at mile 123 on the Dempster Highway, which will help to open up new road links for the vast region of the Mackenzie River delta up to Inuvik….

As a stated policy, the Department of National Defence is encouraging young northerners to join the Canadian Forces, and is helping other government departments to train still more for the new era in the north. Recruiting teams from Edmonton, Winnipeg and Montreal visited all major Arctic communities in the spring of 1971 to enrol young northern Canadians who have a knowledge of the Arctic and sub-Arctic regions. The current recruiting target for the northerners is 100 for a variety of trades, and nine had been enrolled by December.

In addition, Training Command provided aircraft mechanic, heavy equipment operator and home-handyman training for 22 young men and women from northern Canada at the request of the Department of Indian Affairs and Northern Development.

Air Forces

With many new tasks assigned to them, the air elements of the Canadian Forces continued to improve their ability to operate in the north, as well their flexibility for the future. The training included familiarization of new crews with the remote Arctic airfields, increased practice in the techniques of air drops of troops and materiel, and a concentration on Arctic meteorology and navigation. The facilities included improved Arctic airstrips, fuel caches for helicopters and detailed studies of the future requirements of long-range aircraft for surveillance.

Air Transport Command continued to provide weekly air service to the Canadian Forces communications stations at Alert (routing from Trenton, Ontario, through Thule in Greenland, to Alert, and back through Resolute Bay to Trenton), and at Inuvik (routing from Namao, Alberta, through Yellowknife to Inuvik, and back through Yellowknife to Namao). The aircraft used was a C-130E Hercules.

Air Transport Command also provided airlift for the annual resupply of Canadian Forces Station Alert with flights staging through Thule, during which a total of 117 loads of fuel oil and general cargo were flown in by Hercules aircraft.

Air Transport Command is also responsible for search and rescue for the whole of Canada, including the north. The four squadrons searched for 98 missing aircraft in 1971 and helped to save 193 lives. A total of 8,628 hours was flown in search and rescue missions. Five major searches were conducted north of the 60th parallel, entailing about 225 flying hours during the year. Search and rescue flights are operational missions demanding skill and determination. An aircraft and eight crew members were lost in an attempt last November to drop supplies to a downed pilot in the Arctic barrens.

A standing detachment of two Twin Otters from 440 Squadron in Edmonton was assigned to Northern Region headquarters during the year. It will provide direct communications with settlements and development sites within Northern Region, and will also augment the search and rescue capability in the north, and perform mercy flights.

Providing a long-term military presence in the Arctic, the DEW Line consists of four main and 18 auxiliary radar sites which are strung across the Canadian Arctic from Cape Dyer in the east to Komakuk Beach near the Alaskan border.

For the first time in many years, Canadian Forces fighter aircraft appeared in Arctic skies. Quite different in both role and capabilities from Canada's long-range interceptors of Air Defence Command, CF-5 tactical fighters of Mobile Command took part in Arctic exercises in February. While a detachment of 434 Squadron from CFB Cold Lake, Alberta, operated out of Whitehorse in the Yukon, four CF-5s from *433[e] Escadrille tactique de combat,* CFB Bagotville, carried out 30 exercise missions over Baffin Island in the eastern Arctic. Supported by a Hercules, four of these attack/photo-reconnaissance aircraft were successfully staged through Fort Chimo near Ungava Bay, to Frobisher. During the four days of missions flown out of this airfield, the CF-5s penetrated some 250 miles beyond the Arctic Circle.

During the summer two Air Reserve squadrons moved north for their annual training. No. 402 "City of Winnipeg" Squadron operated out of a forward base at Yellowknife and 418 "City of Edmonton" Squadron operated out of Norman Wells. In addition, to their training, they flew far ranging reconnaissance and pollution survey missions. They inspected and photographed six abandoned DEW Line sites, oil exploration bases, pipeline routes aid and abandoned airstrips for the Northern Region commander.

To handle all this renewed air traffic, and to help open up Arctic settlements to year-round traffic, work continued on the six new and improved airstrips in co-operation with the Department of Indian Affairs and Northern Development. The airstrips are being built by military engineers and heavy equipment operators from CFB Winnipeg, with the help of local labour. The strip at Pangnirtung, 2,600 feet long and 150 feet wide, will be ready for use in September of this year. The facility at Whale Cove is 4,000 feet long and able to accommodate large military transports. Work there is expected to be finished by August 1972. Similar airstrips at Cape Dorset, Pond Inlet, Igloolik and Chesterfield Inlet will be ready in 1973.

A handover ceremony at Cape Dorset, Baffin Island, where the DND constructed a packed gravel airstrip and turned it over to the Department of Transport. 2 October 1976. (LAC)

Plans for 1972

General

Commensurate with the department's objectives and activities in the Canadian north, a three day conference was conducted during February 1972, to which delegates from eight other governments were invited to attend. One of the major conclusions reached during this conference was the need for close co-operation and co-ordination between various departments in the achievement of the national aim. Similar conferences are planned for 1972-73 but on a reduced scale.

Maritime Forces

Current plans call for a naval task group including Maritime Command aircraft to conduct exercises in northern waters and to continue Arctic and northern coastal patrols on a scale similar to 1971 operations. The Maritime Command will continue to support other federal departments and agencies to the greatest extent possible, consistent with the primary tasks and resources now assigned.

Land Forces

The New Viking series of exercises will continue. In addition several major environmental training exercises will be conducted out of Churchill and Resolute Bay.

Air Forces

Hercules aircraft will continue to fly regularly to Alert and Inuvik and Hercules and Buffalo aircraft will be used extensively in support of land forces environmental training. Two Twin Otter aircraft will continue to be flown from Yellowknife to serve NRHQ.

Two CF-5 Squadrons will support four scheduled FMC land exercises in the north during 1972. In addition the squadrons will occasionally be assigned to operations from northern airfields.

DEFENCE RESEARCH BOARD

Responsibilities

To bring to the Canadian Armed Forces scientific knowledge and experience in solving problems associated with military operations in high latitudes, and to sponsor and undertake research projects aimed at acquiring such knowledge.

Long-term Plans

Research will be conducted both in the laboratory and in the field. Almost every aspect of science is involved, and for convenience the work is categorized as follows:

- Research on the effects of the environment on systems used by the Canadian Forces to generate and transmit information necessary to command and control, and on the effects of the environment on the CF's ability to conduct operations in the north.
- Research directed to protecting the soldier and his equipment from the environment.
- Research directed to the protection of the environment from military operations.

Review of 1971 Operations

Research was conducted at the board's laboratories across the country; these studies are functional and multi-disciplinary. The board also supported research in the north by means of grants and contracts to universities and non-government research organizations, and by providing facilities and goods and services to other government agencies. Close collaboration was maintained with research and development agencies in other countries, especially the United States and Great Britain.

Remote Sensing in the Northern Environment

Two surveys were completed in 1971. One was a statistical study of the distribution of particulates and precipitates in the Arctic atmosphere and their effect on the transmission of those portions of the electromagnetic spectrum used in remote sensing. The other was a survey of the possible application of pattern recognition techniques to the processing of imagery obtained in Arctic surveillance overflights. Both of these surveys bear on longer-term research to determine the spectral properties of background and target materials at ambient Arctic temperatures and to develop devices to give real-time display in aircraft. A Fourier transform spectrophotometer has been obtained for the work on spectral signatures.

Shorter-term work involved direct support for the Canadian familiarization trials of infra-red line scanning equipment (IRLS). Two calibration target arrays have been built, and IRLS imagery over them has been obtained and is being processed in the laboratory to determine the modulation transfer function of the equipment as well as other parameters, such as the temperature difference resolution capacity. A liquid nitrogen transfer unit, which allowed extension of the detector operating time of the Reconofax XIII-A equipment from approximately two hours to 11 hours, was designed for in-flight use. The work on remote sensing is being done at the Defence Research Establishment, Ottawa (DREO) and the Defence Research Establishment, Valcartier (DREV). The research support of Canadian Forces remote sensing work in early 1971 will continue in 1972 and will be extended to include sideways-looking airborne radar. This sensor will become operational in early 1972.

Arctic Acoustics

The gathering of acoustic data in northeastern Arctic waters continued in 1971. Two DRB establishments, the Defence Research Establishment, Atlantic (DREA) and the Defence Research Establishment, Pacific (DREP) were involved. In late summer of 1971 scientists from DREP and DREO, together with those from the Ministry of Transport and the Department of the Environment, sailed aboard the CGS [Coast Guard Ship] *Louis St. Laurent* to Nares Strait where a number of acoustic and other parameters were measured. Acoustic propagation and bottom reflectivity were measured, and data on the water depth and structure (temperature, salinity and oxygen convent) were obtained, as were bottom cores. DREA's research ship CNAV *Quest* sailed as far north as 65°, gathering data on propagation and reverberation, while air-deployed modified sonobuoy were used farther north in Baffin Bay to gather similar data. The ambient noise and reverberation data obtained indicate interesting differences between this area and the open Atlantic. In 1972 *Quest* will go as far north as Smith Sound to check the results obtained by air-deployed sonobuoys using ship-deployed experimental systems that are not only quieter but have greater directivity. Also in early 1972 advantage will be taken of a winter cruise by CGS *Louis St.*

Laurent to the Smith Sound area to obtain under-ice environmental parameters....

Operational Research

Operational research projects in support of military operations saw continuing work on the New Viking detection experiments. Results so far indicate that surveillance flights in good visibility (to 15 nautical miles at 1,000 feet above ground level) may fail to detect a group of 30 men on foot. Detection ranges greater than one or two nautical miles appear very unlikely. However, in reconnaissance flights a creeping line-ahead search with 21/2 nautical mile spacings between legs should find this target. Short detection ranges can be expected, but again ranges greater than one or two nautical miles appear unlikely. During 1972 this work will continue, using a wider variety of spotting aircraft. The work has implications for search and rescue in the north. Other studies were on the financial and technical feasibility for Canada of using satellite surveillance in the Arctic, and an assessment of the possible uses of air lift in developing the north.

6-3. Department of National Defence. *Defence 1971*. Excerpts.

CANADIAN FORCES NORTHERN REGION

Canadian Forces Northern Region was formed on May 15, 1970, with a headquarters at Yellowknife and a headquarters detachment at Whitehorse. Thus 1971 marked the first full year of operations for the Region in the Canadian North.

On the Region's first anniversary, the Minister of National Defence dedicated the Headquarters' site as the Evans Block. It honours Lieutenant Colonel T. D. B. Evans, C.B., the commander of the Yukon Field Force, which in 1898, was the first Canadian military force to serve in the North.

The Canadian Rangers

The Canadian Rangers are direct successors to the Pacific Coast Militia Rangers of the Second World War which were formed in 1942 as a body of coast watchers, aircraft spotters and local defence forces along the British Columbia coast and up to the Yukon. They were expanded in the post war period, reaching a peak strength of approximately 1,600 to include members in many remote areas of the North. The name was changed to the Canadian Rangers at that time.

Unpaid reserve militiamen, the Rangers know how to live, move, and work in their areas and their tasks include guiding regular force troops on exercises, and reporting coastal activities and aircraft in distress.

The Rangers were under the command of Mobile Command until April, 1971, when Maritime Command assumed responsibility for all Rangers in coastal areas, and Northern Region assumed command of the units in the Northwest Territories and the Yukon. At the same time, the Ranger units in northern Alberta, Saskatchewan, Quebec, and Ontario were made dormant.

With the introduction of more sophisticated means of detecting aircraft and improved communications, the need for the Rangers for these tasks has decreased in some areas and studies are now being conducted by Headquarters Maritime Command and Headquarters

Northern Region on how to reconstitute the Rangers to make the best use of their skills and knowledge.

As part of Northern Region's study, two Ranger field training exercises were conducted in 1971, one at the remote Arctic settlement of Holman Island on the west shore of Victoria Island and the other at Frobisher Bay in the eastern Arctic.

...

Assistance to Civil Authorities

On September 1, 1971, a forest fire threatened the safety of Pine Point, a settlement on the south shore of Great Slave Lake. The Commissioner of the Northwest Territories requested the assistance of the Canadian Forces. The Forces response was immediate and meaningful with elements of Mobile and Air Transport Commands, together with Northern Region, responding to the emergency call.

6-4. House of Commons Debates, 12 June 1972.

- Question No. 607 – Mr. [Paul] Yewchuck (Athabaska):

1. To date, what role has the Department of Defence played in the prevention and control of air, water and land pollution in the Arctic?

2. How many members of the armed forces are presently maintained in the Arctic for purposes of policing (a) the pollution-control zone (b) the new fisheries closing lines?

Hon. E.J. Benson (Minister of National Defence): 1. The Department of National Defence has been engaged actively in an anti-pollution campaign in the Arctic for the past several years. Most of the activities have been carried out with other federal departments who have jurisdiction in the area. The main pollution problem is litter and debris. In 1970, air support was provided to Department of Indian Affairs and Northern Development to carry out reconnaissance of four abandoned Distant Early sites. In 1971, this program was continued to include an additional 12 sites. The reconnaissance of the five remaining sites which are located on Baffin Island will be carried out during the summer of 1972. Air reserve squadrons have assisted in these reconnaissance and pollution survey missions. As a result of the findings from these reconnaissance flights, a clean-up of Stokes Point, [Yukon], is scheduled for July 1972. This will be a combined operation between DND and DIAND and will serve as a pilot project to determine the financial and manpower requirements for the clean up of the other sites. The Department of Environment is scheduled to carry out an inspection of selected active DEW line sites this summer to ascertain conditions at these locations. At Canadian Forces' Station Alert, a work party and a drum crusher will eliminate pollution from discarded oil drums. A sanitary landfill operation will also be put into operation to alleviate the solid waste disposal problem. Garbage emanating from exercises and maneuvers in the north is transported out for proper disposal.

2. No members of the Canadian Armed Forces are maintained in the Arctic for the specific purpose of policing (a) the pollution control zone,

and (b) the new fisheries closing line. However, Mobile Command long range patrol aircraft, when flying over the Arctic, report pollution and fishing control zone violations.

6-5. Department of National Defence. Submission for Inclusion in the Advisory Committee on Northern Development Annual Report, "Government Activities in the North – FY 1972/73." Excerpts.

CANADIAN ARMED FORCES

Review of 1972 Operations

Maritime Forces

As in 1971 Canada's northern waters and airspace were again the scene of considerable activity by Maritime Command. Activities included general sovereignty and surveillance flights, search and rescue missions, flights conducted in support of other government agencies, and training exercises.

Argus aircraft flew some 40 missions into the Arctic for a total of 1,681 flying hours, and Tracker aircraft flew a total of 415 hours. The Argus aircraft flew from northern bases at Frobisher Bay, Yellowknife, Inuvik and Thule while the Trackers operated from Goose Bay and Frobisher. Although the primary purpose of these flights was sovereignty protection and surveillance, many sorties were flown in support of other government departments. Examples of this support included ice reconnaissance, photographic missions, a search for Bowhead whales in the Beaufort Sea, and investigation and reporting of off-shore oil explorations and of oil drilling rigs on the archipelago. Also, scientists and observers from other government departments were frequently on board these aircraft to conduct special projects which were beneficial to both the Department of National Defence and to the government department in question.

In August 1972 units of Maritime Command deployed to the vicinity of Hudson Straight to conduct "Norploy 72". Participating units included HMC Ships *Protecteur*, *Fraser*, *Yukon*, *St Laurent* and *Onondaga*; Argus aircraft from VP 404;[51] and Tracker aircraft from VS

51 *Editors' note:* VP is a US/Canadian military designation applied to long range, land based, anti-submarine, maritime reconnaissance aircraft.

880.[52] The deployment included environmental training and tactical exercises en route to, and in Arctic waters; various scientific and biological experiments; the establishment of a significant Canadian Forces presence in the North; and visits to Arctic settlements. In the latter case, visits were made to Port Burwell, Lake Harbour, Cape Dorset, Koartac, and Wakeham Bay. Of particular interest was the support given to a scientific expedition from Acadia University. A scientific team was carried to and from the expedition site on Baffin Island by HMCS *Protecteur*. The team gathered scientific data which was later analyzed at the university.

Land Forces

The continuing series of sub-unit exercises, called "New Viking" has gone on throughout the year. These exercises are designed to prepare ground forces for surviving and fighting in arctic conditions, summer and winter. Apart from providing an almost continuous military presence in the North, these exercises had, by the end of 1972, familiarized more than 4,000 officers and men with the geography, terrain, climate and operating difficulties of Canada's Arctic North. Two "senior officers" serials held each year ensure that staff officers of all three environments land, air and sea, are personally aware of the problems.

... The Canadian Forces continued construction of northern airfields. This joint DIAND/DND-funded program began in 1969 and will continue through until 1976. Engineers from 1 Construction Engineering Unit in Winnipeg provide planning support, supervision and some workers for the project. Local labour is used wherever possible at each site. In 1972 these 1 CEU personnel, augmented by engineers from various bases throughout Canada, completed construction of a 2,600-foot runway in Pangnirtung, on Baffin Island in the NWT. Field Engineers from 1 Airborne Field Squadron in Edmonton carried out runway construction at Whale Cove and Cape Dorset. These airstrips

52 Editors' note: VS is a US/Canadian military designation referring to a Navy Air anti-submarine squadron. VS 880 was shore-based at RCN Air Station Shearwater and continued to fly ASW, pollution, surveillance and fishery patrol operations until it was redesignated as a maritime reconnaissance unit in 1975. Colonel (Ret'd) D.H. Tate, Canadian Aviation Museum Aircraft: Grumann CS2F/CP-121 Tracker," http://www.aviation.technomuses.ca/assets/pdf/e_GrummanCS2F-CP121Tracker.pdf.

will be 4,000 feet long and are scheduled for completion in 1973 and summer 1976 respectively.

Planning began for the construction of a 300-foot single span bridge at Mile 237 of the Dempster Highway in the Yukon. A reconnaissance party inspected the site in September. This project is funded by DIAND, designed by DPW, and will be constructed by Canadian Forces Military Engineers.

A field survey by the Canadian Forces Mapping and Charting Establishment established mapping control for 120 map sheets around the following areas on Baffin Island, NWT: Igloolik, Cape Christian, Pangnirtung, Cape Dyer, Longstaff Bluff, Dewar Lakes, Broughton Island, Cape Hooper. The field party consisted of 13 people and was supported by two light helicopters.

As part of a joint Canada-US project to improve survey techniques, the Mapping and Charting Establishment also manned a satellite observation station at Frobisher Bay between October 1971 and March 1972.

The Canadian Rangers continued to be available for military functions such as land and coastal surveillance, to collect detailed information, to help in search and rescue missions, and particularly to provide experienced guides to other elements of the Canadian Forces when operating in the North. The recent study on the Canadian Rangers confirmed a continuing need for this force but recommended that, in the light of present conditions, change should be made to increase the effectiveness of the individual ranger. Proposals for reconstitution are being prepared for Government approval. Northern Region Headquarters continued its field training exercises for rangers, and it is expected that the results will be used to help shape future training.

Air Forces

Air Transport Command activity in the North was essentially the same as that for 1971. C130E Hercules aircraft provide weekly air service to the Canadian Forces communications stations at Alert and Inuvik and the Northern Region Headquarters at Yellowknife.

Hercules aircraft of Air Transport Command also provide airlift for the annual supply of Alert, during which a total of 193 loads of fuel oil and general cargo were flown in, the flights staging through Thule.

The Twin Otter detachment at Northern Region Headquarters, Yellowknife has proved essential to improved communications for Canadian Forces in the North and adds greatly to understanding the work of Canada's armed forces in the North. The two aircraft are also an essential adjunct to the Canadian Forces search and rescue capability in the North.

Search and Rescue (SAR) for the whole of Canada is divided into four search and rescue regions (SRRs). Each region contains large areas that extend above 60° North.

Administrative control of the primary search and rescue resources in each SRR is the responsibility of Air Transport Command, but operational control is shared by both Maritime Commands and Air Transport Command.

The SAR organization conducted 107 searches for missing aircraft in Canada. There were six major searches conducted above 60° North which took over 3,100 hours of flying. Of these only one missing aircraft, with two persons on board, was not located.

One again CF5 tactical fighter aircraft of 433e Escadrille Tactique de Combat, Bagotville, Quebec, flew Arctic exercise missions from Frobisher Bay during January and February. Aircraft of 434 Squadron, Cold Lake, Alberta, also participated in northern training, including tactical photographic reconnaissance on behalf of other government departments.

Providing a long-term military presence in the Arctic, the DEW Line consists of four main and 17 auxiliary radar sites which are, strung across the Canadian Arctic from Cape Dyer in the east to Komakuk Beach near the Alaskan border.

The Air Reserves from 402 Squadron, Winnipeg, and 418 Squadron, Edmonton, took part in several pollution surveys, as well as the charting of small settlements and Arctic airstrips. In an exercise termed "Flight North of the Ancient Bird", two Otter aircraft of 411 Squadron, Toronto, flew to Eureka on Ellesmere Island in mid-July. This marked the first time the Air Reserve had operated this far north.

PLANS FOR 1973

Maritime Forces

Plans call for continuing the annual exercise in northern waters. Again, participating units will include surface and sub-surface ships, and VP and VS aircraft of the Maritime Command. Northern patrols will continue at a rate similar to 1972. Consistent with the primary tasks and resources now assigned, support will continue to be given to other federal departments and agencies to the greatest extent possible.

Land Forces

The New Viking series of exercises will continue. In addition several major environmental training exercises will be conducted out of Churchill and Resolute Bay.

Construction of the airfields at Whale Cove and Cape Dorset will resume in early June. A 4,000-foot strip will be started in June at Pond Inlet. Whale Cove will be finished in late August, and at that time men and material will be moved to Eskimo Point to begin construction on another 4,000-foot airstrip.

Air Forces

Hercules aircraft will continue to fly regularly to Alert and Inuvik and Hercules and Buffalo aircraft will be used extensively in support of environmental training of land forces. Two Twin Otter aircraft will continue to be flown from Yellowknife to serve Northern Region Headquarters.

Air Reserve Squadron Otter aircraft will conduct settlement and airfield surveys in the Arctic during the period mid-May to mid-June 1973.

DEFENCE RESEARCH BOARD

Review of 1972 Operations

...

Studies continued on the movement of sea ice in channels of strategic-economic interest, and data were obtained on the movement of large ice floes through Robeson Channel. The floes were followed by tracking signals from radar transponders set out on the floes. The transponders were part of an instrument package containing a recording anemometer and sometimes a watercurrent meter to record driving forces in the environment. The data are being analyzed, but some tracks were plotted by direct readout. The data showed a steady net down-channel movement reflecting the net down-channel current and the fact that winds were either also in this direction or of very low velocity most of the time. Water-current direction is influenced by semi-diurnal tides and this effect could be seen in the ice floe tracks. On one occasion, with high southeasterly up-channel winds, the ice changed direction to a course 90° to the down-channel axis and then to an up-channel course. The fastest floe tracked moved down channel at two knots.

Radarscope photography of the ice in Nares Strait continued during reconnaissance flights. Consolidation of ice occurred a month earlier than in the previous year. Successive observation trips showed the persistence of gross features in the ice into spring....

The possible long-term effects of environmental conditions such as climate changes on the mobility of Canadian Forces in the Arctic have been investigated by monitoring the interaction between climate and large permanent and semi-permanent ice masses in Ellesmere. A traverse was made of two small ice caps at Lincoln Bay which had been covered with a dust layer at the point of their minimum retreat in 1959. The accumulation and changes since then could be caused by a mean summer cooling of 1.5°C.

Investigation of ice drift will continue in 1973 with the gathering of further field data and the analysis of present data, and a start will be made on setting up a predictive model relating drift to the environmental driving forces. Monitoring of the equilibrium between ice masses and climate will continue at a low level on the basis of opportunity, and considerable extra direction will be given to vehicle mobility studies, particularly the problem of terrain classification.

Arctic acoustics

The main feature of DRB's investigation of acoustic propagation in the Arctic and the factors interfering with, or degrading, the signal return was the cruise of CNAV *Quest* as far north as Thule. The exercise kept the ship north of the Arctic Circle from 22 August to 19 September and involved Canadian Forces Argus aircraft and the *USNS Sands*, the latter co-operating under the direction of the US Naval Underwater Systems Centre. The objectives of the first phase of the *Quest* cruise to 8 September were to measure ambient sea noise, its level and direction in the Labrador Sea, Davis Strait and Baffin Bay, and to determine the propagating conditions of low-frequency sound in these same areas. The first part of this phase was a follow up on 1971 work that used air-dropped sonobuoys, with quieter, more directional ship deployed systems. A by-product of the acoustics work was the oceanographic data from the large number of bathy-thermograph records down to 2,500 ft. taken along track. For the second phase of the *Quest* cruise a crew change occurred at Thule and from 8 to 19 September the ship on her trip south performed experiments with an experimental automated active sonar aimed at determining bottom, surface and volume reverberation, and back-scatter from ice and icebergs. The strengths of deep scattering layers were measured using a downward directional cone receiver and explosive sound sources.

Other acoustic work consisted of measurements on under-ice noise and measurements of ice and iceberg noises during exercise NORPLOY 72.

Plans for 1973 include continued acoustics work using air and surface platforms and bottom-mounted recording packages left for periods up to one year in channels of interest.

Remote sensing

DRB support to the Canadian Forces sensor evaluation program has continued with in-house and field experiments. The latter included a multi-sensor trial over a flight line from Kingston through Ottawa to Mont Tremblant with short extra legs over Montreal and the St. Lawrence Seaway. Sensors included two infrared line scanners, one with high thermal resolution and one with high spatial resolution, one real aperture sideways-looking airborne radar and one with synthetic aperture, and finally a high-resolution camera. Ground support for these exercises was provided by a number of co-operating universities and interpretation has included these plus other government departments. Both winter and summer imagery was taken and the purpose of the work was to build up a library of characteristic imagery that would help in the assessment of arctic imagery.

Other measurements were made at Resolute using a two-dimensional scanning infrared "camera" to determine the contrast between possible targets and arctic backgrounds as well as to determine effects of the atmospheric path on transmission.

Plans for 1973 call for increased work to determine the effects of snow, blowing snow and ice crystals on infrared transmission as it affects remote sensing coupled with sensor exercise in the north.

Operational research

Operational research on a replacement for the current surveillance platforms used in gathering data in the North continued, along with studies of military operations in the Canadian Arctic. A study of search and rescue operations was begun with the convening of a conference to discuss problems. Some of the immediate tasks are to analyse statistical data to determine the effectiveness of the emergency locating transmitter (ELT) and the cost of operating the present search and rescue system. It is expected that effort on both problems will receive special attention in 1973.

6-6. Department of National Defence. *Defence 1972*. Excerpts.

MOBILE COMMAND

The largest command in the Canadian Forces, Mobile Command had a military strength in 1972 of approximately 20,000 regular force and 16,500 reserve personnel consisting of 15,775 Militia and 725 Air Reserves.

...

Exercises and Training

Mobile Command's exercise program in 1972 continued at a high level of intensity with troops being exposed to a wide range of climatic and topographical conditions, and operational tasks.

...

To exercise Canadian sovereignty and to familiarize the maximum number of troops with the problems of living, moving and fighting in the North, exercise New Viking continued to be the Command's most

New all-terrain vehicles and an artillery piece are tested in the Arctic during Patrouille Nocturne 1972. Frobisher Bay, 9 February 1972. (LAC)

important northern exercise. From advanced bases in Churchill and Resolute Bay, groups of 100 men were successively deployed during the year to forward patrol bases in all parts of the Canadian Archipelago. By the end of 1972, some 4,000 officers and men had taken part in the exercise.

In 1972, the Command also conducted two major group exercises in the North. Exercise Patrouille Nocturne was a 5e Groupement de Combat exercise in Frobisher Bay, running from mid-January to mid-February, and exercise Northern Ramble saw a 1 RCR battalion group with supporting arms and services operating in Churchill during May. Both of these exercises were supported by CF-5 aircraft and CH-135 helicopters from elements of 10 Tactical Air Group.

…

TRAINING COMMAND

Training Arctic personnel

During the year the Command provided "home-handiman" training in conjunction with Maritime Command for 12 students from Northern Canada, at the request of the Department of Indian Affairs and Northern Development.

…

CANADIAN FORCES NORTHERN REGION

Canadian Forces Northern Region, with headquarters at Yellowknife and a headquarters detachment at Whitehorse, also saw an increase in 1972 in Canadian Forces activities, and an expansion of the headquarters staff. The present strength of the headquarters, including supporting air and communications elements, is approximately 90.

…

Assistance to Civil Authorities

Throughout the year, the Canadian Forces maintained readiness to assist civil authorities in emergency situations. For example, as a result of the severe flood threat to a number of communities in the Mackenzie

River valley during the spring of 1972, Northern Region Headquarters was advised by the Commissioner of the Northwest Territories that Forces assistance could be required. Contingency plans were prepared and were co-ordinated with other commands. Fortunately, the weather "cooperated" and while flooding did occur, it was not serious enough for the Forces to be called in to assist.

Search and Rescue

Air Transport Command has the primary responsibility for Search and Rescue throughout the nation. Northern Region supports these operations in the Northwest Territories and Yukon, maintaining a secondary capability both in terms of trained personnel and of aircraft. In 1970, there were 26 Search and Rescue incidents in the North; in 1971 there were 54; and, by November, 1972, the number of incidents for the year had risen to 72 and involved 2738 flying hours. In addition, Northern Region has met Royal Canadian Mounted Police requests for assistance in ground searches.

…

Northern Training

It was a busy year for northern training. Elements from Mobile Command, principally from 5ième Groupement de Combat, took part in Exercise Patrouille Nocturne at Frobisher Bay in January and February. Approximately 1,400 troops participated in this exercise.

An essential ingredient of all northern training is the long-range mobility provided by Air Transport Command, whose Hercules, Buffalo, Cosmopolitan and Twin Otter aircraft are a familiar sight in northern settlements.

During May, 1972, elements of 743 Communications Squadron from CFB Penfold, Alta., conducted a long-range communications exercise to train its personnel in northern communities.

Four ships from Maritime Command came North in August for Norploy 72. In addition to training in northern waters the ships paid port visits to Lake Harbour, Cape Dorset and Port Burwell. During the course of the port visits, personnel from the ships performed a number of valuable community assistance projects.

As elsewhere in Canada, the cadet movement plays an important role in the North in citizenship, leadership and physical fitness. However, the movement has a more significant part to play in the Northern Region because of the limited availability of such youth activities in this developing part of the country.

With the wholehearted support of leaders in territorial governments and communities, the number of cadet units in the North is growing.

To the eight cadet units in the north at the beginning of the year, two new units were added in October, and another two are in the formative stage, giving a 50% increase for 1972.

A number of public service activities gave the cadets an increased sense of purpose, and better training opportunities for the individuals. For instance, cadet units have provided communications and safety organizations for major northern sports events and, in one cross-country ski meet, were credited with saving a contestant who had fallen out. A number of cadets, from various communities, participated in the work to mark the site of Yukon Field Force operations (1898-1900) at the abandoned Fort Selkirk and at Dawson City so that visitors will be aware of the accomplishments of this pioneer Canadian formation, and so that the lives lost on active service will be remembered.

Plans are being made for a regional cadet camp in the Yukon in 1973, which will see cadets from all parts of both Territories working and training together.

6-7. House of Commons Debates, 15 October 1973.

NATIONAL DEFENCE - MARITIME COMMAND, OPERATION ABOVE 60 DEGREES OF UNDERWATER VESSELS

Question No. 2,333 – Mr. [Michael] Forrestall (Halifax)
1. What are the specific plans for developing an underwater capability for Maritime Command, north of 60 degrees parallel?
2. On what date can these plans be expected to be in operational phase, or when will the first of any new series of underwater vessels be put into service?

Hon. James Richardson (Minister of National Defence): 1 and 2. Maritime Command submarines now operate in some waters north of 60 degrees north latitude during certain times of the year. Whether or not this underwater capability will be enhanced or expanded is dependent upon staff studies now in progress.

NATIONAL DEFENCE – SURFACE AND AIR CAPABILITY NORTH OF 60 DEGREE LATITUDE

Question 2,334 – Mr. Forrestall:
1. What are the specific plans for developing a surface capability for Maritime Command, exclusive of aerial reconnaissance, north of 60 degrees parallel?
2. On what date can these plans be expected to be put into operational phase, or when will the first surface vessel be in service?

Hon. James Richardson (Minister of National Defence): 1 and 2. Maritime Command surface ships now operate in some waters north of 60 degrees north latitude during certain times of the year. Whether or not this surface capability will be enhanced or expanded is dependent upon staff studies now in progress.

NATIONAL DEFENCE – MARITIME COMMAND CAPABILITY NORTH OF 60 DEGREES PARALLEL

Question No. 2,336 – Mr. Forrestall:

1. Is consideration being given to Maritime Command capability north of 60 degrees parallel and, if so, in what substantive form?
2. If there is a present capacity, what is it, exclusive of Canadian Coast Guard capability…?
3. If there is no existing capability for operations north of 60 degrees parallel, for what reason?

Hon. James Richardson (Minister of National Defence): 1. As a result of the guidelines set forth in "Defence in the 70's," Canada's military maritime requirements are under review to ensure that the Maritime Command has the capability to meet is assigned roles.

2. Ships of Maritime Command are capable of operating north of 60 degree north latitude during certain times of the year, aircraft at all times.
3. Not applicable.

6-8. Department of National Defence. Submission for Inclusion in the Advisory Committee on Northern Development Annual Report, "Government Activities in the North – FY 1973/74." Excerpts.

CANADIAN ARMED FORCES

. . .

Policy and Plans

To meet these objectives as they apply to Canada's North the Department of National Defence is following the policy developed some years ago of equipping its Forces so far as is practical with materiel suitable for Arctic conditions and then training and using these Forces in actual Northern operations. To this end plans call for several different types of activities to be carried out each year:

- Regular surveillance of Northern land, sea and air space.
- Northern deployments and exercises for land force units including airborne components.
- Training cruises to Northern waters for ships and submarines of Maritime Command.
- Air transport and search and rescue missions in the North.
- Assistance in Northern engineering projects such as the building and improvement of Northern airstrips.

In addition to these activities the Department recruits Northern peoples for the Armed Forces and provides specialized education and training programmes whenever required. Present policy also calls for a continuing review of all of these programmes and activities and the introduction of additional ones wherever warranted. Northern Region Headquarters at Yellowknife plays an important role in co-ordinating Northern operations and collecting information on Northern requirements which Canadian Forces might fulfill.

Maritime Forces

As in previous years, Maritime Forces maintained a significant presence in Canada's Arctic. Activities included sovereignty and surveillance flights, the deployment of ships into Arctic waters, search and rescue flights, flights in support of other government agencies, and training exercises. A permanent detachment has been established at Frobisher Bay to support increasing Maritime Command activity above 60 degrees North.

Argus aircraft maintained a minimum schedule of three 45-hour patrols per month, operating from bases at Frobisher Bay, Edmonton, Yellowknife, Goose Bay, Inuvik and Thule, Greenland. Approximately 1700 hours were flown by Argus operating in the Arctic. Tracker aircraft, reduced in numbers and role, flew approximately 300 hours from Goose Bay and Frobisher. Although the primary purpose of Argus and Tracker flights was sovereignty protection and surveillance, many were flown in support of other government agencies. During the ice-season all northern patrols carried MOT ice observers and conducted ice reconnaissance as a secondary task. Patrols were also assigned photographic tasks on behalf of DIAND, [the Department of the Environment] and EMR, particularly the investigation of off-shore oil exploration and drilling activity on the archipelago. Scientists and observers from other government departments were frequently carried, conducting such activities as investigation of seabird populations in the Beaufort Sea, and ice research along Arctic shores. Maritime Forces also conducted extensive remote sensing trials in the Arctic. Much of the work done was in support of other government agencies.

In August, 1973 HMCS *Protecteur* deployed for six weeks into Arctic waters to conduct exercise "NORPLOY 73." Argus, Trackers and Sea King helicopters operated in concert with *Protecteur* throughout the deployment. Northern deployments are tasked to conduct surveillance, scientific and communications trials, to assist in the replenishment of remote settlements, and to conduct special projects. Visits were made to Resolute Bay, Rae Point, Dundas Harbour Grise Fiord, Pond Inlet, Cape Christian, Broughton Island, Cape Dyer, Payne Bay, Pangnirtung, Port Burwell and Frobisher Bay. In addition to scientists from DREO, DREA and [the Canadian Research Council], a scientific team from Acadia University accompanied HMCS *Protecteur*.

Land Forces

The continuing series of sub-unit exercises, called "New Viking" have gone on throughout the year. These exercises are designed to prepare ground forces for surviving and fighting in arctic conditions, summer and winter. Apart from providing an almost continuous military presence in the North, these exercises had, by the end of 1973, familiarized more than 5,400 officers with the geography, terrain, climate and operating difficulties of Canada's Arctic North....

... A large scale Northern exercise was Exercise Rapier Thrust, a 1 Combat Group exercise conducted in winter conditions in the Fort Churchill area in January 1974. Units from as far apart as Victoria, BC, Calgary, Alberta, and Winnipeg, Manitoba participated.

A field survey party from the Canadian Forces Mapping and Charting Establishment provided control for 118 sheets of 1:50,000 scale mapping covering the following: District of Franklin - parts of Cornwallis and Bathurst Islands; District of Keewatin - areas surrounding Shepherd Bay, Spence Bay and Pelly Bay. The field party consisted of twelve surveyors supported by two CH135 helicopters from 540 Squadron and one CH135 helicopter from 408 Squadron.

The Canadian Rangers continued to be available on a limited basis for functions such as coastal surveillance, to provide information and to help in search and rescue missions. No emphasis has been placed on recruiting of Rangers during the year 1973. The continuing role of the Canadian Rangers is now under active study as part of the Land Forces Policy Review.

Work on the northern airfield. construction program continued this year at three sites: Whale Cove, Cape Dorset and Pond Inlet. This program, which began in 1969, is jointly funded by DIAND and DND. 1 Construction Engineering Unit in Winnipeg provided the Arctic Airfield Operations Centre responsible for technical and logistical support and personnel administration. Weekly airlift support was provided by Air Transport Command Buffalo flights after heavy loads had been prepositioned at Churchill and Frobisher Bay by CC130 Hercules. 1 Airborne Field Squadron from Edmonton completed construction of the 4,400 by 300 foot gravel strip at Whale Cove after two and a half seasons of long hours. 3 Field Squadron from Chilliwack carried on with drilling and blasting at Cape Dorset and after two years operation have completed about 50% of the task. The Pond Inlet airfield was started this year by 2 Field Squadron from Gagetown and is about 20% complete.

Planning continued for the construction of the 300 foot single span bridge over the Eagle River at Mile 237 of the Dempster Highway in the Yukon. This joint DIAND/[Department of Public Works]/DND project to be constructed by Military Engineers is scheduled for completion by the winter of 1975/76.

Air Forces

Air Transport Command activity in the North was essentially the same as that for 1972.

… During the annual Boxtop airlifts Hercules aircraft of Air Transport Command transported a total of 206 loads of fuel oil and general cargo from Thule to Alert.

The 440 Squadron Twin Otter detachment at Northern Region Headquarters Yellowknife continued to provide a service necessary for Canadian Forces communications in the North. The two aircraft again provided a valuable addition to the Canadian Forces northern search and rescue capability.

The Search and Rescue organization conducted 109 searches for missing aircraft in Canada. There were 26 major searches conducted below 60°N which consumed 7446 hours of flying time and five major searches above 60°N which consumed 536 hours of flying time. Of these 31 searches only five aircraft with a total of seven persons on board were not located.

CF5 tactical fighter aircraft of 433e Escadrille tactique de combat, Bagotville, Quebec and 434 Tactical Fighter (Operational Training) Squadron, Cold Lake, Alberta, flew a variety of tactical support missions from northern airfields. These included Goose Bay, Labrador; Churchill, Manitoba; Fort St. John, B.C.; and Whitehorse, N.W.T.

Providing a long term military presence in the Arctic, the DEW Line consists of our main and 17 auxiliary radar sites which are strung across the Canadian Arctic from Cape Dyer in the east to Komakuk Beach near the Alaskan border.

DEPARTMENTAL OBJECTIVES – NATIONAL DEVELOPMENT

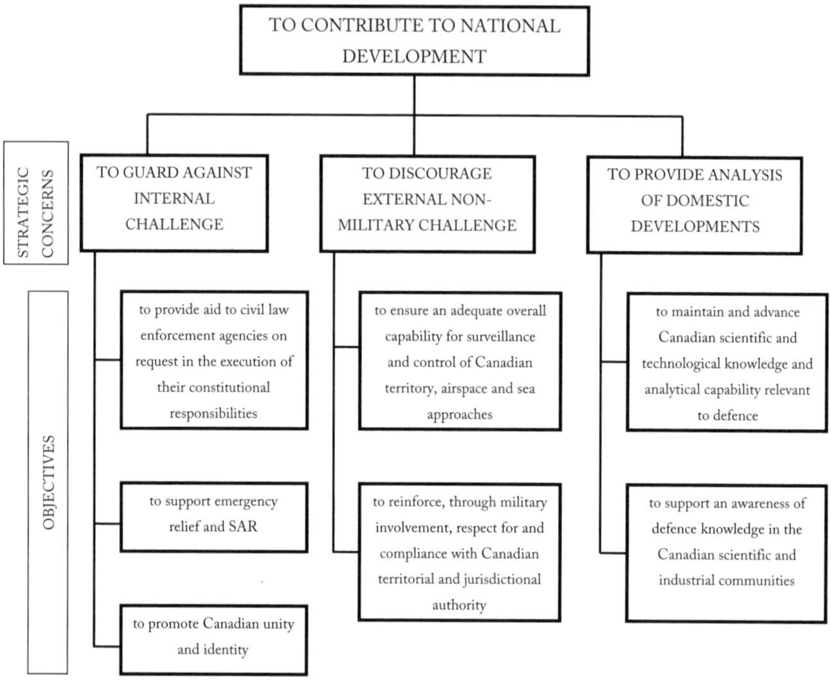

Air Reserve Otter aircraft from 400 Squadron and 411 Squadron, Toronto flew settlement and airfield surveys from Churchill to the eastern Arctic. The western Arctic support was provided by 418 Squadron, Edmonton, for exercise "WAMMOK MAKER 3" in the Fort Selkirk area. Flights were also conducted at Whitehorse in support of air cadet familiarization flying program.

PLANS FOR 1974/75

Maritime Forces

Plans call for maintenance of the present level of air and surface activity, consistent with the primary tasks and resource assigned to Maritime Command. In addition to the regularly scheduled NORPLOY by a fleet replenishment vessel, a surface group of two destroyers will join her to exercise in Hudson Bay for two weeks in August. Support to other government agencies will be increased, consistent with increasing demands for information about, and surveillance of, the Arctic.

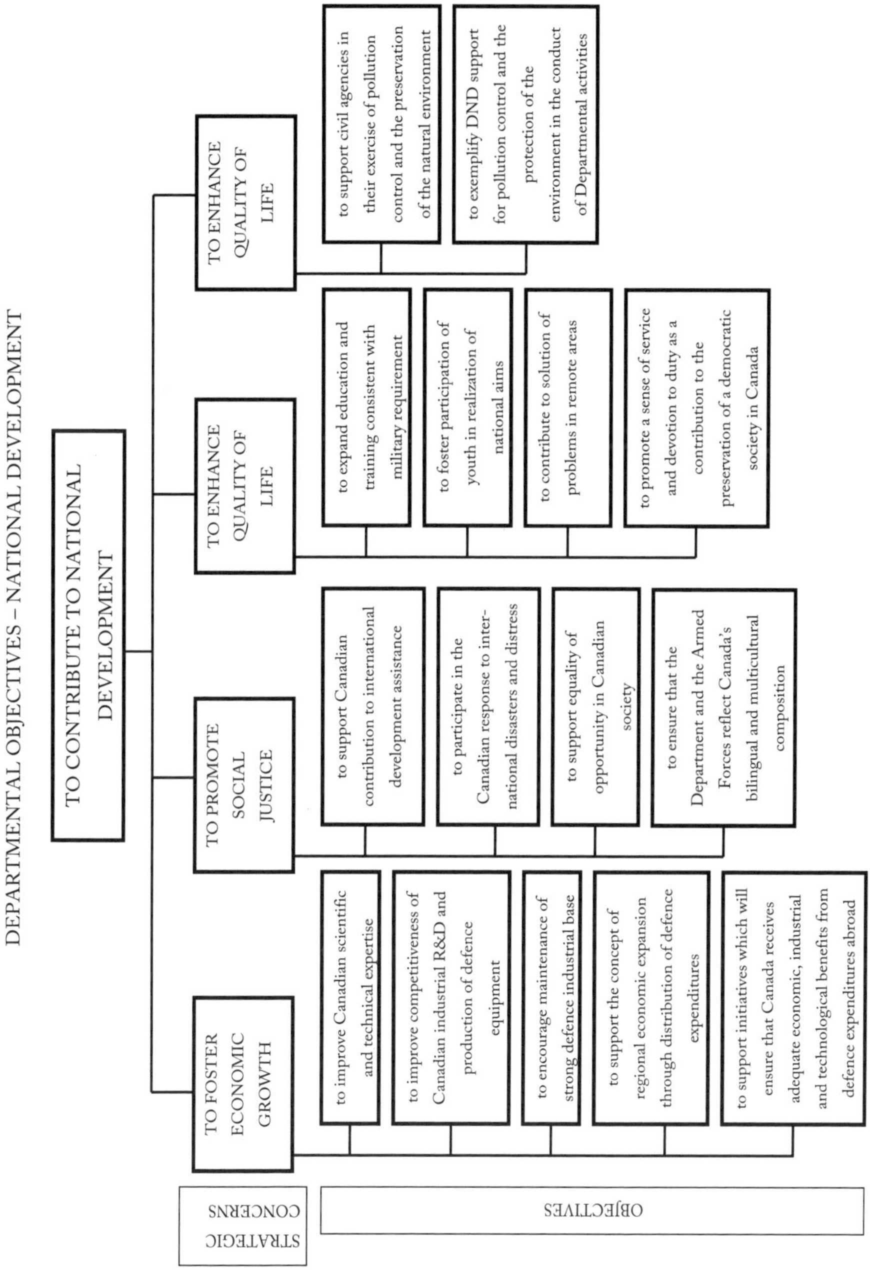
DEPARTMENTAL OBJECTIVES – NATIONAL DEVELOPMENT
TO CONTRIBUTE TO NATIONAL DEVELOPMENT
STRATEGIC CONCERNS
OBJECTIVES
TO FOSTER ECONOMIC GROWTH
to improve Canadian scientific and technical expertise
to improve competitiveness of Canadian industrial R&D and production of defence equipment
to encourage maintenance of strong defence industrial base
to support the concept of regional economic expansion through distribution of defence expenditures
to support initiatives which will ensure that Canada receives adequate economic, industrial and technological benefits from defence expenditures abroad
TO PROMOTE SOCIAL JUSTICE
to support Canadian contribution to international development assistance
to participate in the Canadian response to international disasters and distress
to support equality of opportunity in Canadian society
to ensure that the Department and the Armed Forces reflect Canada's bilingual and multicultural composition
TO ENHANCE QUALITY OF LIFE
to expand education and training consistent with military requirement
to foster participation of youth in realization of national aims
to contribute to solution of problems in remote areas
to promote a sense of service and devotion to duty as a contribution to the preservation of a democratic society in Canada
TO ENHANCE QUALITY OF LIFE
to support civil agencies in their exercise of pollution control and the preservation of the natural environment
to exemplify DND support for pollution control and the protection of the environment in the conduct of Departmental activities

Land Forces

The New Viking series of exercises will continue. In addition a series of no-notice exercises - QUICK VIKING - will also be run. The location for these exercises is also expected to be Fort Churchill.

Exercise READY NOW III will be a Canadian Airborne Regiment exercise, taking place in May 1974, in which the Regiment will deploy on austere summer scales along the Alaska highway.

Exercise PATROUILLE NOCTURNE II will be a 5e Groupement de Combat winter exercise in the Fort Churchill area in February 1975. The Canadian Airborne Regiment and the 1st Canadian Signals Regiment will also take part in this exercise.

As announced by the Minister of National Defence, Canadian Forces Station Churchill will be activated on 1 April 1974. This Station will be the Northern Training Centre for the Canadian Forces. Although the defence facilities will be located in the former military encampment, all permanent residences will be located in the Town of Churchill as part of the Federal-Provincial construction program. The Northern Training Centre will be responsible for conducting the New Viking series of arctic training exercises and instructor courses, as well as providing support for major exercises involving the land forces and tactical air elements.

Canadian Forces personnel pose in front of the igloo they constructed. March 1971. (LAC)

In June, airfield construction will resume at Cape Dorset and Pond Inlet, and a 4,000 foot strip will be started at Eskimo Point. Completion of these tasks is scheduled for 1975. Work on the Eagle River Bridge will commence late in the year.

Air Forces

Hercules aircraft will continue to provide regularly scheduled service to Alert, Inuvik and Yellowknife. Buffalo aircraft will be used during the spring, summer and early fall to provide support for the northern airfield construction program. The two Twin Otters at Yellowknife will continue to provide essential service to Northern Region Headquarters.

CF5 tactical fighters of 10 Tactical Air Group will fly operational training missions including photographic reconnaissance from several northern airfields in support of land force exercises.

Air Reserve Otter aircraft will continue to conduct settlement and airfield surveys in the Arctic. Whitehorse and Yellowknife will see reserve aircraft supporting the National Cadet Camp this summer. Numerous flights will be necessary for cadet field training which includes parachute drops of supplies and air reconnaissance missions.

6-9. Department of National Defence. *Defence 1973*. Excerpts.

CANADIAN FORCES NORTHERN REGION

Canadian Forces Northern Region (CFNR) covering 1.5 million square miles, or 40 per cent of Canada, has its headquarters in Yellowknife and a small detachment in Whitehorse. CFNR has a strength of 47 military personnel, which includes a detachment from 440 Transport and Rescue Squadron, Edmonton, for two Twin Otter aircraft, and detachments from the Canadian Forces Communication Command. Also, there are 43 civilian employees.

In addition to command of assigned forces and particular operations in the north, the Commander's main responsibilities are to:

- maintain liaison with the governments of the Yukon and Northwest Territories' and federal and civil agencies;
- prepare and execute plans for aid of the civil power and assistance to civil authorities;
- support search and rescue operations;
- train and administer cadets in the north;
- collect, collate and disseminate information on the north to support CF operations;
- support other Commands operating in the north;
- maintain liaison with Commander, U.S. Forces, Alaska Command, Canadian commanders at main DEW Line sites, and commanding officers of CFS [Canadian Forces Station] Alert, CFS Inuvik and the Maritime Command Detachment at Frobisher.

Support to Other Commands

Much of CFNR's effort is expended by supporting other commands and the Defence Research Board in operations and exercises North of 60°. One example was the visit of HMCS *Protecteur* to the waters of the high Arctic during August and September. In advance of the visit, one of CFNR's Twin Otters made a comprehensive reconnaissance, including detailed visits to each settlement and community to be visited during the voyage. In addition, a data summary on settlement profiles, photos, communications and aircraft fuel caches were provided.

Northern Region operations staff and ship's underwater clearance divers conducted an underwater clearance investigation at Broughton Island, off the coast of Baffin Island.

Maritime Command is provided with support on a continuous basis in the planning and execution of northern aircraft patrols.

During the summer months, Canadian Forces Northern Region was closely associated with the northern activities of Air Reserve squadrons. Missions were flown to acquire and update information on settlements, exploration activity, wildlife activities, pollution control, and to take aerial photographs of settlements and resource development sites.

During September, in commemoration of the men who perished in a search and rescue Dakota aircraft crash in November, 1971, a memorial cairn was erected at the crash site, 25 miles south of Paulatuk, on the Western Arctic sea coast.

Canadian Forces Northern Region is supporting preliminary work of field engineers of Mobile Command for construction of the Eagle River bridge, on the Dempster Highway in the Yukon, as well as providing air transport. The bridge is an important link in the highway being built to connect Whitehorse, Y.T., with the Mackenzie Delta.

Mobile Command's Arctic airfield construction program, to build improved airstrips at six locations in the north, continued this year with support and liaison from Canadian Forces Northern Region.

Adventure Training

The many adventure training exercises North of 60° emphasized the unique and demanding challenges of Canada's north. One involved a winter overland transit, using light oversnow vehicles, from Tuktoyaktuk to Yellowknife, a distance of 1,240 miles. The journey, carried out by four NCOs serving in Yellowknife, provided a valuable test-bed for the forces advanced Arctic kit and DRB experimental equipment.

During the summer, adventure training exercises included a journey by canoe down the Burnside River, which flows from Contwoyto Lake across the tundra to Bathurst Inlet, on the Arctic Coast. The aim of this exercise was to improve canoeing skills, evaluate military equipment and supplies, and assess the suitability of the river and surrounding terrain for fitness training.

Exercise *Northern Quest* by the 1st Battalion, The Royal Canadian Regiment, traced some of the movements of the ill-fated Franklin expedition on King William Island.

Two other exercises involved boating down the Mackenzie River. Members of 1 Combat Group, in an exercise named *Northern Adventure*, journeyed by canoe from Fort Providence to Inuvik.

The second trip, named Operation *Arctic Whaler*, involved 12 members of the Naval Reserve in two naval whalers. They proceeded under sail from Yellowknife to the Beaufort Sea, and on to Tuktoyaktuk. From there they sailed back to Inuvik, a total distance of about 1,200 nautical miles. The exercise marked the 50th anniversary of the Naval Reserves.

Northern Region Headquarters also participated in many major Canadian Forces' operations. Exercise *WINTEX 73* provided a test of Canadian Forces Northern Region's ability to meet its role. The headquarters was able to assess the effectiveness of three years of careful planning and construction to meet continuing military requirements in this remote and harsh environment.

6-10. House of Commons Debates, 24 October 1974.

Mr. [W.J.] Kempling (Halton—Wentworth): Mr. Chairman, does the Department of National Defence intend to expand the role of our armed forces in northern Canada? I am particularly concerned about the north in view of the remarks the minister made about the environment, road building, and our position in northern Canada. I assume that the plan to procure tracked vehicles is part of an over-all plan to increase our presence in northern Canada. Would the minister comment on that?

The minister spoke about cutting $100 million from our defence budget. Last week, according to *Newsweek* magazine, we lent $100 million to Iran. That country, in turn, bought from the United States tremendous quantities of military hardware. It spent almost twice as much as we spent on our national defence budget. The people of Canada would have been served better if we had not lent Iran $100 million at 7 per cent but kept the money for our defence budget. That was only a comment. Would the minister care to speak to the northern aspect I mentioned earlier?

Mr. Richardson: Mr. Chairman, as I said in the statement I made at the beginning of our examination of my estimates, one of the important roles for the Canadian armed forces is that of participating in the opening of the Canadian north. We are proceeding with what we call the New Viking program, under which 125 men go north, live, and work under northern conditions, and test equipment. Within the last year we opened the Arctic training center at Churchill, Manitoba, and our forces will train there regularly from now onwards. May I mention that ships of the fleet sailed into Hudson Bay this summer for the first time on training exercises, demonstrating that Canada is not bounded by two oceans but by three oceans. We are doing a number of things, as I have mentioned, to make our presence felt in the north, and this, I believe, will increase rather than diminish as we proceed.

6-11. House of Commons Debates, 15 November 1974.

PROPOSAL TO ESTABLISH ARCTIC BASE – GOVERNMENT POSITION

Mr. Elmer M. Mackay (Central Nova): Mr. Speaker, my question is for the Minister of National Defence. In light of the avowed Canadian needs for policing and servicing in the Arctic both to protect our sovereignty and to foster economic development, can the minister tell the House whether he will study proposals for an Arctic Canadian base as proposed by the Naval Officers' Association of Canada?

Hon. James Richardson (Minister of National Defence): Yes, Mr. Speaker.

ADEQUACY OF ARMED FORCES TO PATROL COASTS AND PROTECT SOVEREIGNTY

Mr. Mackay: A supplementary question, Mr. Speaker. Does the minister still hold to his position, as stated in this chamber on November 13 in response to a question by the Leader of the Opposition, that the job of protecting Canadian sovereignty and coastal surveillance is being done adequately at the present time and does he plan to take action on the recommendation for nuclear submarines and icebreakers made by the Naval Officers' Association of Canada?

Hon. Mr. Richardson: Mr. Speaker, in response to the question of the Leader of the Opposition I stated that surveillance of our coasts was taking place. I did not at any time suggest that we could not continue to improve our capability. I have made it known that we are actively studying the acquisition of a new long range patrol aircraft which would greatly increase our capability to survey Canadian coastal waters.

6-12. House of Commons Debates, 19 November 1974.

NATIONAL DEFENCE – EFFECT OF FINANACIAL RESTRAINTS ON OPERATIONAL ROLES OF FORCES

Mr. J.P Nowlan (Annapolis Valley): Mr. Speaker, my question is directed to the Minister of Defence. In view of the increased emphasis on offshore resources, pollution off our coasts and a presence in the north, would the minister explain the rationale for the cutbacks in the operations of Maritime Command which have resulted in one flight every six months in the north, next to no effective coastal patrols, and no joint exercises with our NATO allies?

Hon. James Richardson (Minster of National Defence): Mr. Speaker, I have before me figures for the last month. There were 15 Argus flights in October and 12 Tracker flights. This amounted to 150 flying hours for the Argus and 67 flying hours for the Tracker. We have carried out more flights than this in other months, but these facts confirm that the surveillance flights are being flown on a regular and continuing basis.

Mr. Nowlan: A supplementary question, Mr. Speaker. Could the minister assure the House that the figures he has just read out are flights for training, which has top priority to keep men in a training stance so they can learn; and can the minister confirm that there has not been a flight to the north, about which we talk so much, and that none is intended until after this fiscal year?

To conclude this supplementary question, Mr. Speaker, can the minister tell the House what we are not doing now that we did do before the financial restraints of the minister cut back operations?

Hon. Mr. Richardson: Mr. Speaker, I think my previous answer indicated that surveillance flights are continuing. Some of them are training flights, but there are flights over the Atlantic. Flights to the north have been curtailed and no date has been set for the next flight to the north.

…

EFFECT OF FINANCIAL RESTRAINTS ON STRENGTH OF FORCES IN YUKON

Mr. Erik Nielsen (Yukon): Mr. Speaker, I have a supplementary question for the Minister. In view of the announced intention of the government regarding the cutbacks and the avowed policy of the government to establish and retain Canada's sovereignty in Canada's north through the presence of armed personnel there, is it also the intention of the government to cut back on the existing forces' strength in the Yukon, which is now five to cover 207,000 square miles of Canada's sovereign territory?

Hon. James Richardson (Minister of National Defence): No, Mr. Speaker. I would remind hon. members that the defence budget has not been cut; it has been increased by more than a quarter of a billion dollars this year over last year.

6-13. House of Commons Debates, 20 November 1974.

NATIONAL DEFENCE – POSSIBLE CHANGE IN PRIORITIES OF ROLES OF FORCES – ALLEGED LACK OF PATROLS IN ARCTIC

Mr. J.P Nowlan (Annapolis Valley): My question is directed to the Prime Minister. In light of the fact that the government's white paper on defence set as a top priority that there will be surveillance of our own territory and coastlines, and this was confirmed by the Minister of National Defence as recently as October 15 in the debate on the Speech from the Throne when he said:

> Our first task and our central responsibility are nothing less than to defend Canadian independence and sovereignty.

- can the Prime Minister tell the House whether the priorities in defence have changed in view of the admission by the Minister of National Defence yesterday that all coastal patrols on both the east and west coasts have been substantially reduced and at that time – meaning yesterday – there were no patrols in the Arctic and none contemplated? Can the Prime Minister answer the question keeping in mind that the other three priorities set out in the white paper, that is NATO, NORAD and peacekeeping, have had no cutbacks?

Rt.Hon. P.E Trudeau (Prime Minister): No, Mr. Speaker, the priorities have not changed. The government is doing the best it can within its budgetary limitations to fulfill these priorities in the order that had been stated by the minister.

Mr. Nowlan: Mr. Speaker, I should like to put my next question to the Prime Minister but I think I will put it to the Minister of National Defence. In the light of today's report that Soviet and American armed forces are encroaching on and over Canadian territory in the north, would the minister advise the House what action his department is taking to police, patrol and protect Canadian territory in the high Arctic? At the same time, and with your indulgence, Mr. Speaker, would he clarify the answer he gave to the hon. member for Esquimalt-Saanich when he said that there were flights in the north, having admitted yesterday that there were none and that none were contemplated?

Hon. James Richardson (Minister of National Defence): I did not say yesterday that no flights were contemplated. I said very clearly that patrols were continuing on a regular basis but at a reduced level. I said yesterday that I did not know the date of the next Arctic flight. I can report today that there will be flights next month and the following month. They are continuing on a reduced but regular basis into the high Arctic.

On the hon. member's question concerning the report this morning by the CBC, I can confirm to the House that to the best of my knowledge no Soviet aircraft are flying in Canadian air space or have been flying in Canadian air space.

Mr. Nowlan: Mr. Speaker, I will make this a very direct supplementary question. In view of the fact that there have been no Arctic flights of the Maritime Command either from Comox or any of the Maritime Command bases in Canada in September, or October or until this time in November and yet the Minister said yesterday, as recorded at age 1443 of *Hansard*:

> …no date has been set for the next flight to the north.

- how can the minister say with such assurance that in effect there is no encroachment either from the sky or from the water?

Hon. Mr. Richardson: The hon. member should know that it is not reconnaissance flights that identify foreign aircraft, but rather the radar screen and our interceptory aircraft, which are working at full capacity and have not been reduced in any way.

6-14. House of Commons Debates, 25 November 1974.

NATIONAL DEFENCE: SURVEILLANCE FLIGHTS IN THE ARCTIC – INADEQUACY OF FROBISHER BAY FACILITIES

...

Mr. J.P. Nowlan (Annapolis Valley): Mr. Speaker, my question is for the Minister of National Defence. Last week the minister announced the resumption of two flights in a six month period in the Arctic. Was he aware at that time that the necessary maintenance base at Frobisher Bay had been closed; the doors locked, telephones disconnected and the communications centre run down? Does the minister intend to service these two flights with existing resources or additional help?

Hon. James Richardson (Minister of National Defence): Mr. Speaker, I am glad to tell the hon. member that Canada has two coasts and that we can fly to the high Arctic from Comox without going near Frobisher Bay.

Mr. Nowlan: Mr. Speaker, I am fully aware that Canada has two coasts. I am concerned about this Minister of National Defence. What I am most apprehensive about is that this minister does not know anything about the armed services. He does not know we have three coasts, not two.

Some hon. Members: Hear, hear!

6-15. Department of National Defence, *Defence 1974*. Excerpts.

NATIONAL SUPPORT AND DEVELOPMENT

The Department's role in support of national aims was stated in the White Paper of 1971. Activities and contributions toward the achievement of these national aims have been outlined in annual defence reviews. Where skills, expertise and equipment have been required to serve national purposes, the Department has responded, while at the same time maintaining its readiness for the performance of purely military roles.

...

The Department continues to participate in programs designed to alleviate the social and economic problems of Canadians living north of the 60th parallel. Through representation on the Advisory Committee on Northern Development, and a number of related sub-committees, the Department plays an important role in recommending policy and co-ordinating activities in the North.

As part of the Armed Forces' continuing interest in the employment and training of northern natives, the Department has extended its support for, and will soon participate in, the Northern Career Program. This is a new concept to be administered by the Public Service Commission on behalf of the Department of Indian Affairs and Northern Development. It is designed to increase employment opportunities for native northerners in supervisory and middle-management positions within the federal public service.

In keeping with its policy to assist in the improvement of northern transportation, the Department of National Defence provided representation on the Steering Committee for implementation of policy on air transportation facilities and services for the Yukon and Northwest Territories. In support of this program, the Department is constructing six airstrips across the Canadian Arctic, two of which have been completed.

The Armed Forces in 1974 continued their long-standing involvement in northern survey activities. A major field survey operation was conducted on South Baffin Island to provide the necessary information for large scale topographical mapping.

...

CANADIAN FORCES NORTHERN REGION

Canadian Forces Northern Region (CFNR) ... has a strength of 63 military personnel, which includes a detachment from 440 Transport and Rescue Squadron, Edmonton, operating two Twin Otter aircraft, and a detachment from 742 Communications Squadron, Edmonton. CFNR also employs 17 civilian personnel.

...

CFNR Operations

CFNR participated in a major exercise, *Ready Now III*, with the Canadian Airborne Regiment. It was centered in the Whitehorse-Carcross area of the Yukon Territory and involved 1 Commando Group of that unit, along with elements of other Mobile Command units. CFNR provided liaison support to the exercise commander, and all operational message traffic was passed through the regional headquarters to Mobile Command.

In addition, Exercise *Tuktu Swift* involved CFNR in an emergency operations exercise with elements of the Northwest Territorial Government and other civil agencies. The scenario was designed to test the joint liaison and planning required for an emergency operation in the Northwest Territories.

Maritime Command made a significant deployment into the Arctic in August. CFNR provided liaison and northern information for the NORPLOY 74 squadron, which visited several settlements on the eastern Arctic coastline.

Throughout the year, Argus aircraft of Maritime Command conducted northern patrols, responding in part to CFNR tasking. These patrols involved systematic reconnaissance throughout the Arctic, providing data on northern airfields, resource exploration programs, ice conditions, settlement development programs and maritime shipping activities. The surveillance provided by these over-flights makes a significant

A LCVP (Landing Craft Vehicle, Personnel) pulls alongside a 'growler' in the Bay of Woe, Ellesmere Island. 29 August 1974. (LAC)

contribution to the establishment of a Canadian Forces presence in Canada's Arctic regions.

During the brief northern summer, 12 members of maritime reserve units made up two whaler crews that sailed from Yellowknife to Tuktoyaktuk on the Beaufort Sea. The two small craft sailed across Great Slave Lake, followed the Mackenzie River and reached their destination in just over a month, having travelled approximately 1,000 miles. CFNR provided liaison and support for this challenging adventure training exercise.

Divers from 1 Combat Group, Calgary, provided assistance to the government of the Yukon Territory in exploring the Yukon River for artifacts and conducting a reconnaissance at Herschel Island on the Beaufort Sea coast. It is planned to continue this exploration activity in 1975. CFNR provided support for this adventure training activity, carried out at the request of the commissioner of the Yukon Territory.

There was a large number of search and rescue missions within Northern Region during 1974. CFNR has established effective liaison with all Rescue Co-ordination Centres (RCCs) and provides support when required to assist the RCCs. 440 Squadron Detachment aircraft, based at Yellowknife, participated in several searches, and in two cases, utilizing a float-equipped Twin Otter aircraft, effected the rescue of survivors.

Cadet Activities

CFNR continued to direct and administer 12 cadet corps during 1974, and in November added a 13th cadet corps at Cambridge Bay to its roster. A large percentage of the cadets in Northern Regions are native Indian or Eskimo boys, who bring special skills and interests to the training programs.

Another major summer activity conducted in Northern Region is the operation of the annual National Cadet Camp at Whitehorse, Yukon Territory. Planning and administration for the camp is carried out by CFNR personnel, augmented by specialists from other commands and the cadet organizations. Support for the camp is also provided by CFB Edmonton - more than 1,000 miles away.

Several courses are conducted at the camp, one of which is the two-week introductory cadet course. This is a tri-service course, with cadets attending from all across the country. The two-week course takes full advantage of the surrounding countryside, concentrating on basic canoeing, mountaineering and bushcraft.

Canadian Rangers

Although it remains at a relatively low level, Canadian Ranger activity still generates considerable interest, particularly in the more remote communities.

Exercise *Nanook Ranger II*, conducted in the Yellowknife area in March and April, was designed to train selected Rangers to patrol-leader level. All trainees were Indian or Eskimo Rangers from the Arctic Bay, Holman Island, Lac La Martre and Detah Village patrols.

6-16. House of Commons Debates, 5 June 1975

Mr. H.A. Anderson (Comox-Alberni): …Unfortunately, this high cost of defence is something which is extremely difficult to justify to the public in times of peace. I am speaking of peace in our own area; we all know that somewhere or other wars have been going on for a generation or so. It is very hard for the military to justify the expenditure of many millions of dollars of the taxpayers' money even for such an object as the preservation of sovereignty in Canada. The Canadian people have shown in many ways that they want additional housing, improved Medicare benefits, and so on. All these things are important, of course, but as a member of the committee on defence I am conscious of a moral tug-of-war between the need for expenditure to protect sovereignty and the desirability of spending money in areas of social need.

Looking toward the Arctic, for instance, it is obvious we need to establish surveillance arrangements in this region, one which I regard as an increasingly important part of Canada. This is necessary if we are to claim sovereignty over the Arctic, but as I say, we are dealing with intangible propositions and it is not always easy to convince Canadians that the heavy expenditures are necessary. Nevertheless, it is surely our responsibility to see that a highly effective surveillance capacity exists and that measures can be taken to deal with aircraft entering our airspace. In opposition to the hon. member for Greenwood, I do not believe that Canada should abandon its role of establishing sovereignty over its airspace.

…

Mr. L.D. Hopkins (Renfrew North): During this debate on the Department of National Defence estimates, the question of the requirement to safeguard Canada's sovereign interests must be kept in the forefront of our deliberations. Of great interest in this respect is the government's current review of the need for a new long range patrol aircraft. I would like to comment briefly on this subject which will have such a major impact on DND expenditures.

The potential challenges to Canada's sovereignty and security take both non-military and military forms and arise principally from Canada's vast size and relatively small population, her abundance of natural resources, the length of her shores, the size of the water areas which are of direct concern to her and the fact that historically we have identified and allied ourselves politically and militarily with those nations that share our perceptions of individual freedom and justice and our way of life.

One important component of the military and civilian resources devoted to monitoring and defending against both military and non-military threats has been the Argus aircraft of Maritime Command of the Canadian forces.

The Argus was introduced into service in 1958 and was a good maritime patrol aircraft in its day; its equipment was among the best available at that time and its range made it possible to conduct long range patrols over the far reaches of the Atlantic and North Pacific Oceans. Over the years, more modern and effective surveillance equipment has been developed and the Argus is now limited in capability compared with other aircraft in this role. The capability of its surveillance devices is relatively limited, the aircraft is slow, and the long flight times required for patrols results in high crew fatigue because of noise and vibration. The aircraft engines, and installed equipment are getting old and are expensive to maintain. The standard fuel used by the aircraft is now available at only four locations in Canada.

Therefore, on the basis of the policy outlined in the government white paper "Defence in the Seventies," extensive studies of maritime force capabilities conducted within the Department of National Defence, and the fact that continued operation of the Argus was not effective, the Minister of National Defence obtained cabinet approval in May 1972, to examine in detail the possibility of obtaining suitable replacement aircraft. An interdepartmental office was established in September 1972 and initial studies were concluded with five aircraft companies, including Canadair.

Upon receipt and evaluation of the proposals received, it was recommended that studies be continued with the two most suitable contractors, Boeing and Lockheed, and cabinet agreed. The studies are in their final stage at this time and it is expected that a submission to cabinet will be made in the near future. It is now timely to review the challenges facing Canada which the government weigh in arriving at its final decision on the proposal.

With respect to the non-military challenges to Canadian sovereignty, of paramount interest is the ability of Canada to maintain sovereignty and jurisdiction over land and sea of Canadian interest. The challenge, therefore, lies in an attempt to infringe upon these laws, particularly as infringements would affect the resources of the seabed, and as they would affect the marine environment in waters of Canadian interest, including coastal and continental shelf interests.

While other government departments are charged with the task of policing violations of Canadian law in Canadian waters of interest, DND has the ultimate response to ensure that Canadian sovereignty and jurisdiction are maintained. With respect to these challenges, therefore, it is necessary for DND to conduct surveillance of these areas, to assist other departments in their surveillance tasks, and to provide a control capability to back up other departments in their enforcement of Canadian laws.

The potential for external, non-military challenges to Canada's maritime and Arctic sovereignty and jurisdiction is very real and recent developments have heightened awareness of this potential. The U.S. decision to proceed with construction of a pipeline across Alaska and to ship North Slope oil from Alaska to U.S. West Coast ports in supertankers has increased the prospect of major oil spills off the coast of British Columbia. Current and perspective shortages of energy and other basic world commodities have heightened national and international interest in the resource potential of the Canadian Arctic and the continental margin.

The basic concern, nevertheless, remains that of the possibility of foreign infringements of Canadian laws establishing the extent of and governing the use of Canada's territorial sea, internal waters, enclosed fishing zones, pollution control zones, and regulating exploration for and exploitation of the resources of the seabed subject to Canadian jurisdiction, and of Canada's Arctic territories.

Infringements of this kind are most likely to occur in areas where Canada's right to exercise jurisdiction is not fully accepted internationally and, at least at the outset, would probably be non-military in character.

They would, therefore, be of primary concern to those civil departments and agencies of the federal government to which, under Canadian law, responsibility for regulation and enforcement have been assigned. The possibility, however, cannot be excluded that a determined challenge could be supported by the display or limited use of military force, as occurred in the recent fisheries dispute between Britain and Iceland.

These concerns are growing, as evidenced during the recent Law of the Sea Conference, as a consequence of the concept of an exclusive economic zone or patrimonial sea extending not less than 200 miles off a state's coast. Within this zone the state would exercise the sole responsibility for resource management, and enjoy either exclusive or preferential rights in the exploitation of both living and inanimate resources. The implications for Canada of such a broadening of its rights and responsibilities as a coastal state are important. Law is seldom self-enforcing; it is for consideration whether the greater range of interests and greater geographical extent of the areas subject to Canadian jurisdiction would lead to a larger requirement than at present for surveillance capabilities to detect infringements of Canada's legal rights, and also for control capabilities to ensure that those rights were respected.

An area which must be considered as a special case when discussing challenges to Canadian sovereignty is the Arctic. At first glance there appears to be little possibility of direct threats in Canada's Arctic; far more concern is expressed over the possible unauthorized exploitation of the resources of this area, and of the possibility of pollution which is far more damaging in its ecological effects in the Arctic than it would be elsewhere. The non-military challenge in the Arctic includes such things as unauthorized drilling of oil wells and the unauthorized use of Canadian waters by foreign vessels.

Although a number of federal agencies are on the ground throughout Canada's Arctic, a military force, showing its presence in the area on a regular basis, does much to reaffirm Canada's sovereignty. Further precise definition of the various challenges in Canada's Arctic will evolve in time, but it is evident that the possibility exists for a variety of challenges in this area, and a capability is required to meet these challenges as they arise....

Afterword

What can and cannot be said about Canadian Arctic Security

Rob Huebert

The sub-title of Whitney Lackenbauer and Peter Kikkert's collection should have been - "the more things change, the more they stay the same." This collection of almost all of Canada's key documents on Arctic Sovereignty and Security from 1968-1974 is essential reading for anyone interested in the subject. Both the editors' excellent introduction and the documents themselves create a strong sense of déjà vu. Despite the dramatic changes that are now reshaping the Arctic - climate change, boundary issues, and the development of new resources (including diamonds, iron ore, oil and gas) - many of the arguments and debates that shaped the responses of the Canadian government in the 1960s and 1970s are eerily similar to the arguments that are being put forward today. As the government - then and now - recognizes that the Arctic requires some form of policy, it turns to the Canadian military to "do something!" As the documents make clear, however, Canada's senior military leadership are often unsure of what that "something" is to be.

The documents in this collection provide a clear picture of a government that is focused on "doing something" at a minimum cost. There is a clear sense of urgency, but there is also a sense that the government is unclear if it is facing a political problem or a tangible sovereignty or security challenge in the Arctic. At the root of the concern is the assumption that the United States is the main threat. In particular, the voyages of the ice strengthened oil tanker *Manhattan* through the Northwest Passage without Canadian permission was seen as a direct challenge to Canada's Arctic sovereignty. These voyages were not the only issue with the Americans, but the documents show how they quickly became the most important to Canadian policy-makers at the time. It is fascinating to read through the documents to see how the Department of National Defence was asked to consider and create a defence response to what was really a foreign policy issue centred on questions of international law and not military power. As the documents make clear, unless the Government had considered copying the actions of the USSR in 1967 when it ordered its Navy to stop a similar attempt of the Americans to sail through the Northeast Passage - by force if necessary - there was little that the Canadian Forces could do to respond to the American action. The documents make it clear that the Canadian Forces were at a loss when asked to treat the Americans as the "threat."

Reflecting on the evident discomfort of the Canadian defence officials in making the Americans the main Arctic "threat," what the documents show was not being discussed also makes this collection outstanding. The documents make it clear that Canadian defence officials were focussed on responding to American actions in the Arctic. Even when senior officials from the Canadian Navy considered the possibility (no matter how unlikely) of acquiring American nuclear powered attack submarines (SSNs) in the 1960s, the rationale for such a purchase was placed in the context of "protecting" Canadian Arctic sovereignty from the Americans! (The documents do not mention if the officials appreciated the irony of being allowed to buy what was then one of the most sophisticated weapon systems in the American arsenal for use against the Americans.) On a much more serious note, however, is the complete absence of any discussion of the most important Arctic security challenges of the entire Cold War. None of the documents really discuss a naval engagement between the submarine forces of the United States and the USSR in the Arctic. There is no mention of Soviet submarine development and strategy, nor is there any discussion of what Canada should do either by itself or with its allies and friends to counter the potential Soviet submarine threat. It was as if the Soviet Arctic naval build up was not happening.

The documents paint a picture of Canadian officials ignoring this issue in the understanding that the Americans would take care of it. Yet the activities and actions of the two superpowers in Canada's third ocean were arguably some of the most critical to the real protection of Canadian security and not just limited to the Arctic. Geography meant that the Soviet Navy had to be Arctic capable. Even if they wanted to adopt an alternative strategy, the location of their ports meant that they needed to build vessels that had the ability to operate in Arctic waters.

Geography also meant that the Arctic Ocean was the primary region of naval confrontation between the Soviet Union and NATO. Military technology made the nuclear missile (SLBM) carrying nuclear-powered submarines (SSBN) the key component of nuclear deterrence. The ongoing "games" of cat and mouse played by the Americans, Soviets (and possibly British) under the polar ice cap determined if the unsteady "peace" of the Cold War would be maintained or if nuclear war would erupt.

It is therefore astonishing to find that at no point in the documents did any senior official - civilian or defence - consider the possibility that Canada should develop a policy on its security needs in this context. Canadian officials at that time were willing to face the challenges of sailing Canadian forces and supplies to both the UK and Norway in the event of open conflict with the USSR. They were aware of the need to respond to Soviet aggression, but they were completely mute on what Canada should do to protect its own Arctic waters. They were equally mute on what actions they should take to provide for the common security of NATO. Instead they seemed to leave the issues entirely to the Americans to deal with as they saw fit. In this way, Canadian officials could then tinker with the marginal issues such as the voyages of the Manhattan or other such minor irritants that arose with the Americans in the Arctic.

With the advantage of hindsight, it is bewildering to ask why Canadian defence and government officials were willing to simply let the Americans take care of the North, and why was there no consideration given to supporting their actions either through NORAD or NATO? Why were Canadian officials so incensed by the voyage of one American commercial vessel but seemingly willing to ignore the many voyages of Soviet submarines near and possibly in Canadian Arctic waters? Why was there no serious discussion of what Canada could do to temper Soviet aggression and protect nuclear deterrence - both of which were the core Canadian security requirements of the time. Reflecting on the document trail so ably provided by Lackenbauer and Kikkert, Canadian Arctic security policy in the 1960s and 1970s was simply determined by the headlines. If the public became aware of events like the sailing of the *Manhattan* through the Passage, then defence officials were required to act. Yet the presence of foreign submarines near or in Canadian northern waters did not seem to elicit any response from the same officials. It was as if the Canadian Government would only respond if the public demanded it. Surely the presence of a Soviet submarine (or even an American) in Canadian waters was as serious of a threat (and possibly more) to Canadian Arctic sovereignty and security. How else can one interpret the differences in the Canadian responses? There is the possibility that Canadian defence officials did consider the Soviet strategic threat and may have even acted upon it, but that those documents remain secret. If that is the case, then the full story of Canada Arctic security in this era still remains to be told. Perhaps Canadian defence officials were aware of the need to protect all three oceans but the documents that show this remain classified and hidden.

The current challenges now arising in the Arctic demand that Canadians fully understand what worked in the past and what did not, and there are lessons to be learnt today from this collection. The Canadian government becomes fixated on responding to the public understanding of Arctic issues. When stories begin to appear in the *Globe and Mail* or on CBC, there is a call for action. As this collection carefully documents, this is often met with consternation by the Canadian Forces, which are not always clear on what they need to do. On the other hand, if the issues remain hidden from the public's attention, the Government can rest content to ignore the Arctic. These documents do not give confidence to those who hope that the government is continually examining the issues to achieve a full and comprehensive understanding of the nature of the problem in the Arctic.

This book offers an important warning to Canadian officials who must face security challenges and not run away with the hope that the Americans will protect us. That is not what sovereign states do. The north is once again entering a period in which the circumpolar states are beginning to rearm their military forces for Arctic operations. Demark and Norway have already invested substantially into rebuilding their militaries into a combat capable force that can operate in the north. Russia is in the process of rebuilding its submarine force and is now increasing its operations and training in Arctic waters. The United States Navy recently released its Arctic Roadmap to lay the groundwork for a renewed presence in the region; and the US Air Force is in the process of deploying almost 20% of its newest fighter (the F-22) in Alaska. The question that Canadian defence planners now face is what should they do. Let's hope that when future researchers are carrying the work of Lackenbauer and Kikkert into the twenty-first century, they do not find a similar failure on the part of the government to address complex and demanding security issues that face Canada.

Lackenbauer and Kikkert have provided a critical resource and service to all those who are interested in understanding how the Canadian government responds to Arctic security issues. It is not a reassuring picture, but one that can hopefully be used to ensure that current officials can improve on early efforts as the Arctic continues to evolve as a complex security environment.

Further Reading

Abele, Frances. "Canadian Contradictions: Forty Years of Northern Political Development," *Arctic* 40/4 (December 1987): 310-320.

Bankes, Nigel D. "Forty Years of Canadian Sovereignty Assertion in the Arctic, 1947-87," *Arctic* 40/4 (December 1987): 292-99.

Bell, G.G. "The Armed Forces and the Civil Authority: 2 Aiding National Development," *Behind the Headlines* 31/7-8 (December 1972).

Berger, Thomas R. *Northern Frontier/Northern Homeland: The Report of the Mackenzie Valley Pipeline Inquiry, vol. 1.* Ottawa: Department of Supply and Services, 1977.

Coates, Ken, Whitney Lackenbauer, William Morrison, and Greg Poelzer. *Arctic Front: Defending Canada's Interests in the Far North.* Toronto: Thomas Allen, 2008.

Cohen, Maxwell. "The Arctic and the National Interest," *International Journal* 26/1 (1970-71): 52-81.

Dickerson, Mark. *Whose North? Political Change, Political Development, and Self-Government in the Northwest Territories.* Vancouver: UBC Press, 1992.

Diubaldo, R.J. and S.J. Scheinberg. "A Study of Canadian-American Defence Policy (1945-1975) – Northern Issues and Strategic Resources." ORAE Extra-Mural Paper No. 6. Ottawa: Operational Research and Analysis Establishment, Department of National Defence, Dec. 1978. Copy on file at DHH 79/697.

Dosman, Edgar. *The National Interest.* Toronto: McClelland and Stewart, 1975.

---, ed. *The Arctic in Question*. Toronto: Oxford University Press, 1976

Duffy, R. Quinn. *The Road to Nunavut: The Progress of Eastern Arctic Inuit since the Second World War*. Montreal: McGill-Queen's University Press, 1988.

Elliot-Meisel, Elizabeth B. *Arctic Diplomacy: Canada and the United States in the Northwest Passage*. New York: Peter Lang, 1998.

---. "Still unresolved after fifty years: the Northwest Passage in Canadian-American relations, 1946-1998," *The American Review of Canadian Studies* 29/3 (Fall 1999): 407-430.

Eyre, Kenneth C. "Custos Borealis: The Military in the Canadian North." Ph.D. thesis, University of London-King's College, 1981.

---. "Forty Years of Military Activity in the Canadian North, 1947-87," *Arctic* 40/4 (December 1987): 292-99.

Griffiths, Franklyn, ed. *Politics of the Northwest Passage*. Kingston & Montreal: McGill-Queen's University Press, 1987.

Hamilton, John D. *Arctic Revolution: Social Change in the Northwest Territories, 1935-1994*. Toronto: Dundurn Press, 1994.

Head, Ivan L. "Canadian Claims to Territorial Sovereignty in the Arctic Regions," *McGill Law Journal* 9 (1963): 200-226.

Horn, Bernd. "Gateway to Invasion or the Curse of Geography? The Canadian Arctic and the Question of Security, 1939-1999," in *Forging a Nation: Perspectives on the Canadian Military Experience* ed. Horn. St. Catharines: Vanwell, 2002: 307-32.

Jenness, Diamond. *Eskimo Administration II: Canada*. Montreal: Arctic Institute of North America, 1964.

Kirkey, Christopher. "The Arctic Waters Pollution Prevention Initiatives: Canada's Response to an American Challenge," *International Journal of Canadian Studies* 13 (Spring 1996), 41-59.

Kirton, John and Don Munton, "Protecting the Canadian Arctic: The Manhattan Voyages, 1969-1970," in *Canadian Foreign Policy: Selected Cases* ed. Kirton and Munton. Toronto: Prentice-Hall, 1992: 206-221.

Lackenbauer, P. Whitney. "Canada's Northern Defenders: Aboriginal Peoples in the Canadian Rangers, 1947-2005," in *Aboriginal Peoples and the Canadian Military: Historical Perspectives* ed. Lackenbauer and Craig Mantle. Kingston: CDA Press, 2007: 171-208.

Lackenbauer, P. Whitney and Matthew Farish. "The Cold War on Canadian Soil: Militarizing a Northern Environment," *Environmental History*, vol. 12, no. 3 (2007): 920-50.

Lloyd, Trevor. "New Perspective on the North," *Foreign Affairs* 42/2 (1964): 293-308.

Lotz, Jim. *Northern Realities: The Future of Northern Development in Canada*. Toronto: New Press, 1972.

MacDonald, R. St. J., ed. *The Arctic Frontier*. Toronto: University of Toronto Press, 1966.

McRae, D.M. "Arctic waters and Canadian sovereignty," *International Journal* 38/3 (1983): 476-492.

Morrison, William R. "Eagle Over the Arctic: Americans in the Canadian North, 1867-1985," *Canadian Review of American Studies* (Spring 1987): 61-85.

Orvik, Nils. *Policies of Northern Development*. Kingston: Queen's University, Department of Policy Studies, 1973.

Page, Robert. *Northern Development: The Canadian Dilemma*. Toronto: McClelland and Stewart, 1986.

Pharand, Donat. *Canada's Arctic Waters in International Law*. Cambridge: Cambridge University Press, 1988.

Phillips, R.A.J. *Canada's North*. Toronto: Macmillan, 1967.

Purver, Ron. "The Arctic in Canadian Security Policy, 1945 to the Present," in *Canada's International Security Policy* ed. David B. Dewitt and David Leyton-Brown. Scarborough, ON: Prentice-Hall, 1995: 81-110.

Rea, K.J. *The Political Economy of the Canadian North*. Toronto: University of Toronto Press, 1968.

Rohmer, Richard. *The Arctic Imperative*. Toronto: McClelland and Stewart, 1973.

Sutherland, R.J. "The Strategic Significance of the Canadian Arctic," in *The Arctic Frontier*, ed. R. St. J. MacDonald. Toronto: University of Toronto Press, 1966: 256-78.

Tynan, Thomas M. "Canadian-American Relations in the Arctic: The Effect of Environmental Influences upon Territorial Claims," *The Review of Politics* 41/3 (July 1979): 402-427.

Withers, BGen R.M. "Defence Requirements 'North of Sixty,'" *Canadian Defence Quarterly*, 1/1 (Summer 1971): 37-43.

Wonders, William C., ed. *Canada's Changing North*. Toronto: McClelland and Stewart, 1971.

Zaslow, Morris. *The Northward Expansion of Canada, 1914-1967*. Toronto: McCelland and Stewart, 1988.

About the Editors:

P. Whitney Lackenbauer is associate professor and chair of the Department of History at St. Jerome's University in the University of Waterloo, and a faculty associate with the LCMSDS. He is author or editor of eight previous books including *Arctic Front: Defending Canada in the Far North* (with Ken Coates, Bill Morrison, and Greg Poelzer), which won the 2009 Donner Prize for the best book on public policy. He was an inaugural Canadian International Council Fellow working on Arctic sovereignty and security issues from 2008-09, and his final report entitled *From Polar Race to Polar Saga: An Integrated Strategy for Canada and the Circumpolar World* was published in July 2009.

Peter Kikkert recently completed his M.A. at the University of Waterloo and is a Ph.D. student in history at the University of Western Ontario. He is the author of "The Polaris Incident: 'Going to the Mat' with the Americans," *Journal of Military and Strategic Studies* (2009), and a forthcoming book chapter with Dr. Lackenbauer entitled "Sovereignty and Security: The Department of External Affairs, the United States, and Arctic Sovereignty, 1945-68." He held a Social Sciences and Humanities Research Council (SSHRC) Joseph-Armand Bombardier Canada Graduate Scholarship and a Balsillie Fellowship in 2008-09.

Index